There's one thing tougher than reaching the top— staying there.

It's a rare breed that can reach number one and keep that hungry, fighting attitude that put them there. Rick Mears and the entire Penske team behind The Gould Charge have that winning attitude. That's why we're one of the most successful teams on the circuit—year after year. Because we've learned that the competition is not just the other guy. It's yourself. It means continually setting new goals, meeting new challenges.

This same winning attitude is true of our business. We're determined to be number one in every electronic and electrical market we serve. That's why we put more effort into research and development. That's why we concentrate more on innovative products and technological leadership.

At Gould, we know that once we've reached the limits, it's time to set new limits.

To learn more about how this winning attitude keeps us ahead, write: Gould Inc., Department INDY, 10 Gould Center, Rolling Meadows, Illinois 60008.

THE GOULD CHARGE

1

GOULD

GOULD

Electronics & Electrical Products

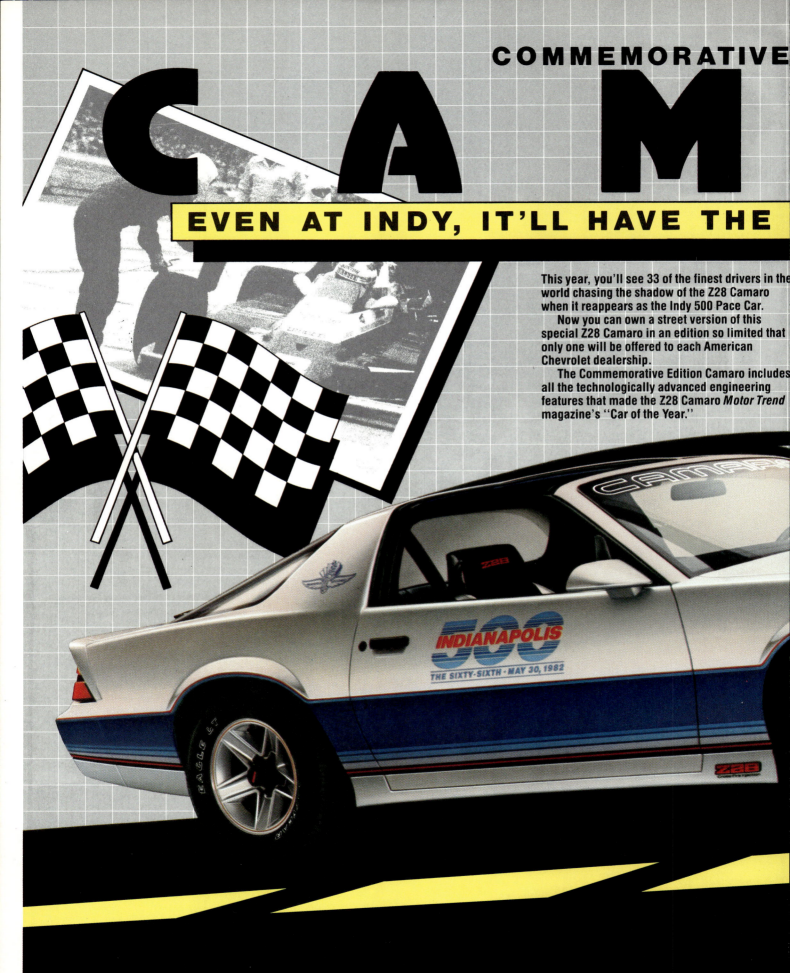

COMMEMORATIVE
CAM

EVEN AT INDY, IT'LL HAVE THE

This year, you'll see 33 of the finest drivers in the world chasing the shadow of the Z28 Camaro when it reappears as the Indy 500 Pace Car.

Now you can own a street version of this special Z28 Camaro in an edition so limited that only one will be offered to each American Chevrolet dealership.

The Commemorative Edition Camaro includes all the technologically advanced engineering features that made the Z28 Camaro *Motor Trend* magazine's "Car of the Year."

INDIANAPOLIS 500
THE SIXTY-SIXTH · MAY 30, 1982

DITION PACE CAR.
ARO

MPETITION CHASING SHADOWS.

Ground Effects technology, similar in theory to rrent Formula One practice, which literally lls the car to the surface in some driving and ad conditions.

A 62-degree windshield rake, which helps the 8 achieve a .369 coefficient of drag, even with wnforce-inducing air dam and spoiler.

otally redesigned suspension, front acPherson-strut-based) and rear (coils, trailing ks, torque tube and Panhard rod), that abled the Z28 to generate .8g-range cornering power on GM skid pads.

• A healthy 305 CID version of the smallblock V8 can be equipped with optional new dual Cross-Fire fuel injection. (Not available in Calif.)

The Commemorative Edition Pace Car Z28 Camaro. At Indy, it'll have the competition chasing shadows.

Some Chevrolets are equipped with engines produced by other GM divisions, subsidiaries, or affiliated companies worldwide. See your dealer for details.

GM

MARK OF EXCELLENCE

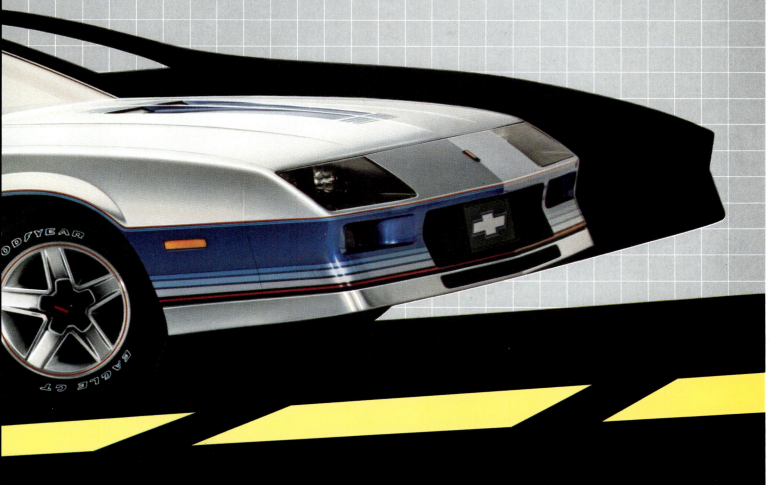

Chevrolet

Indianapolis 500 Yearbook

Whew! How'd you like that race. The closest ever and thrilling even before the green flag dropped. And the best thing about it was the spirit of cooperation between the contestants. The CART boys, headed by Pat Patrick and Roger Penske, gave USAC a chance to present their program under their rules without bickering and, everyone was the better for it. Certainly the fans were. And there might just have been more fans than ever before. At least the gate receipts should have been the biggest in history.

Just a day before the track opened, John Cooper resigned as president and reliable Joe Cloutier was called back for a second term. It was nothing new as he has served the Hulman family for most of his life but we really think that he is beginning to enjoy the job. Very much in the background while Tony was alive and under pressure when he died, this time Joe can be his own man without looking over his shoulder. The reasons for Cooper's departure . . . there have been many rumors as to why he left but none seem any more valid than the official word from the track that he had merely left for what he considered a better position. We in racing don't feel that there can be a better position than President of the Indianapolis Motor Speedway but, while Cooper was a racer, he was also a practical businessman with a family to support which may have outweighted that fact. In any case, GOOD LUCK, JOHN COOPER in whatever you do. Maybe some day you'll be back on the scene.

How about that two-million plus purse. While the Speedway increases the payoff a bit each year, if possible, this was more than a BIT. Of course the drivers put on a helluva show for the money and they deserved every penny of it. But, in any case, it was a pretty fair payoff.

For the first time since the Swede Savage accident, a driver was fatally injured. The track and USAC have done everything within their power to make the race safer and it seems they have been successful . . . to a point. Gordon Smiley was a competent driver but, it seems, at the crucial moment he made the one fatal mistake just as many good drivers had done before him. Ralph Hepburn who had as much experience on the track as anyone in racing, did it as did Chet Miller, with almost as much experience as Hep. We would suppose that it is a normal reaction to try to bring a car under control any way you can without realizing that what feels right might be dead wrong. The Speedway is a very unforgiving taskmaster. Godspeed Gordon . . . you will be missed!

All in all, it was a fine race. Much better than you could ever hope for. The bunching behind the pace car and the manditory pit stops must be given a lot of the credit. It makes each restart a whole new race. Maybe not in the traditional form but as the folk singers used to say, "THE TIMES THEY ARE A CHANGIN'"!

JCF

Volume X

Unequalled In Coverage of The World's Most Famous Automobile Race

Publisher	Carl Hungness	Circulation	Wilma Steffy
Editor	Jack C. Fox	Secretary	Terri Gunn
Staff Photographers	Phil Whitlow	Production	Justyn Blackwell
	Roy Query		Rick Whitt
			Jim Wallick
			Mary Ann Zaban

Our thanks once again to the Public Relations staff headed by Al Bloemker, vice-president of the Indianapolis Motor Speedway and his assistants Bill Donaldson, Bob Laycock, Roger Depe, Bill York and Speedway Photo Department Ron McQueeney and his staff for their continuing assistance in the compilation of this book.

Page 224 photo of a disgruntled Mario Andretti by ace photographer Phil Whitlow.

St. Louis Artist Mike Lynch is a fan of the world of wheels. He draws cars of every conceivable use and proportion. We chose him for the cover of our Tenth Anniversary edition because of his continuing interest in producing the right piece of art for the occasion. We'd say he succeeded.

The opinions expressed herein do not necessarily reflect those of the Indianapolis Motor Speedway Corporation.

Printed by Webcrafters, Inc., Madison, Wisconsin.

Contributing Photographers:
Roy Query
Phil Whitlow
John Mahoney
Don Larson
Dave Scoggan
Rick Whitt
Gene Crucean
Arnie deBrier
Bill Enoch
Bob Mount

Joe Henning
Jack Fox
Carl Hungness
Doug Wendt
Jerry Nolan
Bruce McPherson
Jack Ackerman
Deborah Eckler
Jim Dawson
John Mihalke
Bud Cunningham

IMS — Staff Photographers
Ron McQueeney
Charles Duffy
Jack Householder
Bob Scott
Dan Frances
Steve Snoddy
Harold Bergquist
Dave Dwiggins
John Gray
Harry Goode

Debbie Young
Jim Haines
Steve Lingenfelter
Harlen Hunter
Frank Newman
Dean Sellers
Denis Sparks
Jeff Stephenson
Dave Thomas
Stephanie Bloom
Jack Schofer
Larry Smith

Bill Watson
Van Wildman
Dale Wines
Dave Willoughby
Steve Voorhees
Del Neal
Tom Lucas
Mark Reed
Jim Gabbert
Rick Wall

Contributing Writers:
Jep Cadou
Donald Davidson
Jack Fox
Fritz Frommeyer
Lynda Johncock
Jerry Miller
Dave Overpeck
Paul Scheuring
Dave Scoggan
Al Stilley
Dave Woolford

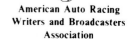

GORDON SMILEY

"Gordon Smiley loved his life. He accepted his life on the terms on which it was presented to him, and, above all he was daring. Every man with an ounce of ambition wants to accomplish something in his stay on this earth, try to excel in some way based on the talents God has given him."

"Its men with hearts like these men who have made the forward steps history. Man has need to excel, to reach out for the unattainable, and reaching out in a racing automobile is symbolic of that spirit that is beating within each of us. Gordon Smiley was daring, and he died while daring greatly."

Paul Page

The Peeled Eye

by Carl Hungness *Publisher*

I don't think I like columnists who write about themselves often. I believe anyone who's ever pecked away at a typewriter for a living is sometimes guilty of injecting themself into their stories and certainly this writer is no different. Thus this is going to be one of those stories and I hope you'll bear with me for I've reached a fork in the road for the tenth anniversary of the Indianapolis "500" Yearbook.

Constant readers will note that our byline doesn't appear in this edition as it has in the past. We haven't given up writing about race cars, but almost. For the time being anyway. Capable journalist and good friends Jack Fox and Donald Davidson are responsible for the bulk of the editorial content of this edition. Per usual however, your writer is responsible for assigning the stories and selling the advertising. The advertising. That's where the problem (or solution) comes in. I can sell.

Some years back, about the time that everyone else was getting ready to receive their driver's license, we "ran away from home." And made it. All the way from Golden, Colorado to New Orleans and a hat store called Meyer The Hatter. Soon I was a high-school drop-out and the best damn hat salesman in the country. I speak fluent hat. Dobbs, Stetson, Mallory, Borsalino, etc. We soon discovered that we had a gift for gab that would often see topless men plucked off St. Charles Street and into the one man show given by yours truly who would steam, block fit and size the perfect ornament to satisfy even the most discriminating. Yes sir, boss, we have got a Homburg that was made just for you. Want me to put your initials in it? Here, I've even got a special box I've been saving just for that hat. Bring your best friend in brother, and tell him to see Mr. Carl.

Hats and books really have a lot more to do with one another than you might think. If I couldn't sell, we wouldn't have an Indy 500 Yearbook. We're always proud to say that yes, our books have won awards. Our writing has won awards. But if there wasn't any advertising in the book you're holding, it would be about half its size complete with all black and white photographs.

One hat store led to another and we were back in Denver. Then we went to a Midget race and it was goodbye hats, hello race cars. A job in a local speed shop proved to me that I was better with my wits than my hands but the employment office said, "Sorry, the best we can get for you is wiper at a car wash." I made pizzas for a couple of months and then convinced the registrar at the University of Colorado that he was being derelict in his duty if he didn't admit me without a high school diploma. Another sales job. They agreed to let me in, for no credit. That was fine, all my friends were in classrooms. It seemed like everyone I sold a hat to was working at the car wash.

A couple of years later the University told me I'd done a good job and they'd formally admit me. Later they told me I was the first guy to graduate without a high school diploma. Along the way I never bothered to get another job. It seemed like there was always something to sell. Since I was a died-in-the-wool hot rodder, I sold space in the local car show and made money. There were always good deals on cars, and with a little rubbing and scrubbing the tuition bills got paid. There were a lot of pool tables in between and one night I won a typewriter from some poor fish who would always choke on the nine ball.

Then I found a racing newspaper in Denver that was floundering and convinced the publisher I could save it. Another sales job. But the paper made money and I was forced to learn to construct a gramatically correct sentence. After the local racing paper (with the memorable name of SPEED WHEELS) we headed for Big Time Auto Racing and Indianapolis. Unknown to anyone in the sport, we made an appointment to see the staid USAC Board of Directors and give a presentation to them. We told them we could change their weekly newsletter into the best full size racing tabloid they'd ever seen ... and we'd do it for a small percentage of the action. They bought it. Trouble was, they only bought it for a year. It was back on the street again.

It took about three years to get it done, with not too many smiles along the way, but we finally convinced enough buyers and advertisers that there should be an Indianapolis 500 Yearbook. Sold. That was back in '73 and along with a little help from my friends, the Yearbook was re-born. Since, it's been one sale after another.

We've been fortunate enough to build a small, but respectable auto racing publishing firm. Sales of the Yearbook climbed steadily and soon we were wheeling and dealing for printing presses, a building, etc. But it was no Hugh Hefner story. We peaked out at a level that was considerably lower than I anticipated. We always thought that if we could tell the entire world about the Indianapolis 500 Yearbook we'd sell a zillion of them. The best way to inform the racing world of your existence is by buying time on the Indianapolis Motor Speedway Radio Network. We convinced the Speedway officials to give us $37,500 worth of radio time for a percentage of sales. We then convinced Johnny Rutherford that he would sound great as a pitchman for the Yearbook and soon I was counting the dollars that would come rolling in thru the mail and dreaming about the Duesenberg I've always wanted. We sold a few books but the Duesenberg remained a picture on the wall. Rutherford's still a friend but the people at the radio network were walking around asking themselves who talked them into the deal.

Alas, the hardest one to sell was myself. I was sure there was a market for at least a quarter of a million Indy Yearbooks world-wide. I'm convinced there isn't. I've been convinced for a few years now and have been looking for some other things to do.

Last August we left our publishing business to our trusted employees and moved west to finish writing "The Tinley Park Express," a biography on the Bettenhasuen family. About four weeks from the completion date we stumbled across another deal to sell. Since I figured the Bettenhausen book would best be finished just after the 1982 race, I agreed to sell the new deal my brother had approached me with. He's a genius. He's got more ideas on how to make money than there are pebbles on the beach. But he never follows through. I took the idea and ran with it.

(Continued on P. 198)

[6]

The Contents

Car owner Roger Penske saw his car finish an eye blink behind Gordon Johncock this year. For a complete feature story on Roger see page 130.

Schlitz . . . Josele Garza

Our friend from South of the border became a full-fledged race car driver this year. Josele Garza encountered more problems than he'd care to remember trying to make this year's "500" but the popular Mexican was in the field on race day. Along with help from Bobby Unser and chief mechanic Ronnie Dawes, Josele figured out what it was really like to be in tune with the handling characteristics of a race car. We'd be hard-pressed to find a more popular sophomore Indy driver and happy to see he's blessed with determination.

MEET OUR DRIVERS!

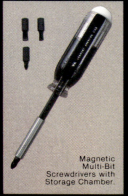

Magnetic Multi-Bit Screwdrivers with Storage Chamber.

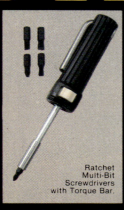

Ratchet Multi-Bit Screwdrivers with Torque Bar.

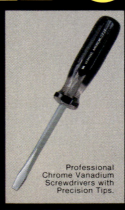

Professional Chrome Vanadium Screwdrivers with Precision Tips.

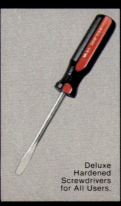

Deluxe Hardened Screwdrivers for All Users.

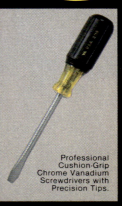

Professional Cushion-Grip Chrome Vanadium Screwdrivers with Precision Tips.

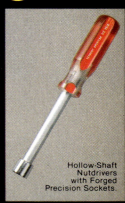

Hollow-Shaft Nutdrivers with Forged Precision Sockets.

VERMONT AMERICAN PROFESSIONAL DRIVERS MAKE EVERY TURN COUNT

Smooth performance in the turns makes the difference. That's why so many 'pit crews' like A.J. Watson's prefer 'drivers' made by the highest technology standards.

Choosing the right size and type screwdriver for any job is easy when you choose VERMONT AMERICAN — slotted and Phillips; special screwdrivers including hex, square recess, clutch and Torx heads; or insert bits which can be used in magnetic and ratchet drivers or in your power screwdriver or drill.

Because 'drivers' are the tools you use most often, it just makes sense to turn with VERMONT AMERICAN. Each 'driver' has been crafted to the same exacting quality specifications as our full line of other hand tools and power-tool accessories: saw blades, router bits, drill bits, taps and dies, tool boxes, plus many more. Your VERMONT AMERICAN retailer is the place to start any job that you want done right.

VERMONT AMERICAN
WHEN THE JOB REALLY COUNTS ™

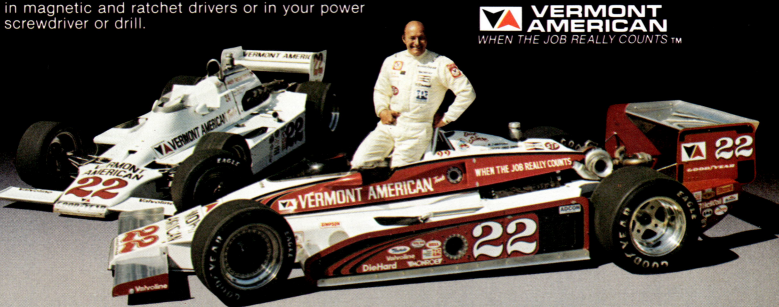

"Look for me on the track and A.J.'s crew in the pit . . . we all drive with VERMONT AMERICAN." *Dick Simon*

Genesee Beer Racing Team

The beautiful machines belonging to car owner Dick Hammond were back in Gasoline Alley when the green flag dropped for this year's running of the "500". Hammond and his capable chief mechanic Galen Fox were among those taken by surprise at the sharp jump in speeds for the 1982 event. The Hammond machines are as finely detailed pieces of equipment as you'll find at the Speedway, but this year the very latest in chassis was mandatory. We're sure they'll be back next year and among the starting line-up. Joe Saldana drove for the team.

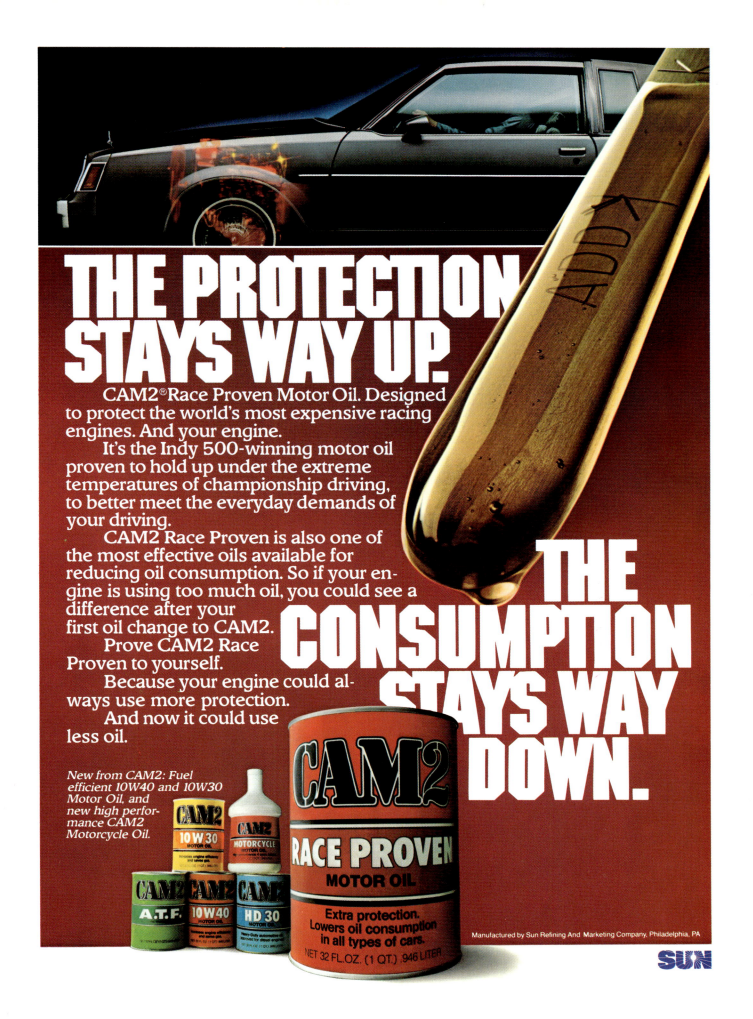

Longhorn Racing Team

The Longhorn racing team, owned by the ever smiling Texan Bobby Hillin, is one of the most professionally run operations at Indianapolis. It is surprising that this assemblage of talent, spearheaded by three-time winner Al Unser, is running without major sponsorship. Overall, they may be described as a group of veterans, each capable of cracking the combination to win at Indy, but who simply haven't been rewarded with a trip to victory circle yet. Once they arrive you can imagine they'll be ahead of the competition by a Texas mile.

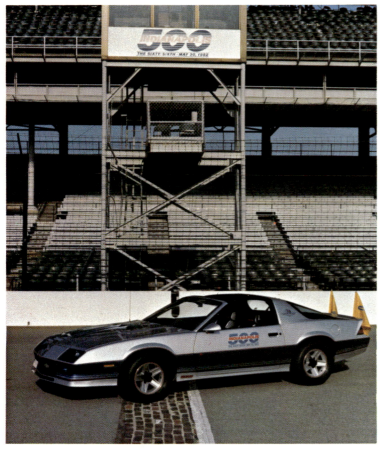

DAY-BY-DAY

by JACK C. FOX

Many thanks to Jep Cadou and his crew who wrote and produced the day-by-day trackside reports. Their information was concise and accurate and helped recall incidents we would have otherwise missed.

The Chevrolet Camaro pace car was used by the officials to inspect the track.

Pancho Carter leads a bunch of practicers through the first turn. That's Al Unser in No. 10 followed by Bobby Rahal, Johnny Rutherford, Gary Bettenhausen and Don Whittington.

Gary Bettenhausen and Pete Halsmer have the first race of the month . . . to see who will be first on the track. Gary won!

May, 1982! A repetition of an old story for some and a whole new one for others. But always a fascinating and dramatic month for all. Intermingled with the quest for speed and the elation of victory can be periods of stark tragedy and disappointments which can wipe out fortunes and ruin careers. For every winner there are a hundred losers. Three weeks in May will see every hand played out. This is the story of May, 1982.

SATURDAY, MAY 8
Warm, Late Afternoon Rain

"What a beautiful day in sunny Indianapolis" was the opening remark by Mayor Bill Hudnut as he greeted the crowd gathered for the attendant ceremonies of the inaugural day. Unfortunately Bill's remarks held true only until late afternoon when the clouds began to gather and the track had to be shut down because of moisture . . . from the sky rather than an errant motor.

Johnny Rutherford ready to go in the Chaparral.

Chief Steward, Tom Binford, Mari Hulman George, and Joe Cloutier take part in the opening ceremonies.

Rick Mears is this year's favorite.

[17]

With the opening ceremonies out of the way and the local politicians finished with their traditional tour of the track following the Mayor's Breakfast, Chief Steward, Tom Binford, opened the track officially at 1:13. Usually there is a big rush to see who will be the first car/driver on the track and while the competition was not quite so great this year as in years past it was still an interesting race. One year, when the race was more intense it resulted in the subsequent death of Referee Walt Meyers. He was struck by one of the race cars trying to be first out on the track. This year it was Gary Bettenhausen edging Pete Halsmer for the honors; Gary in Lindsey Hopkins' No. 8 Cosworth and Halsmer driving the multi-sponsored Colonial Bread/Payless Markets Chevy.

Rookie Tests were the order of the day for those intrepid young (or reasonably so) drivers who have their sights set on the gold(?) and glory(?) of big time auto racing. This year the crop of rookies came almost entirely from the sports car ranks with only one or two rookie sprint drivers represented. Sammy Swindell and Neil Bonnett, from the World of Outlaws and NASCAR Grand Nationals, respectively, were entered but their cars did not arrive at the track. Starting on their tests were Hector Rebaque, Bobby Rahal, Chip Ganassi and Desire Wilson. Of the group Hector and Desire have the best credentials with some international competition to their credit.

Rick Mears' older brother, Roger, was the fastest practicer of the day in the Machinists Union No. 31 with a 190.5. There were no other spectacular speeds to report although there were 19 cars on the track. 50 cars are now housed on the grounds with 51 drivers having passed their physicals. Bill Vukovich is the first driver to "jump" his assigned car, moving into the Kraco No. 18 which is a Penske/Cosworth and a fine looking job with its attractive yellow and blue paint. The California-based Kraco Team (Vern Schuppan is the other member) is masterminded by Ken Balch, the son of former Indy car-owner Johnny Balch (circa 1954).

Among the others on the track were racing writer Patrick Bedard, Greg Leffler, Tom Frantz, Herm Johnson, NARC sprint champ, LeRoy Van Connett, and Ken Hamilton, in one of the stranger cars in Gasoline Alley. It was designed by an aeronautical engineer and boasts a wheelbase of 140 inches. The wheels are enclosed in spats which gives it the appearance of an elongated version of Frank Lockhart's LSR car of 1928. It is painted white with blue and red trim and carries No. 63 ... the name is the Eagle Aircraft Flyer but it was immediately nicknamed by railbirds "the Crop Duster."

Bob Lazier, Howdy Holmes, and Chip Mead were also on the track with Mead's 186.1 being second best of the day. Closest call of the afternoon came when Pete Halsmer "peeled" some of his car's body up over the rear wing. He stopped and later borrowed some pieces from Herm Johnson who has a similar Eagle.

Off the track everyone was buzzing with the announcement that Speedway prexy, John Cooper, had resigned his post for a public relations job. Many conjectures as to why he had done so just as the track was opening were heard but the Speedway stuck by their story that it had been his decision and that while the job was not so prestigious it was a financially better deal for him. Joe Cloutier, for the second time, has been named track president.

SUNDAY, MAY 9
Warm

38 cars were on the track (a record number for the second day of practice) and it was Rick Mears, Captain of the Roger Penske Team, who set every one talking with a speed of 203.620, and that after only 11 laps of practice. What was more amazing was that it was run with three of Rick's fingers in splints. Was it a racing accident? "No" said Rick. He, it turned out, had been putting a water pump on a Model A Ford, the pliers slipped and his hand had gone into the fan.

Mears wasn't the only driver over 200 this afternoon as Mario Andretti turned 200.133 in Pat Patrick's No. 40 STP Wildcat/Cosworth. Fast but nowhere near as impresive as Rick and Mario were Al Unser and Danny Ongais with 197s and Bill Whittington and Kevin Cogan in the 196 bracket. Slightly slower but still over 190 were Geoff Brabham, Pancho Carter, Roger Mears and Herm Johnson who was doing a fine job in his Chevy with 191.1 Gordon Smiley had a brush with the wall near turn-3 when he got too high. He scraped along about 40 feet before bringing the car back to the pits. He was still able to go back out and run just a fraction over 190. Gordon seems to be having a little trouble with the car as his runs are not too smooth.

Drivers happily completing their drivers' tests were Hector Rebaque, Danny Sullivan, Chip Ganassi, and Bobby Rahal.

MONDAY, MAY 10
Warm

Everything seems to be pointing to a brand new qualifying record as both of the Roger Penske drivers, Rick Mears and Kevin Cogan, were running over 200. Rick set a new unofficial mark of 205 while Cogan, a classy second year driver, clocked 202.2. Not to be outdone by the "Penske Boys" was Al Unser who ran 200.9 in Bobby Hillin's No. 10.

Hector Rebaque and Danny Sullivan did excellent jobs for rookies in running over 196 and a half. Others in the 190s were Bill Whittington (with a 199.6), Mario Andretti Tom Sneva, Johnny Rutherford, Roger Mears, Gordon Smiley, Herm Johnson, and Bob Lazier. Bill Vukovich, Chip Mead and Bill Alsup were in the high 1980s.

Chet Fillip, and Desire Wilson were on their drivers' tests with Mrs. Wilson needing only the 175-and up performance

One of the nicest looking cars in the field was the Genesee Spl. It looked particularly attractive from a low angle.

Query

before the jury of veteran drivers to receive her final OK. Fillip completed his 165 phase.

TUESDAY, MAY 11
Warm and Humid

It appears that the run for the pole, Saturday, will be a hot one as five drivers were running over 200 mph. Six cars (including the Rick Mears backup driven by teammate Kevin Cogan) have already run over that magic mark. Fastest of the day was the junior member of the Penske Team, (Cogan) with a 204.5 in the Mears backup, No. 1T. Mario Andretti was right behind Cogan with a 203.4 just to add interest to the speed chase. Mears ONLY ran 202.2 for third best time of the day while Bill Whittington was fourth with 201.4. Just under the charmed circle was Al Unser with a 199.9.

Ken Hamilton, driving the No. 63 "Crop Duster" got out of shape coming out of the 4th turn but was able to make it to the pits without hitting anything. Equally lucky were Dean Vetrock and Bob Lazier. Vetrock, a rookie from Wisconsin, lost a rear wheel on his No. 71 Lightning/Chevy while going through the second turn. He slid some 200 feet but got it down in the infield, making no contact with the wall. A little later in the day, Bob Lazier broke a rear half-shaft and blew a tire on the Wysard No. 34. This happened in the backstretch. He was able to make the fourth turn before the emergency equipment brought him in. Desire Wilson in No. 33 and Jim Hickman in No. 42 passed their drivers's tests and Patrick Bedard completed his refresher in No. 36.

WEDNESDAY, MAY 12
Warm and Humid

Speed and crashes highlighted the day of practice with Kevin Cogan blistering the track surface with a new unofficial practice track record of 206.3. As usual Cogan was followed by Rick Mears at 205.8 and these speeds were made when the day was the hottest. Once again Mario Andretti was third-fastest with 202.6 and Don Whittington clocked 201.5. A big surprise was the 199.4 run by rookie Bobby Rahal in his Red Roof Inns March/Cosworth. Geoff Brabham was just a tick slower than Rahal with a 199.2. A J. Foyt, who has had very few laps on the track in his new No. 14 Gilmore March/Cosworth, ran a 197.8 just to show that they can't forget 'ol Tex when racing for the pole. Others with laps in the high 190s were Hector Rebaque,

Even when the going gets rough there's always time for a joke among friends. A.J., Josele and Bobby Unser relax during the month of May. Josele had a difficult time getting up to speed but came through like a veteran.

Danny Sullivan (who later crashed), and Gordon Johncock who has been a low-profiled driver this year.

There were opportunities for the emergency equipment to show their stuff when three cars became involved in accidents during the afternoon. Roger Rager looped coming out of the fourth turn and made contact with the inside wall stopping his wild ride just north of the pit entrance. He was treated for a sore shoulder at the track hospital and then released. His No. 72 Wildcat/Cosworth was pretty badly damaged.

Danny Sullivan, late in the afternoon, got out of shape in the third turn in the No. 53 March/Cosworth and clobbered the wall. The damage to the car was minor as it slid to a stop on the fourth turn grass.

Tony Bettenhausen, running 190, had a half-shaft break on the backstretch. When the car had stopped gyrating it had hit the fence and stopped at the top of the track in the third turn. Tony was uninjured and the car had damage to the left rear.

Pat Patrick's cars "shine like the pants of a blue serge suit."

What makes this radar detector so desirable that people used to willingly wait months for it?

Anyone who has used a conventional passive radar detector knows that they don't work over hills, around corners, or from behind. The ESCORT® radar warning receiver does. Its uncanny sensitivity enables it to pick up radar traps 3 to 5 times farther than common detectors. It detects the thinly scattered residue of a radar beam like the glow of headlights on a dark, foggy road. You don't need to be in the direct beam. Conventional detectors do. Plus, ESCORT's extraordinary range doesn't come at the expense of more false alarms. In fact, ESCORT has fewer types and sources of false alarms than do the lower technology units. Here's how we do it.

The unfair advantage

ESCORT's secret weapon is its superheterodyne receiving circuitry. The technique was discovered by Signal Corps Capt. Edwin H. Armstrong in the military's quest for more sensitive receiving equipment. ESCORT's Varactor-Tuned Gunn Oscillator singles out X and K band (10.525 and 24.150GHz) radar frequencies for close, careful, and timely examination. Only ESCORT uses this costly, exacting component. But now the dilemma.

The Lady or The Tiger

At the instant of contact, how can you tell a faint glimmer from an intense radar beam? Is it a far away glint or a trigger type radar dead ahead? With ESCORT it's easy: smooth, accurate signal strength information. A soothing, variable speed beep reacts to radar like a Geiger counter, while an illuminated meter registers fine gradations. You'll know whether the radar is miles away or right next to you. In addition, the sound you'll hear is different for each radar band. K band doesn't travel as far, so its sound is more urgent. ESCORT keeps you totally informed.

The right stuff

ESCORT looks and feels right. Its inconspicuous size (1.5Hx5.25Wx5D), cigar lighter power connector and hook and loop or visor clip mounting make installation easy, flexible, and attractive. The aural alarm is volume adjustable and the alert lamp is photoelectrically dimmed after dark to preserve your night vision. And, a unique city/highway switch adjusts X band sensitivity for fewer distractions from radar burglar alarms that share the police frequency while leaving K band at full strength.

Made in Cincinnati

Another nice thing about owning an ESCORT is that you deal directly with the factory. You get the advantage of speaking with the most knowledgable experts available and saving us both money at the same time. Further, in the unlikely event that your ESCORT ever needs repair, our service professionals are at your personal disposal. Everything you need is only a phone call or parcel delivery away.

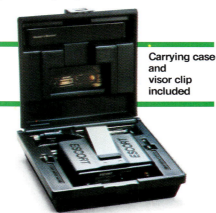

Carrying case and visor clip included

Corroborating evidence

CAR and DRIVER . . . "Ranked according to performance, the ESCORT is first choice . . . it looks like precision equipment, has a convenient visor mount, and has the most informative warning system of any unit on the market . . . the ESCORT boasts the most careful and clever planning, the most pleasing packaging, and the most solid construction of the lot."

BMWCCA ROUNDEL . . . "The volume control has a 'silky' feel to it; in fact, the entire unit does. If you want the best, this is it. There is nothing else like it."

PLAYBOY . . . "ESCORT radar detectors . . . (are) generally acknowledged to be the finest, most sensitive, most uncompromising effort at high technology in the field."

PENTHOUSE . . . "ESCORT's performance stood out like an F-15 in a covey of Sabrajets."

AUTOWEEK . . . "The ESCORT detector by Cincinnati Microwave . . . is still the most sensitive, versatile detector of the lot."

The acid test

There's only one way to really find out what ESCORT is all about. We'll give you 30 days to test it for yourself. If you're not absolutely satisfied, we'll refund your purchase as well as pay for your postage costs to return it. In fact, try an ESCORT and any other detector of your choice. Test them both for 30 days and return the one you don't like. We're not worried because we know which one you'll keep. As further insurance for your investment, ESCORT comes with a full one year limited warranty on both parts and labor. This doesn't worry us either because ESCORT has a reputation for reliability. We know that once you try an ESCORT, radar will never be the same again. So go ahead and do it. Order today.

You don't have to wait

Just send the following to the address below:
☐ Your name and complete street address.
☐ How many ESCORTs you want.
☐ Any special shipping instructions.
☐ Your daytime telephone number.
☐ A check or money order.

Visa and MasterCard buyers may substitute their credit card number and expiration date for the check. Or call us toll free and save the trip to the mail box.

CALL TOLL FREE. . . . 800-543-1608
IN OHIO CALL. 800-582-2696

ESCORT (Includes everything). . . . **$245.00**
Ohio residents add $13.48 sales tax.

Extra speedy delivery

If you order with a bank check, money order, Visa, or MasterCard, your order is processed for shipping immediately. Personal or company checks require an additional 18 days.

RADAR WARNING RECEIVER

☐ CINCINNATI MICROWAVE
Department 025
One Microwave Plaza
Cincinnati, Ohio 45242

Whitlow

It wasn't a particularly happy month for either Billy Vukovich or Vern Schuppan. Here they confer with chief mechanic Haffenden.

THURSDAY, MAY 13
Warm and Humid

With only two days of practice left before the first day of qualifying Rick Mears and Mario Andretti were almost even in their quest for speed. Rick had a 206.8 and Mario, 206.6. It looks like a battle between the two most influential

Publisher Hungness seems to be in very ornamental company.

Whitlow

men of CART, Roger Penske and Pat Patrick, for the prestige of the pole (with Penske having the edge). Kevin Cogan was among the missing, today, as he was given the day off by his team after doing so well earlier in the week.

The 200 mph mark which gives the drivers an "elite" rating was gained by "newcomers" A. J. Foyt (201.3) and Danny Ongais (200.3) both of whom only recently recovered from extensive injuries suffered on last year's circuit. Also joining this group for the first time was Gordon Johncock (202.1) and Tom Sneva, who is always a good qualifier and a so-so practicer, with 202.5. Don Whittington, who has been running well most of the month came in with a classy 204.5. It now looks like there will be close to a dozen qualifiers over 200. There are an even 33 cars practicing at over 190 which made most of the marginal crews start thinking of yellow flags for any speed under a 192 average (or possibly even more).

One driver who had a little more to worry about than running over 192 was 1981 Rookie-of-the-Year, Josele Garza. The wealthy, 23-year old from Mexico City ran his No. 50 Schlitz March/ Cosworth into the third turn wall and the car sustained moderate damage although the popular driver was uninjured. The team, this year, is being managed by last year's winner, Bobby Unser, who says he has no intention of competing in this year's race. While he hasn't exactly announced his retirement the three-time winner has shown no indication that he will take over the driving chores on any car (even Roger Penske's).

Ken Hamilton once again got out of shape, this time in turn-one. While he

made no contact with the wall, he did slide 300 feet before bringing the car around into the pits. Despite being unorthodox the car exhibits good workmanship and a revolutionary concept in race car design.

FRIDAY, MAY 14
Warm and Humid

Unofficial records were the order of the afternoon and, as usual, it was the "Penske Kids" who set them. When things had settled down after traditional 5:00 to 6:00 "Happy Hour" Rick Mears had the honors with a blazing 208.7 and Kevin Cogan had to settle for a "slow" 207.8! It was the fifth day out of six that the unofficial track record has been broken. Whew!

Both of the Pat Patrick drivers, Mario Andretti and Gordy Johncock had the same average at 203.2; Johncock has been coming along about four days behind Mario and appears to be pretty much of a "sleeper" when it comes to qualifying. There is no chance that, barring mechanical problems, he will fail to qualify near the front of the pack although his runs have attracted little enthusiasm or interest.

As usual Foyt, Don Whittington and Tom Sneva were over the 200 mark. It appears almost a certainty that Sneva's official track record has only one day to live as, undoubtedly, 203.620 will be bested ... by four or five drivers.

After the track shut down for the day the drawing was held for qualifying position with Bill Alsup drawing "first out". The Penske back up car, No. 1T drew second spot and Bobby Rahal third. Rick Mears drew No. 4 and Andretti No. 37, and Foyt No. 58. Of course not all of

Mike Chandler's worrying how to make a Chevy run with the Cosworths.

Whitlow

[22]

the cars which drew will make qualifying attempts.

Jim Hickman and Joe Saldana added their cars to the "crunch list" during "happy hour". Neither driver was hurt. Hickman looped down the short chute in his dark red No. 42 Stroh's March/Cosworth, finally stopping in the second turn after hitting the inside wall with the right rear. Saldana merely spun in the first turn and continued on to the pits. He was driving the Genesee Beer Penske/Cosworth No. 58 which sports one of the most attractive paint jobs of all the entered cars. It is metallic blue and white with silver leaf numbers and lettering.

One of the largest practice day crowds ever was on hand for the afternoon's activities. Once during the day traffic extended three abreast down to Lafayette Road from the Sixteenth Street gate. The tower Terrace grandstand was full as was the first turn "Snake Pit". While the latter is traditionally a disorganized territory, someone did present Randy Roberts, a longtime resident thereabouts with a hat on which was inscribed "Mayor of the Snake Pit" which must make his buddy-at-arms, Tom Bacon, "Vice Mayor".

SATURDAY, MAY 15
Warm and Humid

Things were a bit different this year from years past as some new qualifying rules were implemented, designed to give the fans a better and more interesting day. The practice period was from 8:30 a.m. to 10:15 a.m. (longer this year) and then the ceremonies begin. The cars practice in separate groups (odd and even numbers) and then all together for a period which keeps down some of the traffic congestion on the track. Once again Rick Mears was the fastest (207.4)

Strangest looking car in Gasoline Alley was Ken Hamilton's No. 63, dubbed by pitside wags as "the Crop Duster." It had fine workmanship throughout but was withdrawn after two slides.

Gordon Smiley shades himself from the sun during a prolonged stay in the pits.

Larson

practicer followed by Tom Sneva (205.4).

First on deck, when 11:00 o'clock rolled around, was Kevin Cogan in No. 1T, The Norton Spirit Penske/Ford, who started off the action with a second lap speed of 203.851 to break the official track record and then better it by almost one mile per hour on the third round (204.638). He dropped only a tick on the last lap and his average for the four laps was computed at 204.082, ANOTHER RECORD! While he and his crew were receiving the congratulations attendant with setting a new qualifying record, they could not help but see Rick Mears on the track with his No. 1 Gould Charge Penske/Cosworth. This was noted in

A writing desk is where you find one. Gordon Smiley autographs a flag for 13-year old Hugh Waddington.

Mahoney

[23]

Chevrolet leads the pack

The name Chevrolet seemingly has always been associated with the 500-mile race, although not always in the same context. Originally, prior to World War I, Chevrolet was the name of a family of race drivers and constructors. Louis, Arthur and Gaston were the Swiss-born racers who built some fine — and winning — machines. In fact they dominated the racing scene in the first couple of years following the Armistice. Gaston, youngest of the group, won the 1920 race in a radically streamlined green and blue car of family design.

The family had also given its name to a line of passenger cars but that was about their only connection with the "Chevy." Louis, head of the family and eldest brother, had worked on its initial development but shortly after its birth, he had quarrelled with Billy Durant, its backer and quit what was to become General Motors. Supposedly the quarrel had been over Louis's preference for cigarettes over cigars. Durant felt that an executive seemed more impressive if he smoked the stogies ... their smaller versions were just too plebian. The volatile Swiss was so infuriated that he disposed of all his General Motors stock which could have made him a millionaire many times over.

The first Chevolet to become a pace car for the 500 was a 1948 model convertible driven by Wilbur Shaw. The cream car marked the start of a long and happy association and with the Speedway. A red and white convertible paced the race in 1955 and a Camaro did the job in '67 and '69. An impressive black and silver Corvette led the pack in 1978 and this year it was a silver and blue Camaro which impressed both the spectators and the contestants. The track's utility vehicles were also Chevys.

IMS Photos

Cogan's speech over the P.A. system: "The car (#1T) felt real good. It's just not as good as the other race car (#4) was. I blew the engine in it this morning in practice. It was quite a bit quicker. If we have a little bit more time, I think that this car will be just as fast though Rick Mears is out there. I think that he is going to beat me. His car has the same engine in it."

Cogan didn't have long to wait and enjoy his record. Mears first lap run was 206.801 which blew Cogan's 204.6 into a memory. The next lap was even faster (207.039) and then the fastest of them all, and the fastest lap ever turned OFFICIALLY on the track 207.612 ... a recorded time of 43.35. The last lap found Rick "relaxing" down to a modest 206.564. The four-lap average was 207.004! Which immediately made him the odds-on favorite to win the race, the pace car and become the King of Tanzania. It was a jubilant crew which greeted Rick, as most conceeded that this would definitely be the speed of the pole. Rick quipped: "The Gould Charge has just worked tremendously all week long. It was a little bit warm this morning and it got a little bit loose and tried to get away but we were fortunate enough somebody was with us to keep us on the track."

Looking like a "family act," the next car out was Roger Mears. While expected to make the race in the cream, blue and red No. 31 Machinists Union Penske/Cosworth it did take some technical help from the Penske crew. He did run an average of 194.154. "It is a very happy moment. I've wanted to do this for about five years. All my life really. Because I've wanted to get here so bad. So we made it and I'm really excited. We

let him do his thing for awhile (Rick Mears.) I need a little more practice."

Gordon Johncock, who will certainly be considered the dark horse in the race, was timed at a very creditable 201.884 in Pat Patrick's blue and red STP Wildcat/Cosworth. Gordy carried his traditional number 20 on the car which is mechaniched by George Huening, one of the sharpest wrench-turners in Gasoline Alley. "We worked night and day trying to get this car ready. I don't think I'll be in the first row but surely the third row."

Bobby Rahal became the second rookie, after Roger Mears, to qualify and his speed was very close to Roger's, 194.700. He was driving his backup car No. 19T, which will drop the T in the race. With so many entries it has been necessary the past several years to give the backup the same number with a T attached. It keeps things from getting too confused and keeps the Speedway from assigning three digit numbers which might not bother the fans, but which might un-nerve the scorers. After the run Bobby said of his first run: "It's pretty slippery out there. I was generally pretty nervous. But I came by and saw my first lap speed and I knew that that was good enough. We kept at it and I think I'm going to have a beer."

Desire Wilson, in No. 33, made the first incomplete attempt when she was flagged after three laps with only a high 190 average. She will have to try again.

Josele Garza only took one lap on the clock, 187.931, before crew chief Bobby Unser brought out the yellow. It must seem funny for Josele who had very few problems last year to have everything he touches turn to the well-known substance

this year. Seemed like he did better with his old operation.

Even less impressive was the performance of Geoff Brabham, Josele's erstwhile teammate, who came in with his March/Cosworth before even taking the green flag. At least he wasn't charged with an attempt as had been Mrs. Wilson and Garza.

Johnny Rutherford, the personable Texan who has been having trouble all month with Jim Hall's Chaparral/Cosworth settled for an average of 197.066 and the knowledge that he had made the race. "We've had some pretty good times and some bad times. We're a little bit disappointed. We've worked awfully hard this month trying to get the car running. That's the hardest I've had to work to qualify."

Danny Ongais, physically recovered from last year's spectacular "wall-job", ran very well to average 199.148 ... a cautious run for him and, while not up among the super qualifiers, still it must be remembered what he went through and realized that it is a miracle that he can even compete ... anywhere. A somewhat mellowed and friendly Ongais greeted the crowd: "We were going to do the best we could. That seems to be it right now. There were no major problems. We had lost a good deal of time. We are basically

A. J. Foyt celebrated his 25th consecutive "500" start this year, competitive as ever.

Eckler

[25]

Whitlow

Sellers

Freddy Agabashian takes a nostalgic ride in his thirty-year old Cummins Diesel. It was the pole setter in 1952 and still seems to get a little speed. The car is housed in the Speedway Hall of Fame Museum where all can see the state of the art. Circa 1952.

Tim Richmond is still a 500 favorite, but has been concentrating on the NASCAR circuit. He didn't attempt Indy this year, but found time to talk with pretty Linda Vaughn.

here with what we had last year. But what was good then is not good now."

Diminutive Howdy Holmes is next away in his No. 30 March/Cosworth and he seems to have a good run with an average of 194.468. Not the best, but it looks reasonably safe.

The third rookie to qualify is Danny Sullivan in the No. 53 Forsythe-Brown March/Cosworth. His run is a classy 196.292. Remarkable when you consider that there was only a .08 difference between his fastest lap and his slowest. Some of the veteran drivers turn in such consistent laps but it is even more phenomenal when a rookie does it. Danny sounds happy during his interivew: "I feel great. We did what we wanted to do. It feels good. Would have been nice to go over 200. But it feels good! We were a little down on RPM. But it feels great. We are an all-rookie team."

It is now 12:15 and while Sullivan makes his remarks to the crowd another driver is on the track in a red and white car with Intermedics written in black on the sides. It is Gordon Smiley, the intense sports car driver from Nebraska via Grapevine, Texas. People in the turns notice that he is a little erratic in his patterns. One photographer in the second turn says to himself, "I don't think he will be around again".

Going into the third turn on his second practice lap the rear end of No. 35 starts to come around and then, instead of letting the car go into the inevitable spin, Smiley attempts to bring the car back

Bob Lazier ran over some debris on the track. It popped his tire going down the back stretch and he coasted into the fourth turn. Lazier returned to Denver when his friend, Gordon Smiley was fatally injured.

IMS-Snoddy

We show the photos of the Gordon Smiley accident without explanation or comment. It is a part of Speedway history.

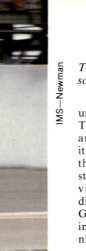

IMS—Newman

Tom Bigelow loses it and spins down the south chute.

under control with a crank to the right. The ground effects of the car take hold and instead of settling back in the groove it makes a sharp right turn and shoots up the bank at near qualifying speed. It strikes the wall almost head-on and virtually explodes on impact. It disintegrates into three major pieces with Gordon's body in one. He is killed instantly; the first Speedway fatality in nine years.

Because of damage to the track surface, the track remains closed for several hours while the maintenance men repair the surface. Pancho Carter and Mario Andretti, the next drivers out to qualify, supervise and ask Jerry Sneva and Don Whittington to test the repairs by taking a series of laps around the track. Jerry and Don report their findings to the official in charge and then go back out for more testing. Finally at 2:32 the track meets the approval of all concerned and it is once again opened.

Pancho makes a fine run in the Alex Foods March/Cosworth No. 3 . . . it is 198.950. Alex Morales, the car's owner and his many brothers, have owned race cars since the Legion Ascot days of the early 1930s. His "Tamale Wagons" have been notable in California sprint car racing for almost 50 years as have his Mexican foods. Pancho eludes to the Smiley accident when he is interviewed: "It was driven under difficult circumstances. But the car performed real well, but we didn't have the opportunity to get the car out. It has some more left in it. The track was different than it was this morning. There are a lot of things that can contribute to that. I'm not sure if it was the incident this morning or not."

Mario Andretti is the next driver on the track in Pat Patrick's dark blue and red No. 40 STP Wildcat/Cosworth. The fans' interest is revived. From his practice sessions Mario has shown himself to be the only driver to consistently be able to run as well as Mears and Cogan. It's a good run but not good enough. The first lap is just over 204 but then it falls down to the 202 bracket. A good run but certainly no record. 203.172 is the average and will, undoubtedly, place him well towards the front. Possibly in the front row. "The wind was whipping the car. I am thankful to my crew; for all their good work. We had a little engine trouble yesterday but we got it straightened out."

Al Unser, another top practicer, is up next but his run is not as impressive as would be expected. The first lap is 198 but then it drops down so that the four-lap average is only 195.567. Al is driving Bobby Hillin's Longhorn Racing/Cosworth. Al is obviously disappointed with his performance: "I just didn't have the

Eckler

Danny Sullivan, one of the fine crop of rookies.

Whitlow

Johnny Rutherford, with eighteen races behind him and three victories looks forward to his nineteenth race.

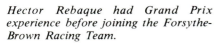

Hector Rebaque had Grand Prix experience before joining the Forsythe-Brown Racing Team.

IMS Reed

A. J. Foyt DOESN'T seem to be having a good day.

Veteran sportscaster, Lou Palmer.

Al Bloemker, author, and historian.

Veteran driver Duke Nalon is interviewed by announcer Jim Phillippe.

Pole-winner Rick Mears.

Josele Garza and his team manager, Bobby Unser have a lot of mechanical problems to work out. This seems to be one of them.

car set right. It started pushing real hard. I just didn't have things together today. I came here to race and race hard and I don't feel that we did today. I don't feel that my speed is competitive."

Don Whittington comes in with a very good 200.725 average in one of the family's March/Cosworths, unsponsored and plain-looking but one of the fastest cars on the track. This year all of the Whittington cars are yellow and as yet they have no trim. Of the run Don says: "I had it sideways for awhile in turn #1 on the 3rd lap. Other than that we had it pretty nice, but that sure took the wind out of my sails. I had to back off a whole lot."

Chip Ganassi, a twenty-three year old rookie from Pittsburgh, qualifies at the most respectable speed of 197.704 in Jack Rhoades Wildcat/Cosworth No. 12 and is elated: "Well I'm sure that when people look at this they'll know that we didn't run this fast all week and all I can say is thanks. I'm glad we hung in there and I'm glad qualifying is over to tell the truth. I graduated from college last week and that checkered flag felt better than my diploma."

Chip's elation isn't shared by Greg Leffler who only gets in two laps in Sherm Armstrong's black and orange No. 43 before his crew yellow-flags him. He was running just over 191.

Another driver from south of the border, Hector Rebaque, the 26-year old with Grand Prix experience stands on the second Forsythe-Brown March/Cosworth to the tune of 195.684. Hector's remarks: "Well it was a bit difficult. We were getting a bit of understeer. The car was handling well but for a little bit of push. I think it's quite a ride. The main thing is to be in the race and of course in the finish."

Blond Herm Johnson, cruises his Eagle/Chevy No. 28 to a speed of 195.929 and remembering how he had been bumped in 1981 quipped: (In response to whether he gets bumped or not) "I don't have any opinion. I think I'll go home and wait until they call me. If I'm in I'm in, and I'm not going through another week sitting on a bubble. Everything was so anti-climatic. The car was running fine and the crew has been just great. GOD BLESS AMERICA AND CHEVROLET ENGINES.

His speed seems to be safe unless a lot of cars which haven't shown much speed up to now suddenly get hot. By now the end of the qualifying line can be seen. Bill

OFFICIAL PROGRAM COVER

For those who didn't attend the race, this is the program cover art work under the coordination of Frederick Junclaus and Bill Donaldson of the Speedway Staff. The photographer was William Tobias. A far departure from the traditional cover art it concisely depicts the Hall of Fame Museum.

First in line for 34 years! This is the van in which Larry Bisceglia shows up at the front gate long before the track opens for practice.

This is one way to announce your car is for sale. When Ray Lipper was denied a driver's test he immediately placed his Eagle/Chevy on the block. It was purchased by the Hall Bros. for Tom Bigelow.

Query

Whittington, roars to a 201.027 average and is quite happy. "It feels good. All the guys that worked on the car have got everything working well. The wind affected Don this morning but my car was pretty well glued down. I just flat footed it all the way around. I'm happy, the crew is happy and it worked out pretty good."

Tom Sneva, who used to hold the track record, p.m. (pre-Mears) makes his run in George Bignotti's Texaco Star March/Cosworth No. 7. The first lap is 203 plus, but then he rubs the backstretch wall. He slowed a bit but still clocked an average lap speed of 201.027. It was a hairy run but particularly successfull. "Goodyear doesn't make whitewalls so

we thought we'd help them out with it. (Tagging wall) I wasn't sure whether I'd cracked a wheel or anything so I had to tiptoe down into #3. It gets your attention pretty good. It's not quite as fast as we were hoping for. We had ran a little bit faster than that and thought we had a little bit left, but there has to be an easier way to get whitewalls on your tires. We'll try something different next time. Thanks to the crew!"

Bearded Chet Fillip, who has supermodified antecedents, comes in after two laps at over 196. Must be some sort of mechanical malfunction as his average was quite safe.

The day's last driver expected to make a good run is "Super Tex", A.J. Foyt.

Seemingly mellowed after his bad accident of last year at Michigan, he is granting interviews, making nice with the media men and generally seems to be a changed person. It is a welcome change! His speed average is 203.332 which is good enough to place him in the front row, at least temporarily. He is driving a car which has seen little practice; one that has white trim along with the "Coyote orange". He has been practicing mostly with the No. 14 which is orange with blue trim. Speculation begins making the rounds whether A.J. will put George "Ziggy" Snider in the backup which is capable of running 200. A.J. had often done this for Ziggy in the past. Says A.J.: "Well, we really didn't get to test

The upper eschelon: Penske and Mears . . .   *Andretti and Bobby Unser.*

Larson

Query

That can't have been a 200 mph lap.

Teddy Pilette is probably the first grandson of a 500 driver.

too much, and you know we didn't have too much time. My engine man Howard Gilbert has done a fantastic job; my whole crew has worked very hard. We have had some oil problems. All I can do is take my hat off to Penske and to Rick Mears."

One of the only Cosworth-powered Eagles in existence is up next with Chip Mead at the controls. His crew accepts an average of 193.819 which looks a bit shaky. The dark blue car seems to be just a little slower than the Chevy-powered Eagles from the Dan Gurney stable.

Chip doesn't sound too enthusiastic: "Well, it's a little slower than we wanted to go but considering the conditions and everying else, I guess we'll have to take it. I'll let you know next Sunday whether or not I feel safe at that speed. I'm going to get out of Indianapolis for the next week.

What do I want to do? Ride the bicycle or drive the race car ponders Howdy Holmes. It must be a slow morning.

Not running fast enough . . . Mario, or was it just a bad slice of pizza?

Tom Sneva and George Bignotti during the hectic qualifying session.

Roger McCluskey, USAC Director of Competition, and Charlie Thompson, Superintendent of the IMS discuss the condition of the track after the Gordon Smiley accident.

I'm going to take a rest. Thanks to my crew. They'll be doing some more work on the car in preparation for the race."

Jerry Sneva runs No. 69 just a wink slower than Mead but his crew doesn't have Mead's optimism so out comes the yellow bunting.

The track is opened for practice as spectators reflect on the afternoon. They have seen blinding speed and a moment of tragedy; perhaps the largest pre-race crowd in history and the fastest field average (198.748) ever.

The end of the long qualifying line is finally here. Geoff Brabham, whose father in 1961 completely revolutionized American Championship motor racing, goes out on the track in No. 21, another March/Cosworth sponsored by Pentax. Before his first lap on the clock is recorded there is a puff of smoke and the car immediately slows with a blown piston. The car is removed from the course and at 4:54 the track is opened for practice. Apparently the fans will have to

John Martin gets sideways and spins in the third turn. He was practicing prior to qualifying.

[34]

Phil Krueger, for the second straight year, crashed Joe Hunt's car in practice.

Two Penskes and a Foyt. The front row with Rick Mears on the pole, followed by Kevin Cogan and A. J. Foyt.

wait for tomorrow to see any further qualifying.

Rick Mears, after the track closed at 6:00, was awarded the $10,000 Budweiser Pole Position Award ... plus other attendant goodies which always come to the pole-setter.

SUNDAY, MAY 16
Warm, Humid and
Late Thunderstorms

After yesterday's hectic day, this afternoon seemed very tame by comparison. In the morning practice period only 12 cars participated with

Gary Bettenhausen clocking the fastest lap speed just over 193. Not particularly impressive. Practice extended until 12:25 since no cars were in line to qualify at the normal time for such proceedures. It looked like it would be a slow day.

Chet Fillip finally pushed his blue No. 39 to the line and then after two laps in the 194's and one in the 192's his crew again hung out the yellow. That will leave him with only one more attempt.

After Fillip's incomplete attempt there was an afternoon of practice well into "happy hour". At 5:18 the day had it's first qualifying attempt with Geoff Brabham making a VERY successful run

... 198.906 in the No. 21 Pentax March/Cosworth. "Well, we had a lot of problems yesterday. There was a mix-up with the green flag at the start of the pit lane which meant that we did not have an official run. I was flat out in turn #2 when the yellow light came on so when I came in I realized there had been a mix-up and then we went to the back of the line. And we went out and unfortunately we lost the engine. I just can't say too much about the guys who worked on the car. We've had a lot of problems the past couple of days and they have just worked really hard. I'm just glad we've got in the race today. And without any problems.

Mitch, the Gypsy, is a colorful member of A. J. Foyt's pit crew.

Michael Warren, from the cast of "Hill Street Blues", clowns with a young fan, Joey Boren.

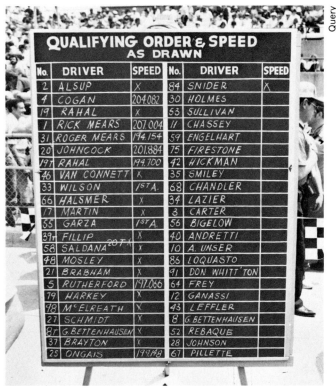

QUALIFYING ORDER & SPEED
AS DRAWN

No.	DRIVER	SPEED	No.	DRIVER	SPEED
2	ALSUP	X	84	SNIDER	X
4	COGAN	204.082	30	HOLMES	
19	RAHAL	X	53	SULLIVAN	
1	RICK MEARS	207.004	11	CHASSEY	
31	ROGER MEARS	194.154	59	ENGELHART	
20	JOHNCOCK	201.884	75	FIRESTONE	
19T	RAHAL	194.700	42	HICKMAN	
46	VAN CONNETT	X	35	SMILEY	
33	WILSON	1ST A.	68	CHANDLER	
66	HALSMER	X	34	LAZIER	
17	MARTIN	X	3	CARTER	
55	GARZA	1ST A.	56	BIGELOW	
39T	FILLIP	X	40	ANDRETTI	
58	SALDANA	201? X	10	A. UNSER	
48	MOSLEY	X	86	LOQUASTO	
21	BRABHAM	X	91	DON WHITT'TON	
5	RUTHERFORD	197.066	64	FREY	
79	HARKEY	X	12	GANASSI	
98	McELREATH	X	43	LEFFLER	
27	SCHMIDT	X	8	G. BETTENHAUSEN	
8T	G. BETTENHAUSEN	X	52	REBAQUE	
37	BRAYTON	X	28	JOHNSON	
25	ONGAIS	199.148	67	PILLETTE	

This board on the starting line gives ready information as to the success or failure of qualifying runs.

AVERAGE SPEED
FAST ENOUGH!

The signboard over the garage tells the story.

And now we're just going to get the car ready for race day. The car was pushing pretty badly and I had to get off at just about every corner. We felt that it didn't matter if we qualified at 196 to 200. We were still going to be in the same row."

Greg Leffler was unsuccessful trying to qualify his No. 43 with three laps just over 193 but Dennis Firestone got in a fine run of 197.217 in his dark red Eagle/Milodon Chevy. His remarks relate to yesterday: "I wanted to do a 200 lap for my good friend Gordon Smiley, but I couldn't do it."

Rookies Jim Hickman is the last driver away in the maroon No. 42 March/Cosworth but after a promising lap of 195 he drops down to two 192 laps and out comes the yellow.

In the few minutes remaining before the 6:00 deadline the track is, once again, open for practice. Five minutes later the track shuts down because of a rainstorm and there is feverish action for the first time of the day with crews trying to get their cars and equipment back into Gasoline Alley. The field average is a phenominal 198.685!

Gordon Johncock's No. 20 is ready to race.

MONDAY, MAY 17
Warm and Partly Cloudy

It was a quiet day after the weekend's hectic activity with most of the better speeds set by cars which have already qualified. Mario Andretti was fastest with an "unspectacular" (by the weekend's standards) speed of 199. Perhaps the biggest news of the day was the shakedown ride of Bobby Unser in the Schlitz No. 50. Was he test hopping for Josele Garza or planning to drive himself after announcing that he had "retired" for the year? This gave everyone at the annual Monroe Rookie Recognition banquet at the Columbia Club, something to talk about besides the fabulous food, entertainment and gifts (steak and lobster, The Lettermen and suitably inscribed mugs). Not to be outdone by Monroe, Budweiser held a Salute to Rick Mears, the pole winner, in the Speedway Motel.

TUESDAY, MAY 18
Warm, Partly Cloudy, Thunderstorms

Action picked up, today, but not too much. There were 25 cars on the track with both qualified and unqualified drivers running. Danny Ongais (198.938) was fastest of the qualified boys and Chet Fillip, of the unsuccessfuls, had a 194.258. The track shut down at 4:30 due to a thunderstorm.

Bobby Unser was again out in Josele Garza's ride which seems to be having a little front end trouble. He maintains that he is "retired" but who knows? Race drivers are funny people.

Bob Lazier has announced that he is returning to Vail, Colorado and will no longer attempt to qualify. He was affected by the death of his good friend, Gordon Smiley. Temporarily, at least, his place in the Wysard No. 34 has been

[36]

Joe Cloutier is once again serving as President of the Speedway after John Cooper's resignation. Unassuming and with a great sense of humor, Joe will be in full charge.

taken by veteran Steve Krisiloff. In another change, John Mahler has decided to drive his own car, No. 92, leaving Jan Sneva walking.

Among those cars still struggling are Vern Schuppan and Bill Vukovich in the highly-touted yellow and blue Kraco Specials. They are both Penske/Cosworths but they just don't seem to be finding enough speed to qualify. Bill Alsup, usually a good qualifier, has also

been having trouble getting speed out of his No. 2, A. B. Dick Penske/Cosworth.

WEDNESDAY, MAY 19
Warm, Partly Cloudy, Thunderstorms

On a slow day, Desire Wilson livened things up a bit with an 883-foot loop down the south chute. It even diverted some of the "Snake Pit" habituees (or "sons of habituees") from fighting, slinging frisbees and asking to see parts of

ladies' anatomies which are usually hidden. Desire was uninjured and on the track later in the day before it shut down because of rain late in the afternoon. Al Unser was fastest of the day (198.281) in Bobby Hillin's No. 10 which has qualified and second fastest, with a surprising 197.4, was Greg Leffler, in the Armstrong No. 43 which has not.

Touring in the 191 bracket was Bobby Unser, still testing Josele Garza's car. Doesn't look like Bobby is running fast enough to make the race either, although he may get things sorted out by the weekend. One of the happier drivers was Pete Halsmer who finally got up to 195. The week has been frustrating for Pete with a pile of blown engines being all that he has to show for his month's work.

Steve Chassey, who replaced Bill Vukovich in the Hubler No. 11 when Vuky moved to the Kraco No. 18 was running laps at 185 which was about the same speed as Vukovich.

Once again the track had to shut down early due to rain but this time there was a pizza party in garage No. 33 hosted by Domino's Pizza, sponsors of Howdy Holmes' No. 30.

THURSDAY, MAY 20
Warm, Partly Cloudy, Thunderstorms

It is getting very late in the game to get up to speed for qualifying but certainly Dale Whittington made it and it would appear that the first-ever three-brother team will be starting in a "500". Of course, the Unser and Chevrolet brothers have competed before but never have all three been in the same race. Dale's average for one lap was 198.8 and if he can do it on the weekend, it will get him in the race.

Jim Hickman has also been running well in the No. 42 and Bill Alsup got near to qualifying speed.

Drivers' tests ran out for three hopeful rookies. Rusty Schmidt couldn't finish the 175 mph phase in Rolla Vollstedt's white Offy and Teddy Pilette couldn't get enough speed to make the 175 either. Teddy's late grandfather, Theodore, did qualify for the 1913 race in his Mercedes-Knight and his father, former Formula I Grand Prix driver Andre Pilette, was in Teddy's pit. It is quite a heritage of speed.

The Miller Pit Stop Contest has been holding elimination matches and next Thursday will present the finalists. The crews selected will include those of Rick Mears' No. 1, A. J. Foyt's No. 14, Gordon Johncock's No. 20, Mario Andretti's No. 40, Bobby Rahal's No. 19, Bill Alsup's No. 2 and Tom Sneva's No. 7. There is a lot of money posted for the winners.

Greg Leffler leads Pete Halsmer down the front chute as the two try to get up to speed.

Crucean

Spike Gehlhausen and Jerry Sneva seem to have found something to laugh about.

Wendt

Sometimes racing gets a little boring. Doesn't it, Hector?

Crucean

Larry "Boom Boom" Cannon and Sprinter Chuck Amati.

Whitlow

After a few laps it gets kinda' hard to hear.

Whitlow

Could he be a Bobby Unser fan?

Scoggan

Jerry Karl's car was one of the better looking cars to fail to qualify.

de Brier

Two-time winner, Rodger Ward.

[39]

Circle Bar Truck Corrall

A race fan walked up to new Indy car owner Tom Mitchell and said, "Say, why'd you buy one of these things?" Mitchell replied in a deep Texas drawl, "Well sir, this young fella come by my truckstop with his Supermodified hitched up behind his truck. We got to talking, and pretty soon I found myself in Phoenix, Arizona and I owned one of these here Indy cars. Sure like it." Driver Chet Fillip and tech man Bill Hite kept a low profile while running their new Eagle at Indy and owner Mitchell kicked around Gasoline Alley in his Levi's and boots. They had a good time, made the show and proved that running in the Indianapolis 500 can indeed be fun.

The winner of the Louis Schwitzer Award for race car design was announced and it is Geoff Ferris, who produced the Penske Pc-10, of which a bit has been heard lately. The award was given by the Indiana section of the Society of Automotive Engineers.

The only incident of the day was John Mahler's crash in the first turn. He was driving his own Offy No. 92 which hit the wall with the right side of the car, damaging it considerably. "S.T.W. Bat" was uninjured.

It was announced that Intermedics, sponsors of Gordon Smiley's ill-fated No. 35, had decided to sponsor Gordon Johncock and Mario Andretti's machines in the race.

FRIDAY, MAY 21
Warm and Rainy

What was to be the last day of practice before the final qualifying weekend was all but washed out by a rain which fell until early afternoon and kept the track from opening until 4:00. Young blond Mike Chandler, son of L.A. Times publisher, Otis Chandler (who would have liked to be a race driver himself) ran 197.238 for the day's fast time. He barely nosed out Tony "Toto" Bettenhausen

Whitlow

Bill Alsup looks happy as Chris Economacki interviews him after his qualification run. The happiness was only temporary.

Josele Garza loses it and clobbers the wall adding to his woes. This was just not his month.

Mahoney Photos

[41]

Billy Scott's No. 88 had one of the most attractive paint jobs on the track. Unfortunately, the car didn't run as well as it looked. Billy failed to qualify.

who ran a respectable 197.152 in the Provimi Veal No. 16.

Two other drivers who have been lagging in the quest for speed are Josele Garza and Jerry Sneva. Josele, after some help from Bobby Unser was able to run 194.5 and Jerry, 196.078, in No. 69.

Johnny Parsons was finally signed to drive the Wysard March/Cosworth after Bob Lazier and Steve Krisiloff had shots at it. Supposedly Krisiloff will go into the Patrick backup car which Mario Andretti is testing.

In a tearful statement to the media Bobby Unser reiterated that while he is not retired he has a committment to Josele Garza and will honor that. Had Joesle qualified last weekend with ease, as he had done last year, Unser had plans to accept rides in either a Penske or Patrick car. "I got myself into whatever I got myself into, and I must make the best of it . . ." said a misty-eyed Unser. "I never had any intentions of retiring." Obviously he is disappointed that he will not be among the starting field but it is his decision. The Saturday lineup is announced with Dale Whittington first out to be followed by Jerry Sneva and Steve Chassey, (if they are ready).

SATURDAY, MAY 22
Partly Cloudy, Warm

The track opened for practice and there were no incidents in the pre-qualification periods other than the normal amount of yellow flags for tow-ins, and track inspections. Of the unqualified cars, the fastest lap was run by Chet Fillip at 196.121 with Rick Mears test-hopping No. 1 at a conservative 199.689. Just before the runs began the Joie Chitwood Thrill show did their act in front of the front-stretch stands. Among the exhibitions was Tim Chitwood driving down the stretch with J. L. Martin Jr., standing on the side of the car. Nothing to get excited about?? Tim was driving the car on two wheels. He did it for 9/10ths of a mile which is, apparently, a new record.

Dale Whittington was first out of the slot and the 22-year old from Florida made a very consistent run of 197.694 in one of the family's yellow March/Cosworths. Quoth Dale: "Great! I received quite a bit of help from Don and Bill. I'm quite a bit excited. Come race day it's just whatever works out. We just want to race."

Jerry Sneva wants to race too, and it looks like he will with the 195.270 which he averages. The car is the Hoffman No. 69, a white job with blue and red trim. Just as he heads for the checker, there is a big puff of smoke. He is going so well and so near the end that he just keeps going and with no power to speak of he takes the flag. Jerry tells the fans about it: "Thanks for the new rule that you only get 2 warmup laps. I come off of 4 and the crew is waving the green flag and Sweeney is waving the checkered so I'm smiling, thinking everything is fine and all of a sudden the motor blows up. I tried to get it out of gear to coast it to the line cause it was pulling it down bad. I guess we practiced just the right amount of laps

this morning. I think the time will be safe. I'm going to celebrate my birthday early. One of these days there will be four of us. We'll have the field covered." It turned out that even with the blown engine, Jerry's last lap was 193.175 which averaged with the other good laps was enough to qualify him.

Bill Alsup doesn't do too well but it seems to be as fast the car can run. He has a borderline 193.123 and sounds dejected in his interview: "I don't feel safe with this speed right now, I tell ya. I guess we lost a valve on the motor or something. It kind of went soft. And I feel terrible cause the guys worked so hard and we owe a lot to the Penske crew. My guys just busted their hump to get this one for us. I sure hope it holds but I don't feel good about it. I could feel it getting softer and softer. There's not much you can do. Just flat to the floor and hold on. I'm afraid all we can do is just set back and wait."

Chet Fillip, 194.879, better than Alsup is still close to the "bubble" but as this is his first year at the track he doesn't seem to mind: "I'm the happiest person here. They say that Texans don't waste anything. We had our other two attempts and used the last one. Well, I've been nervous all week but I don't think I told anybody. The car got kind of squirrely coming off of four on my last lap. Where is Ozona? Down in the middle of nowhere in southwest Texas."

A 191 first lap for Gary Bettenhausen obviously isn't going to be enough so the yellow comes out right away and then Billy Vukovich, Gary's long-time buddy, takes a 185 and a 196. He comes in on his own to await something or other. The 196 lap is the best any Kraco car has done all month. There may be hope for the team yet.

Tom Bigelow blows the engine of No. 56 after only a 185 lap and it takes a half-hour to clean off the track.

Garza is still unsuccessful. 193 and a half is the best he can do and he pulls in after only two laps. This time he is in the Schlitz No. 55.

Johnny Parsons does about the same in the Wysard car and he, too, is yellow-flagged. Jim Hickman is more successful and boots the Rattlesnake Racing's No. 42 to an average of 196.217. A good average for the rookie: "We struggled first part of the session here and I'd like to come out and say that it would be refreshing for somebody to come and say "Well, just real good driving". Those that think it is just the driver is in error. The crew worked overtime, they put in an 18-20 hour day. The owners gave me what I needed to go fast. The folks from Stroh's supported me. It takes that kind of united effort to go fast around here. There's a lot of work to be done there."

Vern Schuppan tries the Kraco backup car, but it can do no better than 188 on two laps; actually the laps are identical

Johncock takes Indy. Bosch takes pride.

Gordon Johncock owned Indy '82 from that split second when he roared past the checker in a battle-scarred Wildcat Mark 8B. In the belly of the beast, a Cosworth V-8 engine—700 thundering horses in harness to the firepower of eight Bosch spark plugs.

Yes, Bosch takes pride. But we also take notes. We're not in racing for the glory or the money (those belong to Gordon). We're in it for the know-how. That's why the plugs that won Indy were carefully packed and on a plane almost before Johncock's engine had cooled. A Bosch research team in Stuttgart is even now putting each of those winning plugs through the kind of painstaking chemical and physical analysis NASA once lavished on moon rocks.

Why? Because discovering just how well Bosch plugs survived the hairiest, most gut-wrenching 500 miles in the world will help us do better what we already do so well. Make spark plugs that perform. Beautifully. On the track and on the street.

 ROBERT BOSCH

which may indicate that is all the car can do.

Mike Chandler makes it, and makes it in very good shape, when he runs the Freeman Gurney Eagle/Chevy No. 68 over 198. His average is 198.042 which sets a new record for normally aspirated engines. "The extra miles per hour wasn't me. It was the car. This was the easiest four laps I've had. With a crew of Dan Gurney working so hard, my job is the easy job. I wish I could lie a little and say that it was a flat out ride all the way around, but the car has quite a bit left and I'm not in a position to set up front row and take a chance and run it flat. So I just ran it comfortably and I'm in the show. Well this is our race motor, our race set-up and I guess I don't have anything to do. We're ready for the race. I just also had the guys on Dan Gurney's crew put so much time into this. It is really astounding. Wayne Leary and Steve Frase and Dan Gurney and the sponsors — I mean I have the easy job. Without the people I just listed, I wouldn't be here."

These seem to be the only cars interested in qualifying now so the track opens for practice at 12:45. About two hours later Phil Kruger hits the wall in the fourth turn, badly damaging the car and giving him a slight concussion which must be treated in Methodist Hospital. He was first checked in the infield hospital which is named for Dr. Thomas Hanna, long time official track physician who has recently passed away. The car, badly damaged, is owned by Joe Hunt, of magneto fame. It is a Crysen McLaren/Chevy. Last year Phil also bent one of Joe Hunt's cars, an elderly Eagle. It got more elderly in short notice.

When the Kruger wreckage was cleaned up Johnny Parsons made a successful run in the Wysard No. 34. It is 195.929, certainly NOT chopped liver. "I didn't plan it that way (waiting until the last minute to find a ride). I'm just happy to be an Indy driver again. Well not too many chassis adjustments, we been working with the engine. Davey pumped the engine up a little bit. It seems like we were down on power a bit. I'm not sure. I'm just getting used to this race car. It's a fine race car. And I'm very appreciative to have the opportunity to qualify. It was pretty close to a flat out run all the way around. I haven't really noticed much of a change in track conditions since this morning. But when the heat rises it usually slows it down a little bit. But we really didn't notice much of that. I'm going to have the best seat in the house this race day."

The track opens for practice again but then closes when Tony Bettenhausen decides to make his run. It is close to Parsons' 195.429 and the Provimi Veal crew is ecstatic. "Thank you very much. This one belongs to the crew. They did

the whole job. And I'll tell you what. We've had a tough last three months and they haven't stopped working yet. They get 99% of the credit. Well we didn't lose an engine yesterday. We ran 197 and we thought that we would be happy with that, come out this morning, do a little practice and then put it in line. But our first hot lap today, when we were getting up to speed, our gear box broke. So the crew, for about the 15th time went back and went to work. They fixed it and made it right and it's all theirs. I want to thank my sponsors, car owners and crew. They did a hell of a job. I think that we might just happen to have a spare engine that would fit into Gary's car, if he needs it." With as much engine trouble as there has been this year this is a particularly altruistic statement. Wonder if Gary will need one?

The last run of the day comes a little past 4:00 and it is "Ziggy" Snider driving the Gordon Smiley backup. It is the exact duplicate, name, number, and color. It will not run that name in the race, however, should it qualify as the Intermedic sponsorship has gone to Pat Patrick's cars. Rather, it will be named after owner Bob Fletcher's Cobre Tire operation in Phoenix. Ziggy's speed is 195.493 ... GOOD ENOUGH. A. J. Foyt can take most of the credit for arranging the deal.

The rest of the day is for practice as there are no other cars which seem ready to qualify. The field's average for the 31 qualified cars is 197.832. Also not chopped liver.

SUNDAY, MAY 23
Cloudy and Mild

This is the day everyone has been waiting for so far, with joy or trepidation, to see just who will make the final lineup. With several competitive drivers still awaiting their runs this day usually is packed with drama. During the practice period there were two incidents which added even more spice to the day.

John Martin spun Rolla Volstedt's yellow No. 17 Offy in the third-turn and came to rest down in number-four with nothing more than a flat tire. And later, Steve Chassey driving the No. 11 Hubler/Q 95 Rattlesnake/Cosworth spun and hit the wall in the first turn causing enough damage to the right side and rear of the car to put it on the sidelines for the day. Steve took the manditory trip to the infield Hanna Medical Center and was treated for minor chest contusions and abrasions and then released. The car was a fine piece of workmanship but never really got up to a safe qualifying speed. It had, however, had the second fastest practice speed of the day ... 192.802. Pete Halsmer lead the practicing contingent with 196.635 and it would appear that he

has an excellent chance of making the starting lineup.

Despite his morning spin, graying John Martin became first out to qualify at noon but he came in on his first lap after taking the flag. Just not enough speed apparently.

Josele Garza was next away in his white and reddish-brown No. 55 March/Cosworth. With Bobby Unser calling the shots he gets his hoof in it and scores with a 194.500 average which looks close. It is in the race although bumping won't start until one more car qualifies. It was Josele's third, and last, qualifying attempt.

Tom Bigelow tries a new car, which has been purchased for him ... an Eagle/Chevy but his time is short of what is required and he is flagged by his crew. The same is true of Pete Halsmer in No. 66 and Roger Rager in No. 72 and then the track is opened for practice. A few minutes later Halsmer pushes his yellow mount to the line once again and this time he is successful. 194.595! It isn't red hot but it does fill the field. There are several cars with slower speeds.

Tom Bigelow comes up about an hour later and the car has been renumbered 27 and renamed the H.B.K. Racing Eagle which seems to do the trick ... 194.784. Better than either Garza or Halsmer, and good enough to bump Bill Alsup whose discouragment is evident when he says, "Going to head home, not much chance for another ride today."

Along about 4:00 p.m. Gary Betten-hasuen pushes Lindsey Hopkins" blue No. 8 to the line. It is a Lightning/Cosworth. Gary, a veteran who use to drive for Roger Penske and might have had it all had he not decided to run sprint cars, makes a very consistent run and his average is good enough to bump Chip Mead. It's 195.673! Gary says: "Well I'll tell you what. It's been a long bumpy road. We've had a lot of little things happen to us and a lot of big things. We had a couple of engines that only ran a lap or two. But this engine that is in this car right now, it must have 700 miles on it. We've run every day with the two cars. We kept switching back and forth. If it wasn't for my crew chief, Chuck Buckman and Ronnie and my car designer and my car builder ... believe me, we were so far off. About an hour ago we were stuck at about 189 mph. And we just made some changes and stumbled onto it. We had the wing down low. When Roger built the car he built the back end so that we could have the choice of running the wing down low or up high. And we hadn't tried it up high so we figured we were stuck we might as well do something. So we moved it up and immediately picked up about 3 mph. Our car designer and chassis man decided to run some more tow-in in the right rear and put more stagger across the rear tires.

[44]

And immediately we picked up another 3 mph. So, you know, it's just crazy little things that make a big difference around this place. Lindsey let me take the cars last September and I've had them home in my shop for the last 6 months. My two boys, Gary & Tod have been working their butts off for 6 months on it. And a neighbor boy that is 18 years old has been working his butt off. It was a family deal. It looked bad up until about the last fifteen minutes. I didn't do it intentionally (run faster laps than Tony) but I'm not going to cry about it. Because this way if I get bumped, he gets bumped too. It looks like there's a lot of brothers that like to race. I'd just like to say thanks to my car owner, Lindsey Hopkins, for having faith in me six months ago, for letting us take the cars and work on them. Believe me, I'm so happy right now I could cry. Everything started out good and then we broke a couple of engines. And everything just went wrong. We ran the old car for the first week and then switched the engine and put it into this new car. This car had never been started until we got here. No wind tunnel tests, no dyno for the engines. So it was just kind of a guess deal. I guess we got it all together right at the end."

Practice resumes and apparently everyone is awaiting "happy hour". Bill Whittington runs into the wall in turn-one and is taken to Methodist Hospital in downtown Indianapolis suffering chest contusions. He is soon released. The crew announces that it will rebuild the already qualified car and Chief Steward Tom Binford OK's the plans provided the car still meets the same specifications as the wrecked one. Methodist Hospital announces that Phil Kruger, who had crashed yesterday and sustained head injuries is due to be released so long as he does not attempt to drive any more this May. "Happy Hour" arrives and Roger Mears, who is on the bubble, undergoes the tortures of the damned. But no one attempts to qualify. Bill Alsup gets into one of the Kraco cars and sits there while his crew makes some final adjustments but time runs out before they can get him going. He has his engine running but is not ready to pull away when the gunshot from high in the tower sounds the time of 6 o'clock. Mears is finally able to breathe.

As an aftermath A. J. Watson pretty well sums it up: "The biggest problem we had is the 3.2 million dollars we didn't have. Our operation had a couple hundred thousand and that's not enough anymore. I think our sponsor Vermont American has seen the light that we need more money for next year."

And the controversial Salt Walther, who wasn't around much this year, echos Watson: "We ran short of money and couldn't afford a PC9 or other ground effects car. I ran as fast as they did here

"Welcome To Indy, 'Lil John"

This prematurely gray gentleman is known throughout one segment of the world of wheels as 'Lil John. His full name is John Buttera and his work prior to coming to the Indianapolis Motor Speedway has been featured, praised and disected by every hot rod and street rod magazine on the stands. John Buttera is one of the nation's premier builders of cars known as street rods, those pre-1949 wheeled-vehicles that defy the adage "form follows function." Buttera's eye for design coupled with his innovative craftsmanship hasn't yet been seen at Indy, but we hope he reaches a point whereby circle track fans will be accorded an opportunity to see his creativity in action.

He came to Indy as a neophyte along with partner Ronnie Capps and enlisted the services of driver Dennis Firestone. Amidst the world of hand-formed, beautifully flowing metal Buttera was like a kid in a great new neighborhood. He knew he wasn't at home, but he wanted to be. Judging by the help he received from the veterans coupled with his own talent, we'd say Indianapolis now has a new pair of welcome hands working back in Gasoline Alley.

Whitlow
Hungness

three years ago, and that's the best we can do. If I can find a ride in a ground effects car, fine, if not I'll just pass it again this year. I've seen Mosley and Spike, they're using their heads, they're smart, if you can't get a good grounds-effects car, there is no sense getting yourself in the hospital for nothing. I've been doing some acting in some TV shows, and I'm going to wait until I have a good car, no sense getting into trouble with a car that isn't even close."

The bottom line is MEGA BUCKS. If you have 'em it is a whole lot easier and without them you really have to scratch. They won't guarantee success (the Kraco team is a good example of this) but they sure improve the chances.

WEEK OF MAY 24
Warm, Rainy and Humid

This is the time for garage work. If it runs; you tear it down. If it doesn't run you tear it down. And if you don't know if it is running or not you tear it down anyway, maybe two or three times. The Oldtimers' Club Barbeque is on Monday night in the infield for those who have been closely associated with the race for more than 20 years ... drivers, owners, officials, riding mechanics, Speedway employee's (full time) and us writers, photographers and various media representatives who have been lucky enough to con Al Bloemker out of a pit badge.

Wednesday night is the annual Press Club party for the last row of qualifiers.

[45]

Hubler Chevrolet

Indianapolis based Chevrolet dealer Howard Hubler annually makes sure his company's name is involved with the world's most famous auto race. His sponsorship this year started out with WFBQ 95 on the car No. 11 driven by Steve Chassey. When it was wrecked beyond repair, Howard found a couple of new car owners, Bob and Bill Hall, who had purchased an Eagle only days before the last qualifying weekend. The Hall scenario was storybook. With virtually no practice time and a driver who had never been in a new Eagle, Tom Bigelow, they put the vehicle in the program. They jokingly said, "What's the big deal . . . you come here, buy a car, drum up some good help and go racing." Mechanics Rolla Vollstedt, Grant King and Wayne Leary assisted the teams' 11th hour effort and once again Howard Hubler had a car in the Indy 500. Nice job.

Kevin Cogan stands on the gas for Roger Penske.

There were racing-oriented ads all over town. This is a particularly good one. The car is Geoff Brabham's March in full racing colors.

Pete Halsmer, Tom Bigelow and Josele are honored (?) with a "roast". Robin Miller is roastmaster and he does a fine job of needling. Garza, who was among the missing, got some of the more barbed comments but Tom and Pete came in for their share. Seems that Josele who was so accessible last year when he won most of the popularity awards, has been a bit of a recluse this year with his appearances being restricted by either Schlitz or Bobby Unser. Wrong way to go, Josele. Robin also needles Janet Guthrie saying, 'she was Denny Zimmerman in drag."

The "carburetion tests" held on Thursday give the drivers one last chance to test their cars and scuff in some tires. There are no particularly noteworthy incidents but it gives the fans one more chance to see the cars running before the race The Miller Pit Stop Contest follows with Rick Mears' crew besting A J. Foyt's for the money ... $20,000 to the winner out of a total purse of $43,750.

Saturday is the "drivers' meeting" in front of the tower (although the REAL one was held Thursday UNDER the tower). It's main purpose, I guess, is to introduce the drivers and the "celebrities". The drivers then are escorted down to the 500 Festival Parade for their appearances there.

Others in the downtown area go over to the Howard Johnson's Motel for the annual Auto Racing Collectors Convention of which Jack Middleton is president. Racing memorabilia of all kinds is displayed and much sold (Dr. Tom Lucas, for example, bought giant-sized scrap books dating from 1946 to date which have photos of the starting fields of cars, newspaper articles, etc., They will be an interesting addition to his dental office over on Tibbs Ave.) There are photos, ticket stubs, old race cars, magazines, programs, pit badges, et al.

And then there is the race.

As an aftermath, the Victory Banquet is held at the Indianapolis Convention Center. There are only a few no shows, which is much better a turnout than last year. Some even have good excuses ... Garza apparently does not.

So there you have the month of May. It was thrilling, it was tragic; it was rewarding and it was heartbreaking. It was AUTO RACING!

Racing publisher (Speed Sport News) Christ Economacki interviews Josele Garza for Wide World of Sports for which Chris moonlights as a commentator.

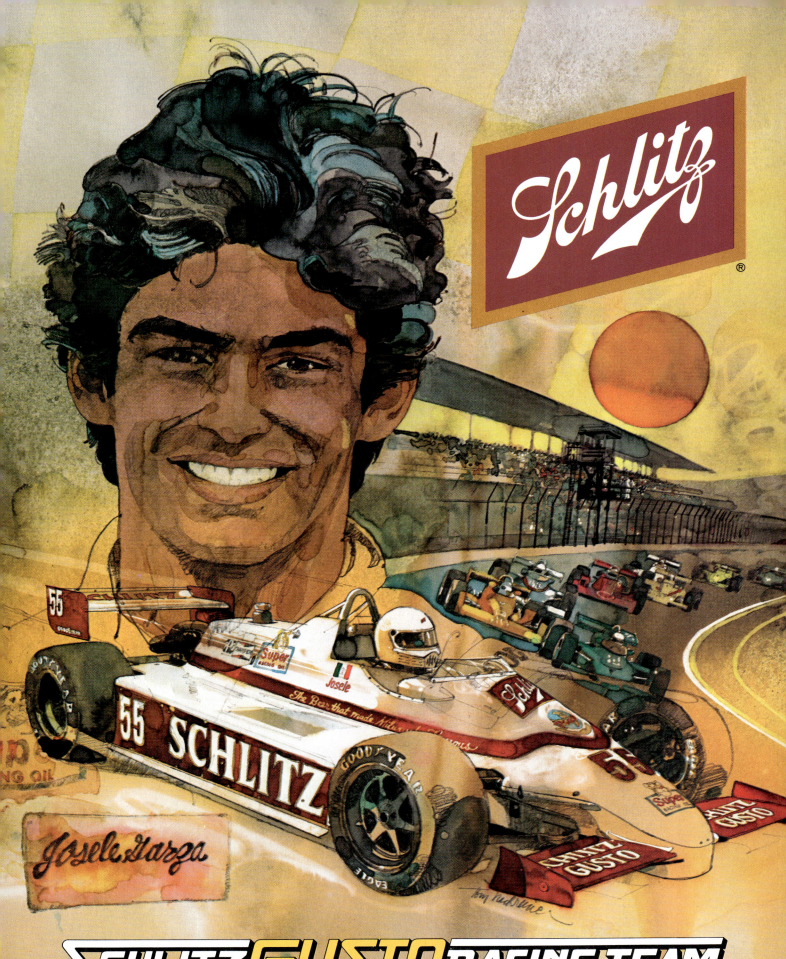

Josele Garza

SCHLITZ**GUSTO**RACING TEAM

Our track stars make us street wise.

Goodyear Racing Eagle

"Racing improves the breed" is a pit-row truism that's older than Nuvolari or Barney Oldfield. Three great examples of that great truth are the Goodyear Eagles for the street, the performance tires with real race breeding.

Because what we learned on all the race tracks of the world, we use in building the Eagle ST, GT and NCT.

And we learn a lot. Goodyear races more often than any other tire manufacturer. And we win more often.

Since 1971 alone, Goodyear race tires have won over 2,000 international events, including the biggest prizes in the racing world.

We've won in NASCAR, NHRA, IMSA GT, SCCA Can-Am, Trans Am, Formula One. The past ten

Indianapolis 500's. And more. In sheer race experience, nothing flies like the Eagles.

TAMED FOR THE STREET. BUT FAR FROM TAME.

Race breeding for street tires comes naturally to the world's leading racer. Our Eagle street radials even *look* like they're ready to fly.

All three have an aggressive low-profile stance and a tread pattern derived straight from the track.

On our Eagle NCT and GT, the tread pattern was inspired by our Formula One racing rain tire. On Eagle ST, the tread is a direct descendant of our two-time IMSA RS Champion tire.

All three Eagles are designed to deliver precise handling, cat-quick steering response and tenacious traction in both wet

and dry.

And our Eagle radials are available in a wide selection of sizes. Which means there's an Eagle radial that can give your car the race-bred performance that's made Goodyear a winner all around the world.

On the track or on the street, nothing flies like the Eagles.

Goodyear Street Eagles

Available in the Eagles' Nest at your Goodyear Dealer or Store.

COME UP TO GOODYEAR

GOOD/YEAR

QUALITY & INNOVATION

GOOD/YEAR

QUALITY AND INNOVATION

Query

deBrier

THE RACE

by Donald Davidson

Was bad weather going to interfere with the "500"?

After a glorious month with hardly any interruption by the elements, it all started to come apart. The Drivers' Meeting, usually held in bright sunshine in front of the control tower on the day before the race, had to be relocated because of rain for one of the very few occasions ever, and was moved to a huge marquee erected northeast of the tower behind the flag lot. Fortunately, concrete had been poured to form a mud-free platform this year; otherwise, it would have been quite miserable in there. Hundreds of spectators filed inside, trying to get a look at the drivers, but without much success, except for those who were able to elbow their way to the front of the throng.

When the meeting was over, the drivers departed, umbrellas in hand, on their way to the buses which would take them downtown for the Five Hundred Festival parade. Overcast skies with occasional showers was the scenario for the afternoon until quite late, when the sun broke through to add to the humid discomfort. Then, in the early evening, the heavens darkened and a blinding storm of torrential rain hit the Speedway.

Race morning dawned grey, cool and overcast. The track had dried, but it felt as if rain was lingering in the air. An enormous crowd, perhaps the largest ever, filed into the track at a steady rate. There did not appear to be so much of a jam-up this time, indicating that people were arriving at a more even flow than in some recent years.

Four retired race drivers, Sam Hanks (above), Freddy Agabashian (left), Rodger Ward (center) and Troy Ruttman (right) had a ball reliving memories of glory.

Mahoney Photos

[51]

One of the excellent bands which entertained before the race.

George, The T-Shirt Man. One of racing's most colorful entrepreneurs.

One amusing item, noted this year for the first time, was that several enterprising youngsters had shown up on West 16th Street with little red toy wagons. In return for some financial consideration, they were delighted to assist you in transporting your cumbersome cooler to the corner of Georgetown Road!

The bands played and the celebrities waved, and then, at about 9:15 a.m., the sun briefly broke through the watery skies. It quickly disappeared for a while, but then patches of blue began to appear. The skies cleared, and to everyone's delight by 10 a.m., there was hardly a cloud to be seen.

A delightful pre-race ceremony, unfortunately unnoticed by many, saw Troy Ruttman, Sam Hanks and Rodger Ward take a parade lap in their winning cars of 1952, 1957 and 1962 respectively, joined by Freddie Agabashian in the Cummins Diesel, with which he won the 1952 pole position. Nineteen sixty winner Jim Rathmann, runner-up both to Ruttman and to Hanks as well as to Ward's first of two winners in '59, stood by ready to drive the pace car.

As Louis Sudler sang the National Anthem, Bobby Unser was seen walking alone down the track. Dressed in a bright red firesuit, he walked along the grass verge, head down, arms swinging, body swaying from side to side, perhaps pondering over the fact that he would be spectating for the first time since 1962. He had been in every race since 1963, frequently starting from the front row. This time he had come through Gasoline Alley as a team manager instead of a driver, then had had to turn right instead of left as he strolled the considerable distance to where Josele Garza's car was placed, far to the north on the outside of the last row.

Then there was Mario Andretti, deeply hurt over being named runner-up to Unser rather than winner of the only-recently resolved '81 "500". He, too, walked alone down the track, having managed, as most veterans do, to appear in uniform at the very last minute. Perhaps working off the tension, he strolled from his own car and down to the fifth row, where he found Hector Rebaque sitting on the wall. His face broke into a smile when he saw the young Mexican, against whom he had driven Grand Prix cars for several seasons. He strolled over, clenched his fist and

Joe Cloutier runs things in the front office.

Tom Binford runs things on the track.

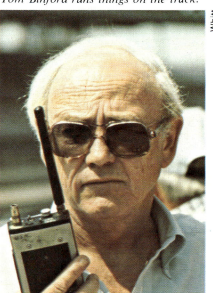

Bob Stemple runs things for Chevrolet.

Race fans or not, the Snake Pit crowd is always interesting.

playfully chucked Rebaque on the chin.

Louis Sudler sang "Back Home Again In Indiana" and the thousands of helium-filled balloons were released into the sky. As soon as the song was finished, the hundreds of black, gold and white-outfitted Purdue University musicians ran from the track, the tubas bobbing in the sunshine. Then Mrs. Tony Hulman commanded, "GENTLEMEN, START YOUR ENGINES!"

Jim Rathmann pulled away in the silver Camaro Z-28 pace car, preceded by two other Camaro pace cars, which also took the warmup and parade laps. One, driven by young Tony Hulman George, carried his mother, Mari Human George, and Bob Forbes of the Speedway Radio Network as passengers. The other was driven by General Motors Vice President Bob Stemple, with his wife as passenger. The pace car driven by Rathmann contained steward, Bob Cassaday, and ABC-TV commentator, Jack Whittaker.

Kevin Cogan and A. J. Foyt moved out behind the pace car several seconds before pole-sitter Rick Mears got underway. Each row took off leaving a single car not yet started. Tom Sneva's engine had not fired. Long after the last row had disappeared through turn one, the crew were permitted to "push start" the car. The engine fired and away he went.

The sun dodged in and out behind the clouds as the field took the warmup and parade laps. Foyt waved at the crowd with his right hand, as did Rutherford. On the next lap Mears and Bill Whittington were seen to be saluting the crowd.

Jim Rathmann picked up speed as the George and Stemple Camaros returned to the pits, and the tension mounted.

The cars were not perfectly lined up. In fact, everyone from the fifth row on back lagged behind by perhaps a hundred yards or more. Row four had cleared the last turn before row five even appeared. Rathmann, far ahead of the field, came down the pit lane and starter Duane Sweeney clutched the green flag.

The front couple of rows were fairly well aligned, but the distance between rows four and five made a start questionable.

Past the pit entrance they came, Mears holding the pace well down from the normal rate at this point. Cogan and Foyt obediently lined themselves perfectly in line with Mears as much of the attention was turned to Sweeney. Would it be a start?

Tom Sneva blows out a puff of that $25000 smoke very near to the finish. Although stopping he was able to salvage fourth spot.

Jim Sullivan manufacturers a myriad of racing pins.

[53]

Early in the race Foyt and Rick Mears duel it out before 400,000.

The general consensus was that Cogan had come down the straight riding the brake and pressing the throttle at the same time, and was caught off guard when the turbocharger kicked in. Cogan contended that he had either been hit from behind (which was not the case) or that something may have malfunctioned (which possibly could have been). He later claimed that he was the victim of a "disintegrating velocity joint" which, if so, was not generally circulated by Penske's spokesmen. The fact remains that Cogan, innocent or not, was going to have to carry this one with him for some time, possibly for the rest of his career. If nothing else, it served as an eye-opener for the newer drivers and perhaps next year's aspirants, stressing that the notoriety one can gain by competing at the Indianapolis Motor Speedway is not always of the type most desirable, and coupled with the Gordon Smiley accident during qualifying, a graphic reminder that motor racing is still a very dangerous and unforgiving sport.

Plenty of criticism was aimed at Cogan's teammate, Rick Mears, who was criticized by several of the drivers for pacing the race too slowly. Mears was adamant about his prerogative to set whatever pace he chose. He stated that he had been asked by Chief Steward Tom Binford to maintain a steady pace and not speed up and slow down as some previous pole sitters have done, insisting that he had honored this request.

And criticism at the ragged condition of the lineup was deflated by an interesting counterthought. Had the field been tightly bunched up as it should have been, there might have been quite a few more cars eliminated than four!

At 11:48 a.m., some fifty minutes after the accident, the 29 undamaged cars were lined up once more, having been topped off with fuel. The pace car set off once more for a complete restart, Mears and Foyt alone in the front row, Johncock and Bill Whittington together in the second.

Once again, the field became spread out, and there was a considerable distance between the fifth and sixth rows. This time it was a start, and Foyt, apparently with fire in his eyes, went for the lead.

The incredible Foyt, belying the fact that he was participating in his twenty-fifth consecutive Indianapolis "500", had moved to a huge lead of one-and-one-half seconds over Rick Mears at the end of the opening lap. It was the first time he had ever led lap one. Gordon Johncock was almost four seconds behind in 3rd position, while Tom Sneva, having started on the inside of the third row, but with a clear shot at the front because of the absence of Mario Andretti, was able to move through to 4th. Bill Whittington was 5th, ahead of his brother, Don, in the

Whether it would have or not will never be known, as such a decision became a moot point. Perhaps one hundred yards from the start/finish line, Kevin Cogan's Norton Spirit veered to the right and struck Foyt's car, leaving a huge tire mark (from Foyt's left front) halfway down the right side of Cogan's car. The exact force of the blow appeared to vary from at least two different television camera angles. Video footage shot from the outside upper deck of the grandstand of the accident "going away" gave the impression that Cogan was not veering all that much off course and that his contact with Foyt was slight. Conversely, a telephoto lense perspective from turn one pointing directly up the track showed Cogan's maneuver to have been quite sudden, and the contact with Foyt quite violent. From this angle it appeared miraculous that Foyt was even able to maintain control.

Having struck Foyt, the Cogan car then turned around to the left at a ninety degree angle, passed behind Mears and struck the inside pit wall head on. No sooner had it done so, in a cloud of shattered fiberglass, than Mario Andretti, accelerating in anticipation of a green flag, came upon Cogan and had no alternative but to tee-bone the Norton Spirit in its left side. Andretti's car went into a reverse half spin and slid backward to the start/finish line. Cogan's car was spun around again, almost into the proper direction, and rolled across the track, bearing right toward the outside wall. Johnny Rutherford, starting on the outside of the fourth row, was just able to get clear before Cogan slid behind his

rear tires, hitting the outside wall with a bump.

Meanwhile, back in the pack, there was further confusion as Dale Whittington's car broke away for an inside spin, clobbering the rear of Roger Mears' car, which happened to be in the row ahead.

Cogan's car sat against the outside wall, its left side tires flattened, suspension broken, and left side body work smashed. Andretti's car, with a crunched front end, sat backwards at the start/finish line with smoke smoldering from the tires. Dale Whittington's car came to rest some distance up the track, sideways, with the nose pointing to the outside wall. Roger Mears, perhaps in disbelief of what had just occurred, allowed his car to roll far on down the track next to the inside wall, and did not come to a stop until he had reached the electronic scoring pylon.

The red flag was displayed and all of the other cars came to a stop.

Cogan climbed from his badly damaged car and walked across the track to the inside wall. He and Andretti vaulted it together, and, still wearing their helmets, walked together down the grass verge, gesturing with their arms to each other as they went.

Foyt, understandably angry at first, quickly assessed the damage and discovered that a front left steering rod had been bent by the impact. Although it had been carefully calibrated upon installation, it was now simply a matter of "a couple of applications with a blunt instrument and hope for the best". Within a few minutes, Foyt was ready to go.

PRIDE...

Pride helped build America into the greatest nation on earth.

Pride helped build the Machinists Union into one of the largest, most progressive organizations for workers in the world today.

Now, that same pride is helping to build a new race team—the Machinists Union Racing Team. We're the only team on the championship racing circuit owned, operated and maintained by American workers.

Pride, tempered with patience, perseverance and determination, will one day help make the Machinists Union Racing Team one of the top contenders on championship race car circuit.

You can count on that. And you can count on us.

**International Association of Machinists
and Aerospace Workers, AFL-CIO
William W. Winpisinger,
International President**

A sequence of the the Cogan-Andretti scramble that caused the event to be stopped before it began . . . and more than a little speculation as to what happened.

identically painted yellow March, Don having hooked on behind Sneva in coming up from the third row.

Pancho Carter was 7th, followed by "rookie" Danny Sullivan, who had made a great start (8th from 13th), Chip Ganassi and Johnny Rutherford completing the first ten. Danny Ongais was next, ahead of Al Unser (up from 16th), Herm Johnson, Hector Rebaque, Bobby Rahal, Howdy Holmes, Johnny Parsons (17th from 25th) Geoff Brabham, Dennis Firestone (The two second-day qualifiers hanging right together) and Michael Chandler in 20th. Then came Jim Hickman, Jerry Sneva, Tony Bettenhausen, George Snider, Chet Fillip, Gary Bettenhausen, Pete Halsmer, Tom Bigelow and finally, poor Josele Garza, having a thoroughly miserable year as a sophomore, running dead last and with smoke pouring from the exhaust, indicating that something serious had already occurred within his power plant.

In recent years, an incident such as Garza's would almost certainly have guaranteed that a yellow would be flashed on momentarily, since drivers have elected to stop on the track in precarious positions to more or less force the officials to have them towed in. Fine for them, but annoying to the other participants (unless it happens to be time for a pit stop anyway), and certainly an irritant for spectators, who possibly have to see a wheel-to-wheel battle interrupted because of the ensuing caution period. Such was not the case today, and young Garza, realizing that he was through, pulled his brown and white Schlitz Gusto March to the inside of the back stretch at reduced speed, then sportingly steered it off into the grass at the north end, safely vacating the track without interrupting the action.

Foyt's first lap, at 194.342 mph, was faster than a couple of qualifiers and it smashed Danny Ongais's 1978 track record by almost nine miles per hour!

Even as Garza was still in motion, bumping through the infield grass to retirement, Foyt had already completed a second lap and smashed more records. He'd done 197.585 (the fastest ever turned in competition, although this one would be topped many times throughout the day), and had raised the average for two laps to 195.950, knocking Wally Dallenbach's 1974 mark out of the book by eight miles per hour.

Mears was still about one-and-a-half seconds behind Foyt, but Johncock had fallen to more than four seconds from 1st place. Sneva was still 4th, but the Whittingtons had swapped positions, Don moving to 5th. Sullivan had passed Carter for 7th and Rutherford had replaced Ganassi in 9th. Rebaque had passed Johnson for 13th, and Rahal had dropped from 15th to 17th, giving up the

positions to Holmes and Parsons.

Ganassi lost 10th to Ongais on the 3rd lap, while Parsons, making a great advance in the Wysard family March, made up two more spots to 14th.

Mears, who has frequently admitted that he prefers to let others set the pace in the early stages, maintained an almost equal pace to that of Foyt's, right at 195 mph or higher. Foyt was building on his lead so slightly that it was undetectable without the use of a stop-watch, and the gap was still under two seconds at the completion of four laps. Foyt travelled the distance seven seconds faster than Bobby Unser had a year ago, so another record, 195.993 mph, became Foyt's property.

There were no changes among the first ten but Al Unser came up to 11th as Ganassi bowed to the veteran three-timer winner, and Brabham came up to 14th running 190 mph laps, to pass the fast-rising Parsons.

Gary Bettenhausen and Tom Bigelow, two fine Sprint Champions, sadly found themselves running in the last two spots, and as they entered turn one a few yards apart, Foyt was already boiling through turn four and into the straight.

The average climbed to 196 mph under trouble-free conditions as Foyt continued to lap faster than any one had in the history of the Speedway.

Brabham made the best progress of the next couple of laps, passing Ganassi and Rebaque on the sixth circuit to run 12th. Mears stayed within a couple of seconds of Foyt, but Johncock had fallen to six seconds in arrears and Sneva was almost ten seconds back. Don Whittington was right behind Tom, but Bill Whittington in sixth was 18 seconds behind!

Ongais passed Rutherford for 9th and Carter took 7th from Sullivan. Brabham grabbed 11th from Al Unser and Parsons returned the 14th as Foyt lapped Bettenhausen inside of ten laps! Carter kept coming and took 6th from Bill Whittington, but was still darn close to half a lap behind Foyt.

Foyt's average for 10 laps (25 miles) was 194.966 mph, to erase Al Unser's 187 mph clip with the Pennzoil Chaparral in 1979.

The complete rundown for 10 laps had Foyt, Mears, Johncock, Tom Sneva, Don Whittington, Carter, Bill Whittington, Sullivan, Ongais and Rutherford running in the first ten, followed by Brabham, Al Unser, Rebaque, Parsons, Holmes, Ganassi, Johnson, Rahal, Chandler, Hickman(20th), Jerry Sneva, Tony Bettenhausen, Firestone, Snider, Fillip, Halsmer, Bigelow and Gary Bettenhausen.

Foyt and Mears both lapped Halsmer and Bigelow by the time one dozen laps were on the board and Mears had been able to close to within half a second of Foyt as they wove their way through traffic. Ongais passed Sullivan for 8th, and Brabham, having tried for a couple of laps to overhaul Rutherford for 10th, came into the pits with clouds of thick white smoke erupting from the exhaust.

George Bignotti's crew conferred with Brabham for a few moments before the attractive black and silver Pentax-sponsored entry was wheeled away, the second car to be eliminated by mechanical failure.

Ongais overtook Bill Whittington for 8th at 16 laps as Foyt and Mears lapped both Chet Fillip and Dennis Firestone. After the rousing start the race had settled in nicely, with the pace having dropped to the mid-180's and the average still over 192.

The lapping process continued as Foyt took Snider and Ganassi, but for the next several laps Mears was unable to find a way around Snider. While he was working at it, Johncock made up some deficit and passed Mears for second!

Johncock was second across the line at 20 laps, just over five seconds behind Foyt, who had established another record. The fourth-time winner had traveled 50 miles in 15 minutes 40.66 seconds, for an average speed of 191.355, dispensing with another 1979 Al Unser record.

The regular pit stops began with Parsons, Halsmer and Fillip the first to come in, thus causing some position shuffling and dropping Halsmer and Fillip to last. The top ten were Foyt, Johncock, Mears, Sneva, Don Whittington, Carter, Ongais, Bill Whittington, Sullivan and Rutherford.

Mears was the first of the front runners to come in, stopping after 22 laps to be followed a lap later by Foyt. Johncock assumed the lead on the 23rd lap, only to

Roger Mears had a little to say about being gored by Dale Whittington.

Wonder what Andretti and Cogan are saying to each other?

Kevin Cogan tries to explain why his car eliminated Andretti and ALMOST eliminated Foyt. Does anyone believe him? Was it mechanical failure or inexperience?

McPherson

Ackerman

Howdy Holmes...is he resting, meditating or could he be PRAYING!?

give it up when he came in next time around. Pit activity was frantic for the next couple of minutes as just about everybody zipped in and out, making quick stops under the green. Don Whittington stayed on the track to lead laps 24 and 25 and then Ongais led for a lap as Whittington came in. By the 26th lap, just about everyone had completed their initial stops and the standings were fairly well returned to where they had been. Foyt led by less than one second over Mears, while Johncock was back to 3rd, about eight seconds behind. Sneva, Whittington and Ongais were next, while Firestone's Chevrolet-powered car which had not yet stopped, was 7th. Carter, Rutherford and Unser filled out the first ten as Parsons was back in for what proved to be a lengthy stay.

Firestone made his stop and Bill Whittington returned to the top ten as 30 laps approached with no sign of a yellow. Foyt and Mears continued to hover just below 190; better than half of the field had been lapped at least once. Fillip, Bettenhausen and Hickman had fallen to two laps in arrears.

Howdy Holmes in 12th spot was lapped as Foyt and Mears logged in 30 laps in well under 25 minutes, pushing the average, including a pit stop, to over 185, adding five miles per hour to the rate Foyt was travelling at this point in 1977.

At 32 laps, Foyt passed Rebaque, so that only the first ten remained in the lead lap, as Bigelow was lapped for the second time. Another circuit and Bill Whittington was overlapped by Foyt and Mears. Meanwhile, Johncock had been fairing better in traffic and had closed to within four seconds of Mears. Sneva was less than ten seconds out of first place, but fifth place Don Whittington had faded somewhat and was better than half a lap behind.

Steady progress was being made by Jerry Sneva, who was up to 13th, while Danny Sullivan, who had dropped almost two laps back during his first stop, was lapping quickly and beginning to reclimb the ladder.

Ongais passed Don Whittington for 5th place on the 35th lap as Al Unser went a lap down to the leaders.

The lead changed hands, other than for

pit stops, for the first time on lap 36, when Mears outdueled Foyt while they were lapping Gary Bettenhausen and Halsmer. As Mears took first place, Pancho Carter took 6th from Don Whittington, while Bill Whittington picked up 9th from Al Unser.

Once in front Mears began to build on his lead, and had it up to three seconds at 39 laps, but the possibility of one hundred miles without a caution could not quite be realized. Rick was appoximately in turn three when the yellow light flashed on for what could have been a nasty accident.

Tony Bettenhausen was on the mainstraight and heading for the start/finish line when his car suddenly veered one way and then the other as a half shaft broke. He frantically tried to correct against the slides, but the erratically behaving car then turned around and smashed the outside wall with the nose cone. Still travelling at a high rate of speed, it spun around and around on down the straight, banging the wall a couple more times, throwing off debris and finally coming to stop just north of the start/finish line. Tony was shaken, but otherwise apparently unhurt after his wild ride. He was helped from the car and into the ambulance, which seemingly materialized from nowhere. This was joined by a wrecker, which hardly could have arrived any quicker. A hook was attached to the roll bar, the stricken car was hoisted into the air, and the wrecker was removing it from the scene in what could have been no more than sixty seconds from the time of the accident.

The debris strewn down the track was considerable, yet the amazing cleanup crew had the entire job completed in nine minutes!

In the meantime, the second round of pit stops, which had already begun at the time of the Bettenhausen accident, flourished for the next few minutes as everyone took advantage of the opportunity to make a stop without losing a lap in the process. Jim Rathmann paced the field with the Camaro at what appeared to be a crawl but in reality was better than 95 mph!

The furious scramble among the pit crews of the leading teams provided for a new shake-up in the standings as Tom Sneva was able to get out ahead of Mears, Johncock, Foyt, Carter and Ongais. This became the revised order of the leading half dozen, each of whom were separated by only about eight

Johnny Parsons apparently has some mechanical difficulty with the Wysard which causes him to spin.

seconds because of the "pack-up" situation.

The green flag was waved as Tom Sneva headed down the straight to finish his 46th lap, and Ongais out-accelerated Carter to take 5th at the line. Tom was not the only Sneva to have been able to advance through superior pit work. The Cincinnati-based Hoffman family, who this year had induced several friends to enter a car as a limited partnership, had Jerry Sneva in and out so quickly during the Bettenhausen accident that their boy was running 7th, one lap down and directly behind his brother on the race track. Don Whittington passed Jerry soon after the restart, but Jerry continued on in 8th for several more laps.

Pete Halsmer's turbo-charged Chevrolet-powered Eagle was pushed away after having sat in the pits for several minutes. This concluded the initial Indianapolis race for long-time car owner Frank Arciero, known best perhaps for being the entrant of a Lotus driven by Dan Gurney in early 1960's sports car races. This was Frank's third Indianapolis entry, the original, which didn't make it, having been in 1959 with Shorty Templeman, and the second six years later in 1965, when Al Unser passed his "rookie" test before blowing the engine. Both cars, front-engined in '59 and rear-engined in '65, were powered by Maseratis!

The pace had fallen under track record standards at 50 laps because of the Bettenhausen accident, Sneva averaging 167.954 mph for 125 miles, which was about ten miles per hour slower than Bobby Unser had been able to travel in 1974.

Johncock was three seconds behind Sneva at the one-quarter distance, with Mears, Foyt, Carter and Ongais coming next, Danny about 11 seconds out of first place. Don Whittington, Jerry Sneva, Bill Whittington, Rutherford, Chandler,

Rick Mears car was as attractive as it was fast.

Unser, Rahal, Rebaque and Holmes were 7th through 15th, one lap behind. Snider, Ganassi, Bigelow, Sullivan, Johnson and Fillip were next, two laps behind. Gary Bettenhasusen was three laps down, and Hickman four, with Firestone and Parsons, both having been pitted for some time, as the only others still in the contest. The recent sidelining of the cars of Tony Bettenhausen and Halsmer had reduced the field to 25.

During the next few laps Sneva continued to set the pace, Johncock and Mears running close together about one second behind. Michael Chandler in the Bill Freeman-sponsored 1981-style Gurney Eagle entered the top ten by passing Johnny Rutherford, and Ongais wrestled 5th away from Carter.

On the 58th lap, Mears captured 2nd from Johncock and Chandler kept on coming by disposing of Bill Whittington in 9th. Mears completed the next lap just a couple of car lengths behind Sneva, and on the 60th lap he blazed around into the lead most people had expected him to hold for much of the time.

Rick's burst of speed had carried the average to 171.571 mph for 150 miles, still about five miles per hour off Foyt's speed for the distance in 1974, but only about one-and-a-half minutes longer in terms of elapsed time.

The fine top-five run by Danny Ongais came to an end on the 63rd lap, when his car spun out to the outside wall in turn two, directly in front of the V.I.P. suites. The black Interscope racer smashed into the wall and then ricocheted across the track to the inside, leaving a trail of broken pieces in its wake. Chet Fillip slowed as Ongais's car sailed across in front of him and Jerry Sneva, not anticipating Fillip's reaction, was unable to avoid contacting the first time starter's car. Sneva's car spun into the grass, out of the race, while the bearded Fillip was able to keep running and limped with his

IMS-Stephenson Sequence

Whitlow

Al Unser, while never really a contender, was, as usual, a consistent finisher.

Danny Sullivan has a little trouble.

Tony Bettenhausen breaks a half-shaft and the car turns into the front stretch wall. No. 16 was damaged too extensively to finish the race.

turquoise and orange Eagle around to the pit area. The Ongais car was damaged quite heavily, but in marked contrast to the situation of a year ago, the plucky Hawaiian was able to extricate himself without injury. Jerry Sneva was not hurt at all, but his strong run in eighth place was over.

While the debris was cleared from turn two, Mears, Tom Sneva, Johncock and Carter seized upon the opportunity to make a stop, giving the lead to Foyt for a single circuit. Foyt stopped on his 65th lap, but the stop was not a smooth one. Some fuel inadvertently spilled into the cockpit, as he soon was to discover. He felt liquid soaking into the seat of his pants as he left the pit area. It quickly began to irritate his skin as it soaked through his uniform. Performing with skill and presence of mind as few others in the world possess, he loosened the seat belts and shoulder harness and, while bracing his back against the headrest, was able to maintain control with one hand while trying to brush off any excess fuel with the other. He hoisted his body from out of the pool of methanol splashing around on the seat, and even caught the attention of fellow Texan, Johnny Rutherford, against whom Foyt has raced Championship cars for an unbelievable twenty years. Rutherford glanced over in turn four and noted Foyt's predicament as the four-time winner writhed painfully around in the confines of the cockpit on his way down to the pit lane. Foyt's crew dumped a bucket of cold water into the cockpit to ease the irritation. By the time he returned to the competition, Foyt had dropped to 9th place, more than a lap down. It might have been a three-lap or even a four-lap deficit had this occurred under green.

Mears led the field past the 70 lap mark with the average still above 160 in spite of several laps at around 95 behind the pace car. Sneva and Johncock were 2nd and 3rd with Carter 4th, the only other driver in the lead lap following the exit of Ongais and the delay of Foyt. Rebaque had emerged in 5th a lap behind, and was ahead of Unser, Rutherford, Foyt and Don Whittington. Chandler in 10th place was two laps behind.

Chet Fillip's car had suffered enough suspension damage from the Ongais/Sneva incident to prevent the Ozona, Texas modified driver from continuing, and with Dennis Firestone's car also having been pushed away after a lengthy attempt to get it running, the field was reduced to 21. Johnny Parsons' car, stationary for almost 40 minutes, finally rolled back into the contest amidst a great cheer from his fans.

The green was waved as Rick Mears headed down to complete 71 laps and Tom Sneva closed right up behind him as they crossed the line. Mears ran the next

half dozen laps at over 197, to put seven seconds on Sneva and Johncock by the 78th lap. Foyt was really covering ground a lap plus a few seconds behind. He caught and passed Rutherford for 7th on the leader's 75th lap and overhauled Al Unser for 6th on the very next circuit. Two more and the Texan had taken 5th away from Rebaque, but that was about as high as he could hope to climb for the time being, as 4th place Carter was a lap plus 12 seconds ahead of him.

Still running at 196, Mears notched up 200 miles in under an hour and a quarter, only 50 seconds off the record, and averaging 162.294 mph. Sneva arrived just over nine seconds later, with Johncock and Carter both accounted for in less than three more. Foyt, Rebaque, Unser, Rutherford and Don Whittington maintained positions 5 through 9 though one lap back, with Chandler, Rahal, Bill Whittington, Holmes and Sullivan holding 10th through 14th two laps behind. Ganassi, Snider and Johnson were three laps behind, Hickman four, Bettenhausen six, Bigelow eight and Parsons not even to 100 miles, yet, let alone 200.

Pancho Carter dropped back a few seconds during the next ten laps as the skies became overcast, but Johncock remained extremely close to Sneva, the pair of them usually crossing the line about nine seconds behind Mears. Foyt had come to within five seconds of unlapping himself from Carter, but still one minute and ten seconds from the lead. Rebaque held about six seconds advantage over Unser and Rutherford, who were running lap after lap right with each other, struggling for 7th.

Carter peeled off into the pits on his 90th lap, and with such a substantial advantage over Foyt, was able to get back out without losing 4th place.

Foyt was in on his 91st lap, giving 5th back to Rebaque as he came in. Rutherford passed Unser after many laps of their running together, and Mears came steaming in, crossing the line to complete 94 laps just before slithering to a halt in the Penske pit. Just as he did, Johncock passed Sneva on the track to take 2nd right at the line. Just as Mears went back onto the track, the yellow came on, a tremendous break for Sneva and Johncock!

Predictably, both Sneva and Johncock piled into the pits next time around, and Johncock's superb crew got him out ahead of Mears! Sneva was able to pack up fairly close, with only the lapped cars of Rebaque and Unser between him and Mears. A lap later Rebaque also stopped, and Sneva packed up right behind Unser as the skies cleared once more.

Foyt was in again within a couple of laps of his last stop, delayed this time for close to three quarters of a minute. He raced back onto the track, took another

(Top) Gordon Johncock's pit crew kept up with Roger Penske's. It helped win the race in the pits when Rick Mears rear-ended Herm Johnson on pit row. (Middle) Danny Sullivan and Hector Rebaque in the Forsythe-Brown cars running together. (Bottom) Pete Halsmer's crew takes their Colonial-Payless mount back to Gasoline Alley after mechanical problems put them out. This team should be proud for making one of the most competitive fields in history.

[63]

The cars begin to line up as the pace lap nears.

lap and came back in again, obviously furious as he locked a brake, smoke pouring off his right front tire as he slid to a halt. Mechanics frantically looked for a problem to correct as Foyt remained in the cockpit, revving the engine. The seconds ticked away and the stop became longer. Then the engine died. His whole body lurched forward in an angry gesture before he threw off the belts and attempted to clamber from the cockpit. Crew members attempted to help him but he shrugged them off. He removed his helmet and joined some other crew members, who apparently had located something untoward on the right side of the engine compartment. The initial anger subsided from his face as he took a hammer from one of them and took three or four composed wallops at something near the right rear wheel. Then he shook his head and signalled the car be pushed away. Foyt was through for the day.

Coincidentally, the yellow flag which had been displayed throughout the minutes that Foyt's tremendous effort had been collapsing was for a tow-in on the car driven by George Snider, who has qualified a Foyt backup on no less than nine occasions. Snider was to have driven for Foyt yet again this year, but Foyt had had second thoughts, electing instead to concentrate on a single entry. He had helped Snider secure the Fletcher backup after that team had decided to campaign its second car following the death during qualifying of Gordon Smiley. Foyt had even supplied manpower, himself included, to set the car up for Snider and see him safely in the race. Ironically, the two friends were eliminated within moments of each other.

Under caution at 100 laps (halfway) the average had fallen slightly to just below record speed. Johncock cruised under crossed flags, requiring less than a half minute longer than Gary Bettenhausen's record run had a decade earlier, "Gordo's" average speed for 250 miles being 161.286 mph.

Mears, Sneva and Carter each had a lap over 5th place Rebaque, while Rutherford, now 6th, was two laps behind. Unser was 7th and Bobby Rahal had now moved all the way up to 8th. Sullivan had returned to the top ten, running 9th, three laps behind, ahead of Bill Whittington, Howdy Holmes, Don Whittington and Chip Ganassi. The others still running four laps behind or further were Herm Johnson, Jim Hickman, Michael Chandler (no longer in the the top ten after a long stop), Johnny Parsons, Tom Bigelow and Gary Bettenhausen.

Duane Sweeney began waving the green flag as the leaders came by to complete 103 laps.

Johncock retained the lead until the 109th lap at which time Mears passed him with a blaze of speed. Sneva was only one second behind and Pancho Carter, despite the loss of bottom gear, was right behind Sneva, attempting to overcome his handicap by stopping under the yellow whenever possible.

On the next lap, Johncock dropped 2nd to Sneva and fans of his began to fear that his race might be coming to an end. On the 112th lap, still running but at a slightly reduced rate, he was passed by Carter for 3rd. The gap widened. He was two seconds behind Carter, then four, then five, then seven as Carter hung with Sneva while Mears, on a rampage, began to pull away from them all.

At 117 laps, Mears was leading by eight seconds over Sneva with Carter about two seconds further back. Johncock was nine seconds behind Carter and 19 out of the lead he had held only ten laps earlier. Nevertheless, Johncock's crew were unconcerned. They had plotted a strategy for lap times based on their knowledge of the car's fuel consumption. Their boy was right where they wanted him to be.

Carter was the first of the leading quartet to make the next stop, giving 3rd back to Johncock on the 118th lap.

The attrition rate kept up at a slightly higher rate than usual, with Michael Chandler's run in the Freeman/Gurney Eagle after he had logged in 104 laps. He had moved into the top ten at one point, but his final laps followed a long stop that had dropped him back almost to last.

Tom Bigelow's car, an '81 Gurney Eagle/Chevrolet quite similar to Chandler's, was also in the pits and had been there for some considerable time.

The 300 mile mark fell short of Gary Bettenhausen's 1972 record by a full two minutes as Rick Mears raised the recently depleted average speed back over 162. Sneva was seven seconds in arrears, while Johncock had faded to almost 22 seconds (half a lap) behind. Carter, with a stop in hand, was one lap plus six seconds behind Mears, and 28 seconds in front of Rebaque. Rutherford, Unser and Rahal were two laps behind, and Sullivan and Don Whittington were three laps back, completing the first ten. Howdy Holmes was four laps behind, Ganassi five, Johnson and Hickman six each. Bill Whittington and Bettenhausen, plus the badly delayed Parsons and Bigelow, were the only others still around.

Bigelow returned to the event after a thirteen-minute stop, but took only one slow lap before coming in again.

Mears was leading Sneva by 12 seconds at 125 laps, while Johncock was all the way back to 33 seconds behind.

Sneva made his sixth stop of the day as he began his 127th lap and was able to get away just ahead of Carter. Mears came in next time around, and Johncock went to the front for a single lap until he completed the cycle.

Without interruption from a yellow flag, Mears had pulled to an even greater advantage over Sneva, with almost 17 seconds in hand. Carter was 22 seconds out of first place and Johncock was still 33 seconds back.

The separation between each of the first four remained constant at 130 laps as Mears, cranking out 195 mph laps, hauled the average to just over 163. Rebaque who had been running 5th for ages, was in the process of giving it up during a stop. Rutherford and Unser were 6th and 7th, two laps behind, while Rahal, 8th and three laps down, was in turn a full lap ahead of Danny Sullivan.

Mears had just completed 131 laps when the yellow was displayed for the fourth time of the day, this time as Bill Whittington's car stalled on the course. The 16-second advantage built by Mears was about to evaporate.

Poor Rebaque, in his haste to try and recover some of the excessive time he lost during his pit stop, passed too many cars under the yellow and was docked two full laps. This dropped him from 8th to 10th.

Sneva was able to close to within three seconds of Mears under caution, while Johncock advanced to 3rd as the result of a stop by Carter, and Gordon was now 6 1/2 seconds behind Rick. Rutherford had made it up to 5th, although two laps behind. Al Unser was riding along just yards behind him, and Bobby Rahal, who drove in the Canadian and U.S. Grand Prix of 1978 as a teammate to James Hunt on the Walter Wolf team, was all the way up to 7th, three laps down on Mears.

Bill Whittington's stalled car was out of the race, and once the wrecking crews had returned to their stations, the 136th lap was going on the board.

The green had been on for not much more than one minute when the yellow snapped on for the fifth time. This time it was for Johnny Parsons, who spun hairily across the south short chute, gathered it up and limped down the backstretch to retire with a broken half shaft in turn three. Far behind the rest of the field, he was finally credited with completing 92 laps.

Sixteen cars remained with more than 150 miles still to be completed. Tom Bigelow's car was still being worked on, but was far behind the rest of the field, having completed only one slow lap

This is where the majority of the working press views the race.

within the past half hour.

During the latest caution, there were two notable pit stops. Johncock peeled off on the 140th lap to top off his fuel supply, while Mears, Sneva and Carter stayed on the track. A lap later, Rutherford came in briefly, allowing Al Unser to take over 5th place.

Duane Sweeney began waving the green flag as the field came down to complete 142 laps and Mears was apparently caught off guard. Not only did Sneva duck around and lead across the line, but Bobby Rahal, who had been directly behind Mears, also passed.

Sneva took the pace to 197 for the next few laps and Mears quickly disposed of Rahal to run with Tom. They were less than half a second apart at 150 laps, Pancho Carter having fallen to nine seconds behind, Johncock to 12 seconds. Fifth and sixth places were held by Unser and Rutherford, two laps behind. Rahal was three laps behind, Sullivan and Don Whittington four each, Rebaque five (actually three, but five with the assessment of the two-lap penalty for the illegal passing of cars under the yellow); Ganassi, Bettenhausen, Hickman, Holmes, Johnson and Bigelow were still running, but out of the top ten.

Sneva was still lapping at 197 and holding Mears at bay when Danny Sullivan slid through turn four in his Forsythe-Brown entry. He hit the outside wall and spun down to the infield near the pit entrance, sustaining damage but no injury. He convinced the medics that he was not affected in any way and was permitted to walk back to the pits rather

When Hector Rebaque came in for his last pit stop his car burst into flames.

PISTON RINGS

TOTAL SEAL™ runs up front — no other piston ring provides the blow-by protection and stability you get when the **TOTAL SEAL GAPLESS RING™** is in the 2nd groove — That's Right — Stability — the same 2% leakdowns — even after a 500 mile race — think about how much easier it is to control — fuel ratio, oil control and temperature when blow-by rates are stabilized and reduced — this all adds up to longer ring and engine life. And the latest from **TOTAL SEAL™** is a winner too!

The **"RED HEAD"™** top ring will make horsepower — bulletproof, but lighter and with lower tension means reduced friction losses and less tendency to flutter —

Try 'em, and you'll find as many top engine builders already have, that the least expensive way to improve engine output and reliability is a set of **TOTAL SEAL™** piston rings.

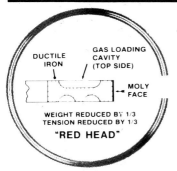

**TOP GROOVE
"RED HEAD"
FIRE RING**

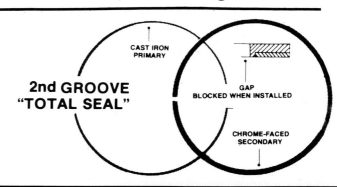

**2nd GROOVE
"TOTAL SEAL"**

Jerry Sneva's car on the wrecker after the Sneva-Ongais-Fillip tangle in turn-2.

Rick Mears makes one of the very fast Penske Stops. Probably at around 14 seconds.

Many new fueling regulations made the pit work more efficient and much safer this year. This is George Bignotti's Texaco crew; one of the best in the business.

than take the ride to the newly-named Hanna Emergency Center for a check-up.

The field reduced its pace again behind the silver Camaro, and Tom Bigelow's crew pushed his disabled white Eagle/Chevrolet away after a game effort. With Sullivan's wrecked car being removed from the course, that left 14!

Mears and Sneva immediately came in, but Sneva had a disastrous stop, or what would have been disastrous had it occurred under the green. The mechanism in the refueling hose malfunctioned,

and by the time he was properly serviced, 54 seconds had elapsed. Mears was away in 14!

Johncock and Carter were in and out a lap later, and Johncock was able to merge in directly behind Mears, who in turn was the first car behind the pace car. After some of the back-markers had stopped, Sneva was able to recover nicely from his frustratingly long stop, and had only Jim Hickman's car, which was painted up like a Stroh's truck, between him and the leading pair.

The green came out just as the leaders

When the Forsythe hoods are not in use they are stacked like surf boards.

Danny Sullivan's car starts to shed its fibreglass.

Larson

A disgruntled A. J. Foyt supervises the re-adjustment of his front end after his encounter with Kevin Cogan. Instead of a minute calibration a few well applied bangs with a hammer did a good, if temporary job. Foyt was able to lead the first few laps after the impromptu repairs.

Cunningham

Gordon Johncock, on his way to victory, races Pancho Carter, who finished third.

Johncock and Rick Mears hooked up in a Trophy Dash to the finish for the race's closest finish in history.

Cunningham

Cunningham

were about to complete their 159th lap, and Sneva quickly disposed of Hickman to turn the lead into a three-way battle (Carter was six cars back in line).

This time it was Johncock who got the jump on Mears, and Gordon was the leader at 400 miles. Mears and Sneva completed the top three in a little over one second, with Pancho about six seconds behind. Of the other survivors, there were Unser and Rutherford two laps behind, Rahal three, Whittington four, Hickman eight and Johnson ten laps behind in 10th! Howdy Holmes was also ten laps down, and Bettenhausen eleven. Ganassi had been in his pit for several laps and suddenly a huge cloud of white smoke from the north end of the pits signalled that Rebaque's pitted car was having a refuelling fire extinguished.

Carter quickly passed the slower cars in front of him, but lost a little ground to the leading quartet. Johncock set the pace, Mears usually within a couple of car lengths. By the 170th lap they had put about five seconds on Sneva, while Carter had dropped back to about 18 seconds. The rest of the top ten remained unchanged as the field diminished to twelve cars. Both Ganassi's and Rebaque's cars were pushed back to the Garage Area. Johncock, Mears, Sneva, Carter, Unser, Rutherford, Rahal, Whittington, Hickman, Johnson, Holmes and Bettenhausen were the only competitors still running.

The attrition continued as Bettenhausen's backmarker was retired and pushed away as the leaders reached 175 laps. A couple of laps later, Bobby Rahal's seventh place car came by with black and white smoke pouring from the exhaust. He pitted next time around.

It was still Johncock and Mears, with Sneva six seconds behind. It remained that way at 450 miles, and Pancho Carter, still 4th, was only about ten

Everywhere there are splashes of yellow as Johnny Rutherford makes his pit stop. Not only is the Chaparral yellow but his pit crew have uniforms to match. Despite a broken engine Johnny was in the top ten.

seconds away from being lapped when he raced in for his last scheduled stop. Johnny Capels and crew had him back out in a hurry, but he was now well over a lap down.

On the 183rd lap, Mears and Sneva came on to the pit lane together, although originally separated by about five seconds. Mears came bombing down towards his pit, but was suddenly faced with Herm Johnson's slower car right in front of him. In Rick's confusion as to what Herm was going to do and vice versa, Rick had to jam on the brakes. He was unable to avoid slamming Herm's right rear tire with his left front spoiler as Sneva came upon the scene. Mears gathered everything up and continued on to his pit. He got away fractionally faster than Sneva, in 18 seconds, and was able

to put a lap on Carter. Johncock, with his final stop still to come, was breathing down Sneva's neck, yards short of putting a lap on the three-time runnerup.

Johncock completed his 186th lap by heading for the pits only to find Hickman running much slower in the fast lane. Gordon passed him on the inside. He braked to a halt and the stop was fantastically executed. He was away in only 13 seconds, screaming out of the pits as members of his crew hugged each other, slapped each other's backs, and raised clenched fists in victory signs in joy for what they had just accomplished. They had calculated the precise amount of fuel that Johncock would need to complete 14 laps, approximately half a tank. They had noted by the elapsed time that as fast as Mears's stop had been, the

Another view of the Rebaque fire. He comes into the pits without incident and the car catches fire. It was the reason for Hector's withdrawal from the race.

Larson

[69]

Gentlemen, choose your colors!

A glass-smooth paint job reduces air drag which contributes to the aerodynamics of an Indianapolis race car. Which is one reason so many entrants this year started with *Ditzler*® paint on their cars. Another reason is a durable deep gloss finish that resists the grueling 500 miles of grit and grime punishment.

And even though you'll never tour the Brickyard with the family car, chances are you've got the same kind of tough finish on your car now. Because PPG Automotive Finishes has supplied the car makers with factory finishes since 1928.

So check with your *Ditzler* Jobber who features the full line of *Ditzler* products the next time your car needs professional refinish work. You're sure to finish a winner!

Ditzler
Automotive
Finishes

PPG
INDUSTRIES

Gordon Johncock on his way out of the pits. The STP team handled his pit stops professionally all day and no doubt aided his win.

Query

Penske crew had given Rick a full supply, which was a good safety measure, but unnecessary. The result was that when Johncock completed his 188th lap, he was eleven seconds ahead of Mears! Mechanical problems notwithstanding, Johncock's people felt they had it in the bag. Sneva was 19 seconds from the lead and Carter better than a lap behind.

The separation was 10.66 seconds at 190 laps as both Johncock and Mears were clocked at 196. Sneva and Carter, a lap apart, were together on the race track, Sneva dropping to 26 seconds from the lead. Al Unser, in 5th place, was three laps behind.

All the clocks were on Mears. He was catching up.

At 192 laps, running at 197, he was 7.9 seconds behind.

In order to catch Johncock he would have to make up one second per lap.

At 193 laps Mears had done better than that. He was 6.4 seconds behind.

First Johncock and then Mears lapped Hickman for the eleventh time, leaving no cars between them. The gap at 194 was six seconds.

Almost unnoticed was the fact that Johnny Rutherford's car, 6th for many laps, was being pushed away. A water line had split, allowing all of the water to drain from the engine, causing it to overheat.

The whole place had come alive! The infield crowd, many of whom probably hadn't cared about anything all day, were now straining up against the fence.

Johncock finished his 195th lap at 193 mph. Mears came by at 199 and had closed to 4.6 seconds!

There had never, ever been a finish as

Jim Hickman drove a steady race to finish 7th. His ride earned him enough votes to secure Rookie-of-the-Year honors. Unfortunately, he was fatally injured at a race in Milwaukee later in the summer.

Crucean

Al Unser leads Pete Halsmer through the turn right in the groove.

Dubbed the "Batmobile", Danny Ongais's Interscope was just about a year outdated.

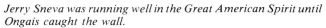

Jerry Sneva was running well in the Great American Spirit until Ongais caught the wall.

Gordon Johncock takes the high groove to pass Gary Bettenhausen.

Pancho Carter had a nice new March for the Morales Bros.

Pete Halsmer leading Johnny Rutherford through a turn.

this one was shaping up to be. Lead cars had dropped out late in the race, lead cars had nursed an ailment in the closing laps, but never, in three quarters of a century of racing at the Indianapolis Motor Speedway, had there been anything such as this.

Johncock lapped Herm Johnson for the 14th time, completing lap 196 at 192 mph. Mears's 196th was clocked at almost 199, and he was three seconds away!

Tom Sneva came by with white smoke trailing from his exhaust pipes. He was off the pace slightly, running in the center of the track, but still running.

One hundred ninety-seven laps completed and Mears was two seconds behind! They had lapped the slowing Sneva, and as Sneva's car smoked quite

heavily, everyone feared that a yellow caution period here could spoil the greatest finish of all time. In fact, a yellow at this point would probably have led to the crowd tearing the grandstands down.

Fortunately, it didn't come.

Incredibly enough, Mears did almost 200 mph on his 198th lap and it pulled him to within three quarters of a second at the finish of this lap. If Johncock had been playing it safe and thought he had the race in hand, that belief had just gone out the window. Mears was about 75 yards behind him and closing fast!

Sneva brought his smoking Texaco Star into the pits, acknowledging a black flag, as his fine 3rd place was about to be taken over by Pancho Carter.

Out of the fourth turn they came, and unbelievably, Mears was right behind

A disgusted and disappointed Garza crosses the infield.

Josele Garza ran only one lap of the race before blowing an engine.

[73]

Tom Bigelow is through as his car emits that wisp of smoke which spells "blown engine."

Rick Mears, in a titanic struggle with Gordon Johncock, comes in for a pit stop and rear ends the slower moving Herm Johnson in the fast lane. This may have cost Mears the race as he lost to Johncock by only a few feet.

Johncock. About one hundred yards in front of Johncock was Don Whittington, several laps behind, but back up to speed and running almost as fast as the leaders. Johncock exited turn four and Mears went right out to the wall, looking perhaps for the opportunity to pass Johncock on the outside. There wasn't enough room. Down for the white flag they came, Johncock edging closer and closer to the inside of the track, Mears reacting to Johncock's every move. Johncock straightened out as he reached about the middle of the track and Mears kept on coming. He came around on the inside and began to catch the full benefit of a NASCAR type slingshot. He crossed the line one-third of a second behind Johncock, but gaining rapidly because of the suction. They headed for the first turn with Mears pulling alongside. Johncock moved out to make the entrance to the first turn and Mears just about dead-heated him. It was an incredible sight.

Johncock had the advantage, and Mears just could not hold him on the inside. He had to lift for just an instant, and lost about ten car lengths in the process. Had Mears lost adhesion, it would have been disastrous for both of them, but the respect these two have for each other is just about unparalleled.

Johncock later admitted that there is probably no other driver he would have run so close to under such circumstances.

Mears was quickly back in it and chasing Johncock.

It happened all over again. Duane Sweeney methodically waved the white flag at the few remaining cars still on the track and reached for the checker as Mears and Johncock came through turn four for the last time. It was as it had been on the previous lap. Rick tried for the outside, couldn't do it, moved to the inside, but Johncock was moving over, too!

They raced for the line, Johncock finally settling for the middle of the track. Mears came around on the inside, but he just didn't have enough time left. He caught the suction and began to come around, but he crossed the line about two car lengths short. Johncock had won it!

The crowd went crazy.

The announced separation between first and second was 0.16 seconds, by far the closest in history.

The yellow came on seconds after Johncock and Mears took the checker as people began streaming onto the track. The remaining cars — and there were only six others — each were given the

checker under caution and given credit for their final lap.

Pancho Carter, a lap down, was flagged in with 199 laps for 3rd, while Sneva, in spite of being out of the race, had completed enough laps to rank 4th. He later explained that the car began to "push" badly in the later stages, necessitating that he "lift" quite frequently, causing the mixture to lean out and burn a piston.

Al Unser, three laps off the pace, came in for 5th, while Don Whittington, who ran some very fast laps near the end, was four laps back in 6th. Then there was quite a drop before Jim Hickman, the highest finishing "rookie", came home for 7th, seven laps behind Whittington and eleven laps down on Johncock and Mears. Rutherford, who logged in 187 laps before dropping out, was credited with 8th, followed by the only other cars running, driven by Herm Johnson and Howdy Holmes, Herm having nosed Howdy out of 9th place with only two laps to go.

The mob awaiting Johncock at the entrance to Victory Circle was so large that Johncock had to stop short of it. He was completely surrounded by well-wishers as Speedway officials frantically tried to get the car placed where it was

Coming down for the white flag Johncock and Mears are almost even.

Larson

[75]

Veteran Johncock used every ounce of his accumulated talent to hold on to first.

supposed to be. After some moments, the crew began to push the car up the ramp onto the checkered carpeted platform where Johncock could be interviewed for radio and television.

It was probably the wildest and most emotional Victory Lane celebration ever seen here. Johncock hugged his crew members, hugged crew chief George Huening, hugged team manager Jim McGee, hugged engine man Sonny Meyer, hugged car owner Pat Patrick, hugged STP's Ralph Salvino, and hugged his sobbing wife, Lynda. It was also probably the *longest* Victory Circle celebration ever seen here. Long after these things have normally run to their conclusions, Johncock was still standing in the cockpit, drinking Mountain Dew, smiling and waving. George Huening, exhausted, sat down on the side pod, rested his right arm on the windshield, and stared down into space with a smile on his face.

Long after the winning car had been pushed away, Don Whittington's car sat in the pits just north of the Victory Circle,

Down the backstretch Johncock leads Mears by just a few feet.

unattended. At 3:30 p.m., more than half an hour after the race had ended, some crew members arrived to push it away. Fully a quarter of an hour after that, Howdy Holmes came strolling down from the north end of the pits with a couple of friends, swinging his helmet on the strap and winding down from a thoroughly delightful month of May.

The finish was one that fans will talk about forever. There had never been, and possibly never will be again, such a close finish here as in 1982.

Rick Mears sitting in his car in the pits for several minutes afterwards, was as gracious a runner-up as there could possibly be. He smiled during the post-race interviews, running his hand through his matted hair, praising Johncock's skill and taking the defeat philosophically. Never once did he complain of how he could or should have won. He sportingly accepted what had happened, then turned to look to the future — and the future for Rick Mears is incredibly bright.

It is conceivable that Bobby Unser might not ever compete again. Foyt,

Rutherford, Andretti, and Johncock, now the second oldest winner at 45, cannot be expected to race for many more years. For as long as Mears continues to race as he does, as one of the two best drivers under the age of 40, and continues to drive for the Penske team, unquestionably one of the two finest in racing, Mears stands to break every major record there is in this brand of racing.

Johncock entered this race still carrying a stigma. He won the 1973 race, the rain-shortened, accident-marred marathon tragedy that everyone wanted to forget. He wanted to win one that went the distance, one that everyone would want to remember. He came close in 1977, leading Foyt by a good distance until a crankshaft broke with only 16 laps remaining. He was only two seconds behind Bobby Unser and three seconds ahead of Andretti when his car failed with only seven laps to go last year. And there have been other occasions. Finally, nine years after his first win, Gordon Johncock won the one that nobody will ever forget.

Coming down for Duane Sweeny's checkered flag ... will it be Johncock or Mears (or could it be a dead heat)?

Larson

[77]

As the checker waves it is Gordon Johncock holding off Rick Mears. It is the closest finish in the history of the race . . . 0.16 of a second. You won't forget that one for a long time!!! Thanks to the pace car bunching up the field, the many pit stops and two evenly matched cars and drivers, the race was almost a dead heat.

Larson

Mihalke

Kevin Cogan gives an interview after qualifying second fastest.

Whitlow

The line to draw the qualifying order. That's Dennis Firestone in the middle.

Whitlow

Pretty, young Lisa Rolf was a press assistant in the Press Box.

Whitlow

A bespectacled Bobby Unser talks with mechanic Ronnie Dawes about Josele's car.

Whitlow

It's been a long time since Johnny Rutherford wasn't a favorite.

Rouem "Haff" Haffenden tried to get the Kraco cars in the race.

Crucean

Andretti and Carter, plus a pit man, keep watch while Jerry Sneva tests the track after the Smiley accident.

Whitlow

Handsome Tim Richmond has deserted the Speedway in favor of NASCAR.

de Brier

Carefree Scott Brayton and a worried Vern Schuppan.

Mechanic, Phil Casey, buckles Danny Ongais in No. 25.

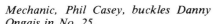

Whitlow

Pretty Vicky Loheider was an interested Tower Terrace spectator.

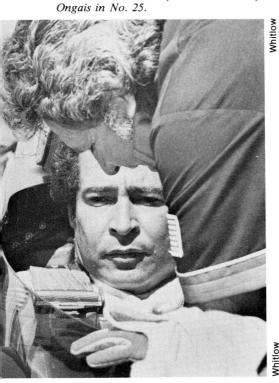

Whitlow

Seems like Howdy Holmes is always good for an interesting snapshot.

Whitlow

Pit Stop Report

Car No.	Stop No.	Lap No.	Reason	Time in Seconds
1st Place — Gordon Johncock, STP Oil Treatment Spl.				
20	1	23	Fuel, RF & RR Tires	15
	2	41	Fuel Only	11
	3	63	Fuel, RF, RR & LR Tires	15
	4	95	Fuel, RF & RR Tires	19
	5	127	Fuel, RF, RR & LR Tires	21
	6	139	Fuel Only	11
	7	155	Fuel Only	10
	8	186	Fuel Only	13
			TOTAL	115
2nd Place — Rick Mears, The Gould Charge Penske				
1	1	23	Fuel, RF & RR Tires	13.5
	2	41	Fuel, RF & RR Tires	12.2
	3	64	Fuel Only	11.7
	4	94	Fuel, RF, RR & LR Tires RF Tire & Tool Unattended	
	5	128	Fuel Only	17
	6	155	Fuel, RF & RR Tires	14.7
	7	184	Fuel	18.4
			TOTAL	104.5
3rd Place — Pancho Carter, Alex Foods Spl.				
3	1	23	Fuel Only	23
	2	40	Fuel, RF & RR Tires	20
	3	63	Fuel, LR Tire	28
	4	90	Fuel, Adjust Lf Wing	21
	5	118	Fuel, RF & RR Tires	25
	6	134	Fuel Only, Loose Tape Removed	17
	7	155	Fuel Only	24
	8	180	Fuel, RF & RR Tires	28
			TOTAL	186
4th Place — Tom Sneva, Texaco Star				
7	1	25	Fuel, RF & RR Tires	19
	2	41	Fuel Only	20
	3	64	Fuel, RF & RR Tires Two Extra people on scoring stand	18
	4	96	Fuel, Adjust Front Wing	21
	5	128	Fuel, RF & RR Tires Car on front hose, air jacked to release hose	28
	6	156	Fuel Only, valve malfunctioned; not cocked properly, four people on scoring stand	54
	7	184	Fuel, RF & RR Tires	22
	8	197	Black Flagged, Engine had burned piston Out of Race	
			TOTAL	182
5th Place — Al Unser, Longhorn Racing Inc.				
10	1	22	Fuel, RF & RR Tires	19
	2	39	Fuel Only	13
	3	42	RF & RR Tires, LR wheel nut problem	25
	4	65	Fuel, RF, RR Tires	21
	5	93	Fuel RF & RR Tires	24
	6	124	Fuel Only	19
	7	153	Fuel, RF & RR Tires Trouble with RR wheel nut-replaced	36
	8	180	Fuel Only	21
			TOTAL	178
6th Place — Don Whittington, The Simoniz Finish				
91	1	26	Fuel, RF & RR Tires	22
	2	43	Fuel, RF, RR & LR Tires Engine stalled, restarted	76
	3	67	Fuel, RF, RR & LR Tires six men over wall	29
	4	68	LF Tire	33
	5	91	Fuel, RF & RR Tires, Engine stalled electric restart, driver needs neck collar	84
	6	121	Fuel, adjust front wing	27
	7	136	Fuel Only	12
	8	182	Fuel Only, car pushed back	27
	9	184	Fuel Only	22
			TOTAL	332
7th Place — Jim Hickman, Stroh's March				
42	1	24	Fuel Only	17
	2	25	No Work	22
	3	26	Fuel, RF, RR & LR Tires	47
	4	38	Fuel, RF Tire	40
	5	62	Fuel, LF Tire	37
	6	88	Fuel, RF, RR & LR Tires	47
	7	119	Fuel, LF Tire	33
	8	133	Fuel, RF, RR & LR Tires	31
	9	147	Fuel Only	14
	10	176	Fuel Only	26
			TOTAL	314
8th Place — Johnny Rutherford, Pennzoil Chaparral				
5	1	23	Fuel Only	13
	2	40	Fuel Only	11
	3	66	Fuel, RF, RR & LR Tires	18
	4	95	Fuel Only	16
	5	123	Fuel, RF, RR & LR Tires	18
	6	139	Fuel Only	10
	7	153	Fuel, RF, RR & LR Tires	18
	8	178	Fuel, RF, RR & LR Tires	32
	9	187	Out of Race, broken water line, overheated	
			TOTAL	136

Car No.	Stop No.	Lap No.	Reason	Time in Seconds
9th Place — Herm Johnson, Menard Cashway Lumber				
28	1	23	Fuel Only	16
	2	39	Fuel Only	26
	3	62	Fuel, RF & RR Tires	23
	4	89	Fuel Only	18
	5	119	Fuel Only, wouldn't take fuel?	15
	6	121	Fuel Only, engine stalled, restarted	48
	7	145	Fuel Only	22
	8	171	Fuel Only	24
			TOTAL	192
10th Place — Howdy Holmes, Domino's Pizza/Team Shierson				
30	1	25	Fuel Only	16
	2	43	Fuel, RF, RR & LR Tires	21
	3	63	Fuel Only	17
	4	91	Fuel, RF, RR & LR Tires	20
	5	122	Fuel Only	17
	6	137	Fuel, Changed pressure relief valve to spare	270
	7	157	Fuel Only	14
	8	185	Fuel, RF, RR & LR Tires	23
			TOTAL	398
11th Place — Bobby Rahal, Red Roof Inn March				
19	1	27	Fuel Only	26
	2	41	Fuel, RF, RR & LR Tires	27
	3	63	Fuel, Adjust wing	16
	4	97	Fuel Only	22
	5	123	Fuel, RF, RR & LR Tires	25
	6	152	Fuel Only	21
	7	174	Out of Race, engine failure	
			TOTAL	137
12th Place — Gary Bettenhausen, Kraco Spl.				
8	1	23	Fuel, Adjust RF Wing	18
	2	37	Fuel, RF & RR Tires	25
	3	59	Fuel Only, pulled back, pushed out	15
	4	89	Fuel Only	17
	5	93	Fuel Only	11
	6	122	Fuel Only	18
	7	144	Fuel, RF & RR Tires	26
		157	Out of Race, engine failure	
			TOTAL	130
13th Place — Hector Rebaque, Carta Blanca				
52	1	24	Fuel Only	17
	2	42	Fuel, RF & RR Tires	19
	3	64	Fuel Only	14
	4	96	Fuel, RF & RR Tires	37
	5	129	Fuel Only, engine stalled in pit	18
	6	129	Engine stalled, poured water on it to restart six men over wall	97
	7	151	Fuel, RF & RR Tires refueling fire, six men over wall, would not restart, clutch failed Out of race	33
			TOTAL	235
14th Place — Danny Sullivan, Forsythe-Brown Racing				
53	1	25	Fuel Only	38
	2	40	Fuel, RF & RR Tires	27
	3	64	Fuel, RF & RR Tires	21
	4	91	Fuel Only	16
	5	123	Fuel, RF & RR Tires	20
	6	130	Fuel, Adjust front wings	12
	7	149	Out of Race, hit wall near pit entrance	
			TOTAL	134
15th Place — Chip Ganassi, First Commercial Corp. Spl.				
12	1	24	Fuel Only	16
	2	39	Fuel, RF & RR Tires	15
	3	63	Fuel Only	13
	4	92	Fuel Only	16
	5	122	Fuel, RF & RR Tires	20
	6	129	Fuel, LF & LR Tires	17
	7	148	Out of Race, engine failure	230
			TOTAL	327
16th Place — Bill Whittington, Whittington Warner Hodgdon				
94	1	23	Fuel, RF, RR & LR Tires	22
	2	40	Fuel Only	15
	3	63	Fuel, RF, RR & LR Tires	23
	4	93	Fuel, RF Tire, six men over wall	25
	5	96	Adjust front wings	10
	6	98	Inspected car	12
	7	116	Fuel, RF, RR & LR Tires	32
	8	117	Adjust waste gate	43
		123	Out of Race, broken header	
			TOTAL	182
17th Place — Michael Chandler Freeman-Gurney Eagle				
68	1	22	Fuel, RF & RR Tires	27
	2	40	Fuel, RF & RR Tires	25
	3	62	Fuel, RF & RR Tires, refueling valve O'ring replaced, slight oil leak checked	31
	4	91	Fuel, removed cowling, cleaned oil off underpan,	472
	5	104	Fuel-cowl removed, engine shut off, Out of Race, transmission failure	
			TOTAL	555
18th Place — Tom Bigelow, H.B.K. Racing-Vollstedt Eagle				
27	1	22	Fuel, Adjust LF wing	19
	2	39	Fuel, RF & RR Tires	36
	3	58	Black flagged, checked for leak, added fuel, returned to race	414
	4	60	Fuel Only	55
	5	85	Fuel, changed fuel nozzle	162
	6	93	Black flagged, changed Rt. valve cover gasket and RR tire, returned to race	803
	7		Replaced cracked right valve cover	1353
	8	96	Out of Race, Oil pressure problems	
			TOTAL	2842

Car No.	Stop No.	Lap No.	Reason	Time in Seconds
19th Place — A. J. Foyt, Valvoline-Gilmore Spl.				
14	1	24	Fuel Only	18
	2	42	Fuel, RF RR & LR Tires	24
	3	65	Fuel Only, fuel valve on car stuck open, o'ring problems	17
	4	66	Refueling valve repaired, changed valve on hose	95
	5	92	Fuel Only	21
	6	94	Attempted to repair shift linkage	40
	7	95	Attempted to repir shift linkage	97
	8	96	Out of Race, trasmission shift linkage not repairable	300
			TOTAL	612
20th Place — Johnny Parsons, Silhouette/Tombstone/WIFE				
34	1	20	Fuel, RF & RR Tires, air jack hose thrown over wall	19
	2	23	Tape over split in intake log	254
	3	27	Fuel, changed intake log	2195
	4	52	Fuel Only, air jack hose thrown over wall	22
	5	78	Fuel, RF & RR Tires	21
	6	90	Fuel Only	19
		93	Out of Race, broken half shaft	
			TOTAL	2530
21th Place — George Snider, Cobre Tire				
35	1	23	Fuel Only	13
	2	39	Fuel, RF& RR Tires	25
	3	61	Fuel Only	13
	4	63	Rt. side mirror loose, taken off	10
	5	87	Fuel Only	13
		87	Out of Race gearbox problems	
			TOTAL	74
22th Place — Danny Ongais, Interscope Racing				
25	1	27	Fuel Only	21
	2	41	Fuel, RF, RR & LR Tires	21
		62	Out of Race, Accident	
			TOTAL	42
23th Place — Jerry Sneva, The Great American Spirit				
69	1	22	Fuel, RF & RR Tires	27
	2	39	Fuel, RF & RR Tires	18
		61	Out of Race, Accident turn two	
			TOTAL	45

Car No.	Stop No.	Lap No.	Reason	Time in Seconds
24th Place — Chet Fillip, Circle Truck Corral				
39	1	19	Fuel Only	20
	2	41	Fuel, RR & LR Tires	33
		58	Out of Race, Accident damaged Lt. side of car	
			TOTAL	53
25th Place — Pete Halsmer, Colonial/Payless/WISH/Arciero				
66	1	20	Fuel Only	20
	2	38	Fuel, engine stalled, push start tried gearbox would not disengage, out of race	
			TOTAL	20
26th Place — Tony Bettenhausen, Provimi Veal				
16	1	22	Fuel, RF & RR Tires	19
		38	Out of Race, accident on front straightaway, broken half shaft	
			TOTAL	19
27th Place — Dennis Firestone, B.C.V. Racing				
75	1	28	Fuel Only	22
	2	37	Out of Race, broken ring gear	
			TOTAL	22
28th Place — Geoff Brabham, Pentax Super				
21	1	12	Out of Race, engine failure	
29th Place — Josele Garza, Schlitz Gusto				
55	1		Out of Race, engine failure	
30th Place — Kevin Cogan, Norton Spirit Penske				
4			Out of Race, accident on pace lap	
31st Place — Mario Andretti, STP Oil Treatment Spl.				
40			Out of Race, accident on pace lap	
32nd Place — Roger Mears, Machinist Union Racing Team				
31			Out of Race, accident on pace lap	
33rd Place, Dale Whittington, Whittington Warner Hodgdon				
95			Out of Race, accident on pace lap	

10 Lap Run Down

LAP NO. 10

POS. NO.	CAR NO.	DRIVER
1	14	A. J. Foyt
2	1	Rick Mears
3	20	Gordon Johncock
4	7	Tom Sneva
5	91	Don Whittington
6	3	Pancho Carter
7	94	Bill Whittington
8	53	Danny Sullivan
9	25	Danny Ongais
10	5	Johnny Rutherford

Time — 0:07:41.62
Speed — 194.966

LAP NO. 20

POS. NO.	CAR NO.	DRIVER
1	14	A. J. Foyt
2	20	Gordon Johncock
3	1	Rick Mears
4	7	Tom Sneva
5	91	Don Whittington
6	3	Pancho Carter
7	25	Danny Ongais
8	94	Bill Whittington
9	5	Johnny Rutherford
10	10	Al Unser

Time — 0:15:40.66
Speed — 191.355

LAP NO. 30

POS. NO.	CAR NO.	DRIVER
1	14	A. J. Foyt
2	1	Rick Mears
3	20	Gordon Johncock
4	7	Tom Sneva
5	91	Don Whittington
6	25	Danny Ongais
7	3	Pancho Carter
8	5	Johnny Rutherford
9	10	Al Unser
10	94	Bill Whittington

Time — 0:24:18.91
Speed — 185.099

LAP NO. 40

POS. NO.	CAR NO.	DRIVER
1	1	Rick Mears
2	14	A. J. Foyt
3	20	Gordon Johncock
4	7	Tom Sneva
5	25	Danny Ongais
6	3	Pancho Carter
7	91	Don Whittington
8	5	Johnny Rutherford
9	52	Hector Rebaque
10	94	Whittington

Time — 0:32:20.89
Speed — 185.482

LAP NO. 50

POS. NO.	CAR NO.	DRIVER
1	7	Tom Sneva
2	20	Gordon Johncock
3	1	Rick Mears
4	14	A. J. Foyt
5	3	Pancho Carter
6	25	Danny Ongais
7	91	Don Whittington
8	69	Jerry Sneva
9	94	Bill Whittington
10	5	Johnny Rutherford

Time — 0:44:39.30
Speed —167.954

LAP NO. 60

POS. NO.	CAR NO.	DRIVER
1	1	Rick Mears
2	7	Tom Sneva
3	20	Gordon Johncock
4	14	A. J. Foyt
5	25	Danny Ongais
6	3	Pancho Carter
7	91	Don Whittington
8	69	Jerry Sneva
9	68	Mike Chandler
10	94	Bill Whittington

Time — 0:52:27.37
Speed — 171.572

LAP NO.70

POS. NO.	CAR NO.	DRIVER
1	1	Rick Mears
2	7	Tom Sneva
3	20	Gordon Johncock
4	3	Pancho Carter
5	52	Hector Rebaque
6	10	Al Unser
7	5	Johnny Rutherford
8	14	A. J. Foyt
9	91	Don Whittington
10	68	Mike Chandler

Time — 1:05:36.94
Speed — 160.023

LAP NO. 80

POS. NO.	CAR NO.	DRIVER
1	1	Rick Mears
2	7	Tom Sneva
3	20	Gordon Johncock
4	3	Pancho Carter
5	14	A. J. Foyt
6	52	Hector Rebaque
7	10	Al Unser
8	5	Pancho Carter
9	91	Don Whittington
10	68	Mike Chandler

Time — 1:13:56.41
Speed — 162.293

LAP NO. 90

POS. NO.	CAR NO.	DRIVER
1	1	Rick Mears
2	7	Tom Sneva
3	20	Gordon Johncock
4	3	Pancho Carter
5	14	A. J. Foyt
6	52	Hector Rebaque
7	10	Al Unser
8	5	Johnny Rutherford
9	91	Don Whittington
10	68	Mike Chandler

Time — 1:21:46.89
Speed — 165.074

LAP NO. 100

POS. NO.	CAR NO.	DRIVER
1	20	Gordon Johncock
2	1	Rick Mears
3	7	Tom Sneva
4	3	Pancho Carter
5	52	Hector Rebaque
6	5	Johnny Rutherford
7	10	Al Unser
8	19	Bobby Rahal
9	53	Danny Sullivan
10	94	Bill Whittington

Time — 1:33:00.15
Speed — 161.286

LAP NO. 110

POS. NO.	CAR NO.	DRIVER
1	1	Rick Mears
2	20	Gordon Johncock
3	7	Tom Sneva
4	3	Pancho Carter
5	52	Hector Rebaque
6	5	Johnny Rutherford
7	10	Al Unser
8	19	Bobby Rahal
9	53	Danny Sullivan
10	94	Bill Whittington

Time — 1:43:21.03
Speed — 159.651

LAP NO. 120

POS. NO.	CAR NO.	DRIVER
1	1	Rick Mears
2	7	Tom Sneva
3	20	Gordon Johncock
4	3	Pancho Carter
5	52	Hector Rebaque
6	5	Johnny Rutherford
7	10	Al Unser
8	19	Bobby Rahal
9	53	Danny Sullivan
10	91	Don Whittington

Time — 1:51:03.64
Speed — 162.074

LAP NO. 130

POS. NO.	CAR NO.	DRIVER
1	1	Rick Mears
2	7	Tom Sneva
3	3	Pancho Carter
4	20	Gordon Johncock
5	52	Hector Rebaque
6	5	Johnny Rutherford
7	10	Al Unser
8	19	Bobby Rahal
9	53	Danny Sullivan
10	91	Don Whittington

Time — 1:59:31.76
Speed — 163.140

LAP NO. 140

POS. NO.	CAR NO.	DRIVER
1	1	Rick Mears
2	7	Tom Sneva
3	3	Pancho Carter
4	20	Gordon Johncock
5	5	Johnny Rutherford
6	10	Al Unser
7	19	Bobby Rahal
8	52	Hector Rebaque
9	53	Danny Sullivan
10	91	Don Whittington

Time — 2:11:57.04
Speed — 159.150

LAP NO. 150

POS. NO.	CAR NO.	DRIVER
1	7	Tom Sneva
2	1	Rick Mears
3	3	Pancho Carter
4	20	Gordon Johncock
5	10	Al Unser
6	5	Johnny Rutherford
7	19	Bobby Rahal
8	52	Hector Rebaque
9	53	Danny Sullivan
10	91	Don Whittington

Time — 2:21:21.46
Speed — 159.171

LAP NO. 160

POS. NO.	CAR NO.	DRIVER
1	20	Gordon Johncock
2	1	Rick Mears
3	7	Tom Sneva
4	3	Pancho Carter
5	10	Al Unser
6	5	Johnny Rutherford
7	19	Bobby Rahal
8	91	Don Whittington
9	42	Jim Hickman
10	28	Herm Johnson

Time — 2:33:50.01
Speed — 156.013

LAP NO. 170

POS. NO.	CAR NO.	DRIVER
1	20	Gordon Johncock
2	1	Rick Mears
3	7	Tom Sneva
4	3	Pancho Carter
5	10	Al Unser
6	5	Johnny Rutherford
7	19	Bobby Rahal
8	91	Don Whittington
9	42	Jim Hickman
10	28	Herm Johnson

Time — 2:41:27.81
Speed — 157.930

LAP NO. 180

POS. NO.	CAR NO.	DRIVER
1	20	Gordon Johncock
2	1	Rick Mears
3	7	Tom Sneva
4	3	Pancho Carter
5	10	Al Unser
6	5	Johnny Rutherford
7	91	Don Whittington
8	19	Bobby Rahal
9	42	Jim Hickman
10	28	Herm Johnson

Time — 2:49:06.79
Speed — 159.656

LAP NO. 190

POS. NO.	CAR NO.	DRIVER
1	20	Gordon Johncock
2	1	Rick Mears
3	7	Tom Sneva
4	3	Pancho Carter
5	10	Al Unser
6	5	Johnny Rutherford
7	91	Don Whittington
8	42	Jim Hickman
9	28	Herm Johnson
10	30	Howdy Holmes

Time — 2:57:41.82
Speed — 160.687

LAP NO. 200

POS. NO.	CAR NO.	DRIVER
1	20	Gordon Johncock
2	1	Rick Mears
3	3	Pancho Carter
4	7	Tom Sneva
5	10	Al Unser
6	91	Don Whittington
7	42	Jim Hickman
8	5	Johnny Rutherford
9	28	Herm Johnson
10	30	Howdy Holmes

Time — 3:05:09.14
Speed — 162.029

This seems to be one of A. J. Foyt's better days.

Larson

Race car trailers come in many sizes. The big one belongs to the Whittington Brothers and the small one to Joe Hunt.

Mahoney

500 MILE RACE FIELD
Qualified Cars in the Starting Field

#1 Rick Mears — The Gould Charge Penske
2:53.91	207.004
43.52	206.801
43.47	207.039
Qual: 43.35 207.612
5/15 @ 11:06 — 43.57 206.564

#40 Mario Andretti — STP Oil Treatment Spl
2:57.19	203.172
44.11	204.035
44.50	202.247
Qual: 43.39 202.748
5/15 @ 15:24 — 44.19 203.666

#7 Tom Sneva — Texaco Star
2:59.08	201.027
44.24	203.436
44.94	200.267
Qual: 45.05 199.778
5/15 @ 16:08 — 44.85 200.669

#3 Pancho Carter — ALEX Food Spl
3:00.95	198.950
45.17	199.247
45.27	198.807
Qual: 45.21 199.071
5/15 @ 15:18 — 45.30 198.675

#53 Danny Sullivan — Forsythe-Brown Racing
3:03.40	196.292
45.80	196.507
45.85	196.292
Qual: 45.89 196.121
5/15 @ 12:07 — 45.86 196.249

#10 Al Unser — Longhorn Racing, Inc.
3:04.08	195.567
45.43	198.107
46.15	195.016
Qual: 46.19 194.847
5/15 @ 15:29 — 46.31 194.342

#31 Roger Mears — Machinists Union Racing Team
3:05.42	194.154
46.33	194.259
46.09	195.270
Qual: 46.38 194.049
5/15 @ 11:12 — 46.62 193.050

#68 Michael Chandler — Freeman/Gurney Eagle
3:01.78	198.042
45.52	197.715
45.31	198.632
Qual: 45.34 198.500
5/22 @ 12:35 — 45.61 197.325

#34 Johnny Parsons, Jr. — Silhouette Health Spa/Tombstone Pizza/WIFE
3:03.74	195.929
45.90	196.078
45.90	196.078
Qual: 45.99 195.695
5/22 @ 15:30 — 45.95 195.865

#69 Jerry Sneva — The Great American Spirit
3:04.36	195.270
45.94	195.908
45.70	196.937
Qual: 46.13 195.101
5/15 @ 11:06 — 46.59 193.175

#27 Tom Bigelow — H.B.K. Racing/Vollstedt Eagle
3:04.82	194.784
46.12	195.143
46.05	195.440
Qual: 46.32 194.301
5/15 @ 13:55 — 46.33 194.259

#4 Kevin Cogan — Norton Spirit Penske
2:56.40	204.082
44.27	203.298
44.15	203.851
Qual: 43.98 204.638
5/15 @ 11:00 — 44.00 204.545

#20 Gordon Johncock — STP Oil Treatment Spl.
2:58.32	201.884
44.53	202.111
44.56	201.975
Qual: 44.63 201.658
5/15 @ 11:19 — 44.60 201.794

#91 Don Whittington — The Simoniz Finish
2:59.35	200.725
44.73	201.207
44.37	202.840
Qual: 45.17 199.247
5/15 @ 15.35 — 45.08 199.645

#12 Chip Ganassi — First Commercial Corporation Spl.
3:02.09	197.704
45.42	198.151
45.56	197.542
Qual: 45.55 197.585
5/15 @ 15:41 — 45.56 197.542

#28 Herm Johnson — Menard Cashway Lumber Spl.
3:03.74	195.929
45.91	196.036
45.87	196.207
Qual: 45.86 196.249
5/15 @ 15:57 — 46.10 195.228

#19 Bobby Rahal — Red Roof Inns March
3:04.90	194.700
46.31	194.342
46.16	194.974
Qual: 46.14 195.059
5/15 @ 11:25 — 46.29 194.426

#21 Geoff Brabham — Pentax Super
3:00.99	198.906
45.36	198.413
45.22	199.027
Qual: 45.11 199.512
5/16 @ 17.16 — 45.30 198.675

#95 Dale Whittington — Whittington Warner Hodgdon March
3:02.10	197.694
45.58	197.455
45.53	197.672
Qual: 45.46 197.976
5/22 @ 11:00 — 45.53 197.672

#35 George Snider — Cobre Tire
3:04.15	195.493
45.90	196.078
46.15	195.016
Qual: 46.01 195.610
5/22 @ 16:12 — 46.09 195.270

#39 Chet Fillip — Circle Bar Truck Corral
3:04.73	194.879
46.30	194.384
45.90	196.078
Qual: 45.90 196.078
5/22 @ 11:28 — 46.63 193.009

#66 Pete Halsmer — Colonial Bread/Pay Less Mkts/WISH/Arciero Eagle
3:05.00	194.595
45.95	195.865
46.12	195.143
Qual: 46.42 193.882
5/23 @ 12:39 — 46.51 193.507

#14 A. J. Foyt — Valvoline-Gilmore
2:57.05	203.332
44.02	204.453
44.62	201.703
Qual: 44.30 203.160
5/15 @ 16:21 — 44.11 204.035

#94 Bill Whittington — Whittington Warner Hodgdon March
2:58.52	201.658
44.69	201.387
44.62	201.703
Qual: 44.67 201.478
5/15 @ 16:02 — 44.54 202.066

#25 Danny Ongais — Interscope Racing
3:00.77	199.148
45.05	199.778
45.19	199.159
Qual: 44.25 198.895
5/15 @ 11:55 — 45.28 198.763

#5 Johnny Rutherford — Pennzoil Chaparral
3:02.68	197.066
45.61	197.325
45.81	196.464
Qual: 45.56 197.542
5/15 @ 11:49 — 45.70 196.937

#52 Hector Rebaque — Carta Blanca
3:03.97	195.684
45.76	196.678
45.92	195.993
Qual: 46.04 195.482
5/15 @ 15:51 — 46.25 194.595

#30 Howdy Holmes — Domino's Pizza/Team Shierson
3:05.12	194.468
46.26	194.553
46.16	194.974
Qual: 46.18 194.890
5/15 @ 12:01 — 46.52 193.465

#75 Dennis Firestone — B.C.V. Racing
3:02.54	197.217
45.46	197.976
45.59	197.412
Qual: 45.72 196.850
5/16 @ 17:33 — 45.77 196.635

#42 Jim Hickman — Stroh's March
3:03.47	196.217
45.71	196.893
45.89	196.121
Qual: 45.97 195.780
5/22 @ 12:23 — 45.90 196.078

#16 Tony Bettenhausen — Provimi Veal
3:04.21	195.429
45.78	196.592
45.86	196.249
Qual: 46.07 195.355
5/22 @ 15:53 — 46.50 193.548

#8 Gary Bettenhausen — KRACO Spl
3:03.98	195.673
46.06	195.397
46.00	195.652
Qual: 45.95 195.865
5/23 @ 16:01 — 45.97 195.780

#55 Josele Garza — Schlitz Gusto
3:05.09	194.500
46.47	193.673
46.11	195.185
Qual: 46.10 195.228
5/23 @ 12:04 — 46.41 193.924

The average speed of the 33 cars that started the race in 1981 was 191.244 mph.
The average speed of the 33 cars that started the race in 1982 was 197.740 mph.
(6.496 — mph faster)

(Continued on P. 88)

(Continued from P. 87)

QUALIFIED CARS NOT IN THE STARTING FIELD

#49	Chip Mead	3:05.74	193.819
	Arizona Int'l. Travel	46.16	194.974
		46.44	193.798
	Qual: 5/15 @ 16.27	46.49	193.590
	Bumped by car #8	46.65	192.926

#2	Bill Alsup	3:06.41	193.123
	A.B. Dick Pacemaker	46.31	194.342
		46.51	193.507
	Qual: 5/22 @ 11:23	46.75	192.513
	Bumped by car #27	46.84	192.143

1982 GARAGE AREA

NORTH

ENTRANCE TO TRACK

1	Car No. 18 Dick Ferguson Kraco Car Stereo	45	Car No. 28 Herm Johnson Menard Cashway
2	Car No. 99 Vern Schuppan Kraco Car Stereo	44	Car No. 95 Dale Whittington Whittington Brothers
3	Car No. 17 John Martin Vollstedt Enterprises	43	Car No. 94 Bill Whittington Whittington Brothers
4	Car No. 27 Rusty Schmidt Vollstedt Enterprises	42	Car No. 91 Don Whittington Whittington Brothers
5	Car No. 32 Jerry Karl Purcell Racer	41	Car No. 68 Michael Chandler Freeman/Gurney Eagle
6	Car No. 90 Gary Irvin Swingler Chevy	40	Car No. 48 Mike Mosley All American Racers
7	Car No. 78 Larry Rice Lindsey Hopkins	39	Car No. 46 Leroy Van Conett McCray Racing
8	Car No. 8 Gary Bettenhausen Lindsey Hopkins	38	Car No. 86 Al Loquasto Empress Traveler
9	Car No. 64 No Driver Named Jet Engineering	37	Car No. 88 Billy Scott Frito-Lay/Timberwood
10	Car No. 82 Sammy Swindell Jet Engineering	36	Car No. 63 Ken Hamilton Eagle Aircraft
11	Car No. 3 Pancho Carter Alex Foods	35	Car No. 72 Roger Rager Indiana Coal
12	Car No. 3-T Pancho Carter Alex Foods	34	Car No. 12 Chip Ganassi First Commercial
14	Car No. 19 Bobby Rahal Red Roof Inns	33	Car No. 30 Howdy Holmes Domino's Pizza
15	Car No. 16 Tony Bettenhausen Provimi Veal	32	Premier Industrial And D-A Lubricant
16	Car No. 35 Gordon Smiley Intermedics Innovator	31	Car No. 71 Dean Vetrock Vetco Racing/Larrie Ervin
17	Car No. 33 Desire Wilson Theodore Racing	30	Car No. 84 George Snider Valvoline Gilmore
18	Car No. 38 Phillip Caliva C.H.C. Intersec Racing	29	Car No. 14 A.J. Foyt Valvoline Gilmore
19	Car No. 22 Dick Simon Vermont American	28	Monroe Shock Absorbers And Sunnen
20	Car No. 24 Rich Vogler Vermont American	27	Car No. 77 Tom Frantz Burger King
21	Car No. 50 Bobby Unser Schlitz Gusto	26	Car No. 39 Chet Fillip Circle Bar Truck
22	Car No. 55 Josele Garza Schlitz Gusto	25	Car No. 25-T Danny Ongais Interscope Racing
23	Car No. 57 Salt Walther Cognets-Andrews	24	Car No. 25 Danny Ongais Interscope Racing

PREMIER D-A MECHANICAL ACHIEVEMENT AWARD

The Premier/D-A Mechanical Achievement Award recognizes the work of the USAC Championship Division Chief Mechanic for the 500 Mile Memorial Day Race in Indianapolis.

The Award is presented to the Chief Mechanic, who, in the estimation of fellow mechanics and a selected board of judges, has demonstrated the greatest skill, imagination and perseverance in preparing a championship car for the Indianapolis 500 Mile Race.

WINNERS

1981 – Wayne Leary

1980 – Steve Roby
1979 – Grant King
1978 – Jim McGee
1977 – Dave Klym
1976 – Chuck Looper
1975 – Grant King
1974 – A. J. "Tony" Foyt
1973 – Smokey Yunick
1972 – Phil Casey
1971 – Karl Kainhofer
1970 – George Bignotti
1969 – Jim McGee
1968 – Jud Phillips
1967 – Bill Fowler
1966 – Jerry Eisert
1965 – Clint Brawner
1964 – A. J. Watson
1963 – John Pouelsen (deceased)
1962 – Mickey Thompson
1961 – A. J. Watson
1960 – Danny Oakes
1959 – Jean Marcenac (deceased)

TO GARAGE AREA PARKING LOT

46	Car No. 59 Billy Engelhart Beaudoin Racing	89	Car No. 42 Jim Hickman Rattlesnake Racing
47	Car No. 47 Lee Kunzman Jamieson Racing	88	Car No. 11 Bill Vukovich Hubler Q 95
48	Car No. 49 Chip Mead Jamieson Racing	87	Car No. 5-T Johnny Rutherford Pennzoil/Chaparral
49	Car No. 79 Bob Harkey C&H Racing	86	Car No. 5 Johnny Rutherford Pennzoil/Chaparral
50	Car No. 43 Greg Leffler Armstrong Mould	85	Car No. 61 Tim Richmond Mach I Racing
51	Car No. 44 Sheldon Kinser Armstrong Mould	84	Car No. 21 Geoff Brabham Pentax-Super
52	Car No. 10 Al Unser Longhorn Racing	83	Car No. 7 Tom Sneva - Texaco Star/Bignotti/Cotter
53	Car No. 70 No Driver Named Longhorn Racing	82	Car No. 67 Teddy Pilette Mergard's 20th Century
54	Car No. 89 Phil Krueger Joe Hunt	81	Car No. 31 Roger Mears Machinists Union
55	Car No. 40 Mario Andretti STP Patrick Racing	80	Car No. 80 Tom Gloy Machinists Union
56	Car No. 20 Gordon Johncock STP Oil Treatment	79	Car No. 58 Joe Saldana Genesee Beer
57	Car No. 60 No Driver Named STP Oil Treatment	78	Car No. 56 Tom Bigelow Genesee Beer
58	Car No. 98 Jimmy McElreath Giuffre Brothers Crane	77	No Car Assigned No Driver Named Penske Cars LTD
59	Car No. 73 Ray Lipper Center Line	76	Car No. 4 Kevin Cogan Norton Spirit Penske
60	Car No. 75 Dennis Firestone B.C.V. Racing	75	Car No. 1 Rick Mears Gould Charge Penske
61	Car No. 52 Hector Rebaque Carta Blanca	74	Car No. 66 Pete Halsmer Colonial Bread/Payless
62	Car No. 53 Danny Sullivan Forsythe Brown	73	Car No. 34 Hurley Haywood Wysard Racing
63	Indiana Oxygen Welding	72	Car No. 2 Bill Alsup A.B. Dick Pacemaker
64	Car No. 92 Jan Sneva PWS Racing	71	Car No. 36 Pat Bedard Escort Radar Detector
65	Car No. 93 Steve Chassey PWS Racing	70	Car No. 37 Scott Brayton Brayton Racing
66	Car No. 29 Bobby Olivero Hodgdon Racing	69	Racing Associates
67	Car No. 69 No Driver Named Hoffman Auto	68	Racing Associates

Spin & Wreck Report

May 2, 1982 — Sunday
1. Time: 4:38 p.m.

Gordon Smiley in the #35 Intermedics Innovator March/Cosworth got high out of Turn-3 (NE) for 280 feet, brushed wall with right rear tire for approximately 40 feet, continued on into pits.

May 11, 1982 — Tuesday
2. Time: 3:19 p.m.

Ken Hamilton in #63 Eagle Aircraft Flyer DW2/Chevy lost control coming out of Turn-4 (NW), gathered it in and continued into pits.

May 11, 1982 — Tuesday
3. Time: 3:37 P.M.

Dean Vetrock in #71 Vetco Racing/Larrie Ervin Lightning/Chevy lost left rear wheel in Turn—3 (NE); got sideways for 200 feet, stopped on infield grass. No contact.

May 11, 1982 — Tuesday
4. Time: 5:20 a.m.

Bob Lazier in #34 Wysard Racing Team March/Cosworth ran over metal, causing blow-out of right rear tire, in backstretch, continued on to Turn-4 (NW) and stopped. No contact.

May 12, 1982 — Wednesday
5. Time: 1:10 p.m.

Roger Rager in #72 Indiana Coal/Wildcat/Cosworth spun 1 time coming out of Turn-4 (NW) for 440 feet, hit inside wall with left side, scraping 40 feet along wall, then did 3/4 spin away from wall for 200 feet; stopped on track near pit entrance. Driver: Checked and released complaining of sore left shoulder. Car: extensive damage.

May 12, 1982 — Wednesday
6. Time: 5:13 p.m.

Danny Sullivan in #53 Forsythe-Brown Racing March/Cosworth lost control in Turn-3 (NE), slid 440 feet, spinning 1 1/2 times, hit wall on left side; slid along wall approximately 30 feet, car came to stop on infield grass in Turn-4 (NW). Driver: checked and released. Car: very little damage.

May 12, 1982 — Wednesday
7. Time: 5:49 p.m.

Tony Bettenhausen in #16 Provimi Veal March/Cosworth had problem with clutch going into Turn-3 (NE), causing him to slide for 200 feet in a half-spin; slid 240 feet backward into outside wall with left rear hitting; traveled 120 feet, hit wall again, then slid 120 feet away from wall, stopping on track surface, near outside wall. Driver: O.K. Car: damage to left rear.

May 13, 1982 — Thursday
8. Time: 11:38 a.m.

Ken Hamilton in #63 Eagle Aircraft Flyer DW2/Chevy got low in Turn-1 (SW), got sideways and slid 300 feet, dipped into grass infield, gathered it in and continued into pits. No contact.

May 13, 1982 — Thurday
9. Time: 4 p.m.

Josele Garza in #50 Schlitz Gusto March/Cosworth in middle of Turn-3 (NE) lost control and made 1 complete spin covering 480 feet, hit wall, was airborne for 20 feet; made one additional spin for 360 feet away from wall. Came to stop in middle of track mid-way in north short chute. Driver: O.K. Car: extensive damage to right rear section.

May 14, 1982 — Friday
10. Time: 5:35 p.m.

Jim Hickman in #42 Stroh's March March/Cosworth coming out of Turn-1 (SW) lost control, spun 1 1/2 times across track for 820 feet, hit inside steel retaining wall at start of Turn-2 (SE). Stopped against wall. Driver: checked at track hospital and released. Car: damage to right rear section.

May 15, 1982 — Saturday
11. Time: 12:15 p.m.

Gordon Smiley in #35 Intermedics Innovator March/Cosworth in Turn-3 (NE) lost control, overcorrected into a reverse slide for 280 feet to wall. Airborne (vertically approximately 50 feet. Car disintegrated into 3 sections. Engine section sliding 480 feet to middle of north short chute. Driver: died instantaneously (12:15 p.m.) of massive head injuries (Dr. Henry Bock confirmed @ 12:30 p.m.)

May 16, 1982 — Sunday
12. Time: 12:25 p.m.

Tom Bigelow got high out of Turn-1 (SW), making a 3/4 spin for 380 feet to middle of south short chute. No contact. #56 Genesee Beer Wagon Penske/Cosworth.

May 19, 1982 — Wednesday
13. Time: 2:57 p.m.

Desire Wilson in #33 Theordore Racing March/Cosworth lost control coming out of Turn-1 (SW), spun 1 1/2 times for 883 feet, slid across track into infield grass at the east end of the south short chute. No contact.

May 20, 1982 — Thursday
14. Time: 2:02 p.m.

John Mahler in #92 P.W.S. Racing Penske/Offy lost control in Turn-1 (SW), slid 480 feet, making 1 spin; hit wall, slid another 640 feet making an additional spin, car traveled across track and came to stop on apron of Turn-2 (SE). Driver: O.K. Car: extensive damage.

May 21. 1982 — Friday
15. Time: 5:14 p.m.

Greg Leffler in #43 Armstrong Mould Armstrong/Cosworth apparently had right rear suspension problem in north short chute; car slid 460 feet into Turn-4 (NW) making 1 spin, hit wall, went along wall for 100 feet, slid an additional 280 feet to inside of track apron. Driver: O.K. Car: Moderate damage to right side.

[89]

May 22, 1982 — Saturday
16. Time: 2:44 p.m.

Phil Krueger in #89 Crysen McLaren/Chevy got low in Turn-4 (NW), lost control and slid 420 feet, making 1 spin, hit wall, scraped along wall 40 feet, then slid away from wall 440 feet, making 1 1/2 spins to inside of track. Driver: slight concussion, will be sent to Methodist Hospital for further observation. (Krueger was released following day 5/23). Car: extensive damage to rear section.

May 23, 1982 — Sunday
17. Time: 10:28 a.m.

John Martin in #17 Vollsteadt Enterprises Vollstedt/Offy spun one time in Turn-3 (NE) and stopped in Turn-4 (NW) with a flat right front tire. No contact, no further damage.

May 23, 1982 — Sunday
18. Time: 10:54 a.m.

Steve Chassey in #11 Hubler/Q95 Rattlesnake/ Cosworth spun one time in Turn-1 (SW), slid 380 feet to outside, hitting with right front and right rear, continued along wall 60 feet and came to stop 440 feet farther on. Driver: released, had abrasions and contusions to chest. Car: damage to right side.

May 23, 1982 — Sunday
19. Time: 4:15 p.m.

Bill Whittington in #94 Whittington Brothers March/Cosworth spun 1 time in Turn-1 (SW), covering 280 feet; hit outside wall with right side, continued along wall additional 360 feet. Driver: chest contusions, sent to Methodist Hospital for further evaluation. (Whittington was released from hospital that evening). Car: extensive damage.

GOLD CROWN CHAMPIONSHIP SERIES BOX SCORE -- INDIANAPOLIS, IND. -- May 30, 1982

Track: Indianapolis Motor Speedway	Avg. Speed: 162.026 mph.	Basic Purse: $1,643,000
Type Track: 2.5-Mile Paved	Time: 3:05:09.14	Lap Prize: $ 50,000
Organizer: Joe Cloutier	Distance: 500 Miles	Accessory: $ 374,475
Weather: Sunny	Event No.: 6	TOTAL: $2,067,475

66th "Indianapolis 500"

FIN. POS.	ST. POS.	DRIVER	CAR NAME/ NUMBER	PTS. WON	MONEY WON	LAPS COMP.	RUNNING/ REASON OUT
1	5	Gordon Johncock	STP Oil Treatment (20)	1000	$271,851	200	Running
2	1	Rick Mears	The Gould Charge (1)	800	$205,151	200	Running
3	10	Pancho Carter	Alex Foods (3)	--	$ 96,301	199	Running
4	7	Tom Sneva	Texaco Star (7)	600	$ 82,851	197	Engine
5	16	Al Unser	Longhorn Racing (10)	--	$ 55,108	197	Running
6	8	Don Whittington	The Simoniz Finish (91)	400	$ 52,121	196	Running
7	24	Jim Hickman	Stroh's March (42)	300	$ 54,236	189	Running
8	12	Johnny Rutherford	Pennzoil Chaparral (5)	--	$ 45,609	187	Engine
9	14	Herm Johnson	Menard Cashway Lumber (28)	200	$ 48,869	186	Running
10	18	Howdy Holmes	Domino's Pizza (30)	--	$ 44,169	186	Running
11	17	Bobby Rahal	Red Roof Inns (19)	100	$ 43,548	174	Engine
12	30	Gary Bettenhausen	Kraco Car Stereo (8)	50	$ 45,054	158	Engine
13	15	Hector Rebaque	Carta Blanca (52)	25	$ 50,804	150	Pit Fire
14	13	Danny Sullivan	Forsythe Brown Racing (53)	25	$ 42,643	148	Accident
15	11	Chip Ganassi	First Comm. Corp. (12)	25	$ 41,630	147	Engine
16	6	Bill Whittington	Whittington/Hodgdon (94)	25	$ 39,644	121	Engine
17	22	Michael Chandler	Freeman/Gurney Eagle (68)	20	$ 43,935	104	Gear Box
18	31	Tom Bigelow	H.B.K. Racing (27)	20	$ 40,103	96	Engine
19	3	A.J. Foyt	Valvoline/Gilmore (14)	20	$ 66,848	95	Transmission
20	25	Johnny Parsons	Silhouette Health Spas (34)	20	$ 38,970	92	Accident
21	26	George Snider	Cobre Tire (35)	15	$ 37,619	87	Transmission
22	9	Danny Ongais	Interscope Racing (25)	--	$ 37,445	62	Accident
23	28	Jerry Sneva	Great American Spirit (69)	15	$ 36,998	61	Accident
24	29	Chet Fillip	Circle Bar Truck Corral (39)	--	$ 36,728	60	Body Damage
25	32	Pete Halsmer	Colonial Bread/Pay Less (66)	--	$ 37,385	38	Transmission
26	27	Tony Bettenhausen	Provimi Veal (16)	10	$ 36,669	37	Accident
27	21	Dennis Firestone	B.C.V. Racing (75)	10	$ 37,430	37	Rear End
28	20	Geoff Brabham	Pentax Super (21)	10	$ 38,168	12	Engine
29	33	Josele Garza	Schlitz Gusto (55)	5	$ 36,783	1	Engine
30	2	Kevin Cogan	Norton Spirit (4)	5	$ 40,525	0	Accident
31	4	Mario Andretti	STP Oil Treatment (40)	5	$ 40,394	0	Accident
32	19	Roger Mears	Machinists Union (31)	5	$ 38,040	0	Accident
33	23	Dale Whittington	Whittington/Hodgdon (95)	5	$ 36,530	0	Accident

FAST QUALIFIER: Rick Mears (No. 1)--2:53.91 (4-lap time)--207.004 mph. (4-lap average).

LAP LEADERS: Laps 1-22 Foyt, Lap 23 Johncock, Laps 24-25 Don Whittington, Lap 26 Ongais, Laps 27-35 Foyt, Laps 36-41 Rick Mears, Laps 42-59 T. Sneva, Laps 60-63 Rick Mears, Lap 64 Foyt, Laps 65-94 Rick Mears, Laps 95-108 Johncock, Laps 109-127 Rick Mears, Lap 128 Johncock, Laps 129-141 Rick Mears, Laps 142-154 T. Sneva, Laps 155-159 Rick Mears, Laps 160-200 Johncock.

YELLOW FLAGS: Laps 40-45 T. Bettenhausen hit wall on front stretch; Laps 63-70 Ongais-J. Sneva Accident in turn 2; Laps 96-102 Snider stalled; Laps 132-135 Parsons spun in turn 2; Laps 138-141 Parsons stalled in turn 3; Laps 154-158 Sullivan hit wall in turn 4.

**George Snider wins the 1981-82 USAC Gold Crown National Championship.

Teddy Pilette never seemed to find any speed in the Mergard No. 67.

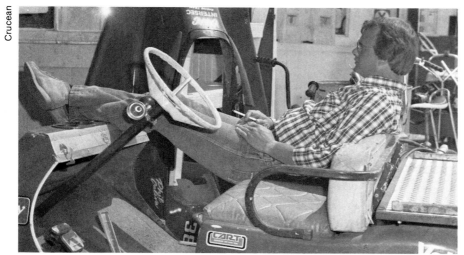

For a change, Spike Gehlhausen doesn't seem worried about putting a car in the race.

Ralph Salvino, STP's man on the scene.

Pancho Carter and Johnny Capels make up one of Championship racing's most compatible teams. Capels was himself a Sprint car driver and can easily relate to most any problem Carter encounters.

Performance Records

Year	Car	Qual.	S	F	Laps	Speed or Reason Out

MARIO ANDRETTI, Nazareth, Pennsylvania

Indianapolis 500 Record (Passed Driver's Test 1965)

Year	Car	Qual.	S	F	Laps	Speed or Reason Out
1965	Dean Van Lines	158.849	4	3	200	149.121
1966	Dean Van Lines	165.899	1	18	27	Engine
1967	Dean Van Lines	168.982	1	30	58	Lost wheel
1968	Overseas Natl. Airways	167.691	4	33	2	Piston
1968*	Overseas Natl. Airways		28	10		Piston
	*(Rel. L. Diclson)					
1969	STP Oil Treatment	169.851	2	1	200	156.867
1970	STP Oil Treatment	168.209	8	6	199	Flagged
1971	STP Oil Treatment	172.612	9	30	11	Accident
1972	Viceroy	187.167	5	8	194	Out of fuel
1973	Viceroy	195.059	6	30	4	Piston
1974	Viceroy	186.027	5	31	2	Piston
1975	Viceroy	186.480	21	28	49	Accident
1976	CAM2 Motor Oil	189.404	19	8	101	Running
1977	CAM2 Motor Oil	193.351	6	26	47	Broken Header
1978	Gould Charge	194.647	33	12	185	Flagged
1980	Essex	191.012	2	20	71	Engine
1981	STP Oil	193.040	32	2	200	Running
1982	STP Oil Treatment	203.172	4	31	0	Accident

GARY BETTENHAUSEN, Monrovia, Indiana

Indianapolis 500 Record (Passed Driver's Test 1968)

Year	Car	Qual.	S	F	Laps	Speed or Reason Out
1968	Thermo-King	163.562	22	24	43	Oil cooler
1969	Thermo-King	167.777	9	26	35	Piston
1970	Thermo-King	166.451	20	26	55	Valve
1971	Thermo-King	171.233	13	10	178	Flagged
1972	Sunoco McLaren	188.877	4	14	182	Ignition
1973	Sunoco DX	195.599	5	5	130	Running
1974	Score	184.492	11	32	2	Valve
1975	Thermo-King	182.611	19	15	158	Accident
1976	Thermo-King	181.791	8	28	52	Turbocharger
1977	Agajanian-Evel Knievel	186.596	21	16	138	Clutch
1978	Oberdorfer	187.324	31	16	149	Blown Engine
1980	Armstrong Mould	182.463	32	3	200	Running
1981	Lindsey Hopkins	190.870	11	26	69	Conn. Rod
1982	Kraco Car Stereo	195.673	30	12	158	Engine

TONY BETTENHAUSEN, Speedway, Indiana

Indianapolis 500 Record (Passed Driver's Test 1980)

Year	Car	Qual.	S	F	Laps	Speed or Reason Out
1981	Provimi Veal	187.013	16	7	195	Flagged
1982	Provimi Veal	195.429	27	26	37	Accident

TOM BIGELOW, Whitewater, Wisconsin

Indianapolis 500 Record (Passed Driver's Test 1973)

Year	Car	Qual.	S	F	Laps	Speed or Reason Out
1974	Bryant Heat-Cool	180.144	23	12	166	Flagged
1975	Bryant Heating	181.864	33	18	151	Piston
1976	Leader Card	181.965	32	14	98	Running
1977	Thermo-King	186.471	22	6	192	Running
1978	Armstrong Mould	189.115	18	21	107	Stalled
1979	Armstrong Mould	185.147	30	14	190	Running
1980	Armstrong/Jiffy Mix	182.547	31	8	198	Running
1981	Genessee Beer Wagon	188.294	14	20	152	Engine
1982	H.B.K. Racing	194.784	31	18	96	Engine

GEOFF BRABHAM, San Clemente, California

Indianapolis 500 Record (Passed Driver's Test 1981)

Year	Car	Qual.	S	F	Laps	Speed or Reason Out
1981	Psachie-Garza Esso	187.990	15	5	197	Flagged
1982	Pentax Super	198.906	20	28	12	Engine

DUANE (Pancho) CARTER JR., Brownsburg, Ind.

Indianapolis 500 Record (Passed Driver's Test 1974)

Year	Car	Qual.	S	F	Laps	Speed or Reason Out
1974	Cobre Firestone	180.605	21	7	191	Flagged
1975	Cobre Tire	183.449	18	4	169	Running
1976	Jorgensen Steel	184.824	6	5	101	Running
1977	Jorgensen Eagle	192.452	8	15	156	Blown Engine

Year	Car	Qual.	S	F	Laps	Speed or Reason Out
1978	Budweiser Lightning	196.829	21	24	92	Header
1979	Alex XLNT Foods	185.806	17	20	129	Wheel Bearing
1980	Alex XLNT Foods	186.480	8	6	199	Running
1981	Alex XLNT Foods	191.022	10	28	63	Lost Comp.
1982	Alex Foods	198.950	10	3	199	Running

MICHAEL CHANDLER, Dana Point, California

Indianapolis 500 Record (Passed Driver's Test 1981)

Year	Car	Qual.	S	F	Laps	Speed or Reason Out
1981	Hodgon	187.568	25	12	192	Flagged
1982	Freeman/Gurney Eagle	198.042	22	17	104	Gear Box

KEVIN COGAN, Redondo Beach, California

Indianapolis 500 Record (Passed Driver's Test 1981)

Year	Car	Qual.	S	F	Laps	Speed or Reason Out
1981	Jerry O'Connell Racing	189.444	12	4	197	Flagged
1982	The Norton Spirit	204.082	2	30	0	Accident

CHET FILLIP, Ozona, Texas

Indianapolis 500 Record (Passed Driver's Test in 1982)

Year	Car	Qual.	S	F	Laps	Speed or Reason Out
1982	Circle Bar Truck Corral	194.879	29	24	60	Body Damage

DENNIS FIRESTONE, Gardena, California

Indianapolis 500 Record (Passed Driver's Test 1980)

Year	Car	Qual.	S	F	Laps	Speed or Reason Out
1980	Scientific Drilling	183.702	24	16	137	Transmission
1981	Rhoades Aircraft	187.784	28	10	193	Engine
1982	B.C.V. Racing	197.217	21	27	37	Rear End

A. J. FOYT, Houston, Texas

Indianapolis 500 Record (Passed Driver's Test 1958)

Year	Car	Qual.	S	F	Laps	Speed or Reason Out
1958	Dean Van Lines	143.130	12	16	148	Spun Out
1959	Dean Van Lines	142.648	17	10	200	133.297
1960	Bowes Seal Fast	143.466	16	25	90	Clutch
1961	Bowes Seal Fast	145.907	7	1	200	139.130
1962	Bowes Seal Fast	149.074	5	23	69	Accident
1962*	Sarkes Tarzian		17	20		Starter
	*Rel. E. George, 127-146					
1963	Sheraton-Thompson	150.615	8	3	200	142.210
1964	Sheraton-Thompson	154.672	5	1	200	147.350
1965	Sheraton-Thompson	161.233	1	15	115	Gearbox
1966	Sheraton-Thompson	161.355	18	26	0	Accident
1967	Sheraton-Thompson	166.289	4	1	200	151.207
1968	Sheraton-Thompson	166.821	8	20	86	Engine
1969	Sheraton-Thompson	170.568	1	8	181	Flagged
1970	Sheraton-Thomp ITT	170.004	3	10	195	Transmission
1971	ITT-Thompson	174.317	6	3	200	156.069
1972	ITT-Thompson	188.996	17	25	60	Engine
1973	Gilmore Racing	188.927	23	25	37	Conn. rod
1974	Gilmore Racing	191.632	1	15	142	Gearbox
1975	Gilmore Racing	193.976	1	3	174	Running
1976	Gilmore Racing	185.261	5	2	102	Running
1977	Gilmore Racing	194.563	4	1	200	161.331
1978	Gilmore Racing	200.122	20	7	191	Flagged
1979	Gilmore Racing	189.613	6	2	200	Running
1980	Gilmore Racing	185.500	12	14	173	Valve
1981	Gilmore Racing	196.078	3	13	191	Flagged
1982	Valvoline/Gilmore	203.332	3	19	95	Transmission

JOSELE GARZA, Mexico City, Mexico

Indianapolis 500 Record (Passed Driver's Test 1981)

Year	Car	Qual.	S	F	Laps	Speed or Reason Out
1981	Psachie Garza Esso	195.101	6	23	138	Accident
1982	Schlitz Gusto	194.500	33	29	1	Engine

CHIP GANASSI, Pittsburgh, Pa.

Indianapolis 500 Record (Passed Driver's Test in 1982)

Year	Car	Qual.	S	F	Laps	Speed or Reason Out
1982	First Commercial Corp.	197.704	11	15	147	Engine

[92]

PETE HALSMER, Lafayette, Indiana

Indianapolis 500 Record (Passed Driver's Test 1981)

Year	Car	Qual.	S	F	Laps	Speed or Reason Out
1981	Hubler/KISS 99/ Colonial	187.705	24	24	123	Accident
1982	Colonial Bread/Pay Less	194.595	32	25	38	Transmission

JIM HICKMAN, Atlanta, Georgia

Indianapolis 500 Record (Passed Driver's Test 1982)

Year	Car	Qual.	S	F	Laps	Speed or Reason Out
1982	Stroh's March	196.217	24	7	189	Running

HOWDY HOLMES, Ann Arbor, Michigan

Indianapolis 500 Record (Passed Driver's Test 1979)

Year	Car	Qual.	S	F	Laps	Speed or Reason Out
1979	Armstrong/Jiffy Mix	185.864	13	7	195	Running
1982	Domino's Pizza/Shireson	194.468	18	10	186	Running

GORDON JOHNCOCK, Hastings, Michigan

Indianapolis 500 Record (Passed Driver's Test 1965)

Year	Car	Qual.	S	F	Laps	Speed or Reason Out
1965	Weinberger Homes	155.012	14	5	200	146.417
1966	Weinberger Homes	161.059	6	4	200	143.084
1967	Gilmore Broadcasting	166.559	3	12	188	Spun Out
1968	Gilmore Broadcasting	166.775	9	27	37	Gearbox
1969	Gilmore Broadcasting	168.626	5	19	137	Piston
1970	Gilmore Broadcasting	167.015	17	28	45	Engine
1971	Norris Industries	171.388	12	29	11	Accident
1972	Gulf McLaren	188.511	26	20	113	Valve
1973	STP Double Oil Filter	192.555	11	1	133	159.036
1974	STP Double Oil Filter	186.750	4	4	198	Flagged
1975	Sinmast	191.652	2	31	11	Ignition
1976	Sinmast/Goodyear	188.531	2	3	102	Running
1977	STP Double Oil Filter	193.517	5	11	184	Valve Spring
1978	N. American Van Lines	195.833	6	3	199	Penalized 1 lap
1979	N. American Van Lines	189.753	5	6	197	Running
1980	N. American Van Lines	186.075	17	4	200	Running
1981	STP Oil Treatment	195.429	4	9	194	Engine
1982	STP Oil Treatment	201.884	5	1	200	Running

HERM JOHNSON, Eau Clair, Wisconsin

Indianapolis 500 Record (Passed Driver's Test 1980)

Year	Car	Qual.	S	F	Laps	Speed or Reason Out
1982	Menard Cashway Lumber	195.929	14	9	186	Running

RICK MEARS, Bakersfield, California

Indianapolis 500 Record (Passed Driver's Test 1977)

Year	Car	Qual.	S	F	Laps	Speed or Reason Out
1978	CAM2 Motor Oil	200.078	3	23	103	Engine
1979	Gould Charge	193.736	1	1	200	Running
1980	Gould Charge	187.490	6	5	199	Running
1981	Gould Charge	194.018	22	20	58	Car fire in pits
1982	The Gould Charge	207.004	1	2	200	Running

ROGER MEARS, Bakersfield, California

Indianapolis 500 Record (Passed Driver's Test in 1980)

Year	Car	Qual.	S	F	Laps	Speed or Reason Out
1982	Machinists Union Racing	194.154	19	32	0	Accident

DANNY ONGAIS, Costa Mesa, California

Indianapolis 500 Record (Passed Refresher Test 1977)

Year	Car	Qual.	S	F	Laps	Speed or Reason Out
1977	Interscope Racing	193.040	7	20	90	Lost Power
1978	Interscope Racing	200.122	2	18	145	Engine
1979	Interscope/Panasonic	188.009	27	4	199	Running
1980	Interscope/Panasonic	186.606	16	7	199	Running
1981	Interscope Racing	197.694	21	27	64	Accident
1982	Interscope Racing	199.148	9	22	62	Accident

JOHNNY PARSONS, Indianapolis, Indiana

Indianapolis 500 Record (Passed Driver's Test 1973)

Year	Car	Qual.	S	F	Laps	Speed or Reason Out
1974	Vatis	180.252	29	26	18	Turbocharger
1975	Ayr-Way/WNAP	184.521	19	19	140	Trans. Shaft
1976	Ayr-Way/WIRE	182.843	14	12	98	Running
1977	STP Wildcat	189.255	11	5	193	Flagged
1978	First Natl. City T.C.	194.280	8	10	187	Flagged
1979	Hopkins	187.813	9	32	16	Piston
1980	Wynn's	187.412	7	26	44	Piston
1982	Silhouette/Tombstone/WIFE	295.929	25	20	92	Accident

BOBBY RAHAL, Columbus, Ohio

Indianapolis 500 Record (Passed Driver's Test in 1982)

Year	Car	Qual.	S	F	Laps	Speed or Reason Out
1982	Red Roof Inns March	194.700	17	11	174	Engine

HECTOR REBAQUE, Mexico City, Mexico

Indianapolis 500 Record (Passed Driver's Test in 1982)

Year	Car	Qual.	S	F	Laps	Speed or Reason Out
1982	Carta Blanca	195.684	15	13	150	Pit Fire

JOHNNY RUTHERFORD, Ft. Worth, Texas

Indianapolis 500 Record (Passed Driver's Test 1963)

Year	Car	Qual.	S	F	Laps	Speed or Reason Out
1963	U.S. Equipment Co.	148.063	26	29	43	Transmission
1964	Bardahl	151.400	15	27	2	Accident
1965	Racing Associates	156.291	11	31	15	Rear End
1967	Weinberger Homes	162.859	19	25	103	Accident
1968	City of Seattle	163.830	21	18	125	Fuel Tank
1969	Patrick Petroleum	166.628	17	29	24	Oil Leak
1970	Patrick Petroleum	170.213	2	18	135	Brkn. Header
1971	Patrick Petroleum	171.151	24	18	128	Flagged
1972	Patrick Petroleum	183.234	8	27	55	Conn. rod
1973	Gulf McLaren	198.413	1	9	124	Flagged
1974	McLaren	190.446	25	1	200	158.589
1975	Gatorade	185.998	7	2	174	Running
1976	Hy-Gain	188.957	1	1	102	148.725
1977	First Natl. City T.C.	197.325	17	23	12	Bent Valves
1978	First Natl. City T.C.	197.098	4	13	180	Flagged
1979	Budweiser	188.137	8	18	168	Running
1980	Penzoil Chaparral	192.256	1	1	200	Running
1981	Pennzoil Chaparral	195.387	4	32	25	Fuel Pump
1982	Pennzoil Chaparral	197.066	12	8	187	Engine

JERRY SNEVA, Spokane, Washington

Indianapolis 500 Record (Passed Driver's Test 1977)

Year	Car	Qual.	S	F	Laps	Speed or Reason Out
1977	21st Amendment	186.616	16	10	187	Running
1978	Smock Material	187.266	32	31	18	Ring & Pinion
1979	Natl. Engineering AMC	184.379	21	31	16	Turbocharger
1980	Hugger's Beverage Holders	187.852	5	17	130	Accident
1982	Great American Spirit	195.270	28	23	61	Accident

TOM SNEVA, Spokane, Washington

Indianapolis 500 Record (Passed Driver's Test 1973)

Year	Car	Qual.	S	F	Laps	Speed or Reason Out
1974	Raymond Companies	185.147	8	20	94	Ring, Pinion
1975	Norton Spirit	190.094	4	22	125	Accident
1976	Norton Spirit	186.355	3	6	101	Running
1977	Norton Spirit	198.884	1	2	200	160.918
1978	Norton Spirit	202.156	1	2	200	161.244
1979	Sugaripe Prune	192.998	2	15	188	Accident
1980	Bon Jour Jeans	185.290	33	2	200	Running
1981	Blue Poly	200.691	20	25	96	Clutch
1982	Texaco Star	201.027	7	4	197	Engine

GEORGE SNIDER, Bakersfield, California

Indianapolis 500 Record (Passed Driver's Test 1965)

Year	Car	Qual.	S	F	Laps	Speed or Reason Out
1965	Gerhardt	154.825	16	21	64	Rear End
1966	Sheraton-Thompson	162.521	3	19	22	Accident
1967	Wagner-Lockhead	164.256	10	26	99	Spun Out
1968	Vel's Parnelli Jones	162.264	29	31	9	Valve
1969	Sheraton-Thompson	166.914	15	16	152	Flagged
1970	Sheraton-Thomp ITT	167.660	10	20	105	Suspension
1971	G. C. Murphy	171.600	21	33	6	Stalled
1972	ITT-Thompson	181.855	21	11	190	Flagged
1973	Gilmore-Racing	190.355	30	12	101	Gearbox
1974	Gilmore Racing	183.993	13	28	7	Valve
1975	Lodestar	182.918	24	8	165	Running
1976	Hubler Chevrolet	181.141	27	13	98	Running
1977	Simon Assoc./ Greenwood Center	188.976	13	24	65	Valve
1978	Gilmore Racing/ Citicorp	192.627	23	8	191	Flagged
1979	Spirit of Neb./ KBHL-FM	185.319	35	33	7	Valve
1980	Gilmore Racing	185.385	21	15	169	Engine
1982	Cobre Tire	195.493	26	21	87	Transmission

DANNY SULLIVAN, Louisville, Kentucky

Indianapolis 500 Record (Passed Driver's Test in 1982)

Year	Car	Qual.	S	F	Laps	Speed or Reason Out
1982	Forsythe-Brown Racing	196.292	13	14	148	Accident

Year Car		Qual.	S	F	Laps	Speed or Reason Out

AL UNSER, Albuquerque, New Mexico

Indianapolis 500 Record (Passed Driver's Test 1965)

Year	Car	Qual.	S	F	Laps	Speed or Reason Out
1965	Sheraton-Thompson	154.440	32	9	196	Flagged
1966	STP Oil Treatment	162.272	23	12	161	Accident
1967	Retzloff Chemical	164.594	9	2	198	Flagged
1968	Retzloff Chemical	167.069	6	26	40	Accident
1970	Johnny Lightning 500	170.221	1	1	200	155.749
1971	Johnny Lightning 500	174.622	5	1	200	157.735
1972	Viceroy	183.617	19	2	200	160.192
1973	Viceroy	194.879	8	20	75	Piston
1974	Viceroy	183.889	26	18	131	Valve
1975	Viceroy	185.452	11	16	157	Conn. rod
1976	American Racing	186.258	4	7	101	Running
1977	American Racing	195.950	3	3	199	Flagged
1978	First Natl. City T.C.	196.474	5	1	200	161.363
1979	Pennzoil	192.503	3	22	104	Transmission Seal
1980	Longhorn Racing	186.442	9	27	23	Cylinder
1981	Valvoline Longhorn	192.719	9	17	166	Flagged
1982	Longhorn Racing	195.567	16	5	197	Engine

BILL WHITTINGTON, Ft. Lauderdale, Florida

Indianapolis 500 Record (Passed Driver's Test 1980)

Year	Car	Qual.	S	F	Laps	Speed or Reason Out
1980	Sun System	183.262	27	30	9	Accident
1981	Kraco Car Stereo	197.098	27	21	146	Engine
1982	Whittington/Hodgdon	201.658	6	16	121	Engine

DALE WHITTINGTON, Orlando, Florida

Indianapolis 500 Record (Passed Driver's Test in 1982)

Year	Car	Qual.	S	F	Laps	Speed or Reason Out
1982	Warner Hodgdon March	197.694	23	33	0	Accident

DON WHITTINGTON, Ft. Lauderdale, Florida

Indianapolis 500 Record (Passed Driver's Test 1980)

Year	Car	Qual.	S	F	Laps	Speed or Reason Out
1980	Sun System	183.927	18	13	178	Running
1981	Road Atlanta	187.237	26	31	32	Accident
1982	The Simonize Finish	200.725	8	6	196	Running

Official Entry List

ENTRY LIST FOR SIXTY-SIXTH INDIANAPOLIS 500

Car No.	Driver	Car Name	Entrant	Chassis/Engine
1	Rick Mears	The Gould Charge Penske PC-10	Penske, Ltd.	Penske PC-10/Cosworth
1T			Penske Cars, Ltd.	Penske PC-10/Cosworth
2	Bill Alsup	A.B. Dick Pacemaker	Alsup Racing	Penske/Cosworth
2T		A. B. Dick Pacemaker	Alsup Racing	Penske/Cosworth
3	Pancho Carter	Alex Foods Special	Alex Morales Co., Inc.	March/Cosworth
3T		Alex Foods Special	Alex Morales Co., Inc.	March/Cosworth
4	Kevin Cogan	Norton Spirit Penske PC-10	Penske Cars, Ltd.	Penske PC-10/Cosworth
4T			Penske Cars, Ltd.	Penske PC-10/Cosworth
5	Johnny Rutherford	Pennzoil Chaparral	Chaparral Racing, Ltd.	Chaparral/Cosworth
5T	Johnny Rutherford	Pennzoil Chaparral	Chaparral Racing, Ltd.	Chaparral/Cosworth
5TT		Pennzoil Chaparral	Chaparral Racing, Ltd.	Chaparral/Cosworth
7	Tom Sneva	Texaco Star	Bignotti-Cotter, Inc.	March 82C/Cosworth
7T			Bignotti-Cotter, Inc.	March 81C/Cosworth
8	Gary Bettenhausen		Lindsey Hopkins	Lightning/Cosworth
10	Al Unser		Longhorn Racing, Inc.	Longhorn LR-03/Cosworth
10T	Al Unser		Longhorn Racing, Inc.	Longhorn LR-03/Cosworth
11	Bill Vukovich	Hubler/Q95 Special	Harry H. Schwartz	Rattlesnake/Cosworth
12	Chip Ganassi	First Commercial Corp. Spl.	Rhoades Racing, Inc.	Wildcat/Cosworth
14	A. J. Foyt, Jr.	Valvoline-Gilmore	A. J. Foyt Enterprise	March/Cosworth
16	Tony Bettenhausen	Provimi Veal	H & R Racing, Inc.	March 82C/Cosworth
16T	Tony Bettenhausen	Provimi Veal	H & R Racing, Inc.	Phoenix/Cosworth
17	Rusty Schmidt		Vollstedt Enterprises, Inc.	Vollstedt/Drake Offy
18	Dick Ferguson	Kraco Car Stero Spl.	Kraco Enterprises, Inc.	PC-9B/Cosworth
18T		Kraco Car Stereo Spl.	Kraco Enterprises, Inc.	PC-9B/Cosworth
19	Bobby Rahal	Red Roof Inns March	Truesports Co.	March 82C/Cosworth
19T	Bobby Rahal	Red Roof Inns March	Truesports Co.	March 82C/Cosworth
20	Gordon Johncock	STP Oil Treatment Spl.	STP Patrick Racing Team	Widcat 8B/Cosworth
20T			STP Patrick Racing Team	Wildcat 8B/Cosworth
21	Geoff Brabham	Pentax Super	Bignotti-Cotter, Inc.	March 82C/Cosworth
22	Dick Simon	Vermont American	Leader Cards, Inc.	Watson/Cosworth
22T			Leader Cards, Inc.	Watson/Drake Offy
24	Rich Vogler	Vermont American	Leader Cards, Inc.	Watson/ Cosworth
25	Danny Ongais	Interscope Racing	Interscope Racing Corp.	Interscope/Cosworth
25T	Danny Ongais	Interscope Racing	Interscope Racing Corp.	Interscope/Cosworth
25TT	Danny Ongais	Interscope Racing	Interscope Racing Corp.	Interscope/Cosworth
27	Jerry Sneva		Vollstedt Enterprises, Inc.	March-Vollstedt/Drake Offy
28	Herm Johnson	Menard Cashway Lumber Spl.	Menard Championship Racing, Inc.	Eagle/Chevy V-8*
28T	Herm Johnson	Menard Cashway Lumber Spl.	Menard Championship Racing, Inc.	Eagle/Chevy V-8*
29	Bobby Olivero	Hodgdon Racing	National Engineering Co./ Warner Hodgdon Racing	Penske PC-7/Cosworth
30	Howdy Holmes	Domino's Pizza/Team Shierson	Douglas Shierson Racing, Inc.	March/Cosworth
30T	Howdy Holmes	Domino's Pizza/Team Shierson	Douglas Shierson Racing, Inc.	March/Cosworth
31	Roger Mears	Machinists Union Racing Team	International Association of Machinists and Aerospace Workers	Penske PC-9B/Cosworth
32	Jerry Karl	Purcell Racer	Purcell Racing, Inc.	Purcell/Chevy V-8*
33	Desire Wilson	Theodore Racing	Theodore Racing	Eagle/Cosworth
34	Hurley Haywood	Wysard Racing Team	Wysard Motor Company, Inc.	March/Cosworth
34T	Hurley Haywood	Wysard Racing Team	Wysard Motor Company, Inc.	March/Cosworth
35	Gordon Smiley	Intermedics Innovator	Robert L. Fletcher	March/Cosworth
35T	Gordon Smiley	Intermedics Innovator	Robert L. Fletcher	March/Cosworth
36	Pat Bedard	Escort Radar Detector Spl.	Brayton Engineering	Wildcat VIII/Cosworth
37	Scott Brayton	Brayton Racing	Brayton Engineering	Penske PC-7/Cosworth
38	Phillip Caliva		CHC-Intersec Racing Team	McLaren-Lightning/Chevy

No.	Driver	Car	Entrant	Chassis/Engine
39	Chet Fillip	Circle Bar Truck Corral Wildcat	Circle Bar Auto Racing, Inc.	Wildcat 3B/Cosworth
39T	Chet Fillip	Circle Bar Truck Corral Eagle	Circle Bar Auto Racing, Inc.	Eagle/Cosworth
40	Mario Andretti		STP-Patrick Racing Team, Inc.	Wildcat 8B/Cosworth
42	Jim Hickman	Rattlesnake Racing Special II	Harry H. Schwartz	March 82C/Cosworth
44	Sheldon Kinser	Armstrong Mould, Inc.	AMI Racing Division, Inc.	S.E.A.-1/Cosworth
45		Armstrong Mould, Inc.	AMI Racing Division, Inc.	Lola/Chevy V-6
46	Leroy Van Conett	McCray Racing	Joel F. McCray	Penske PC-7/Cosworth
47	Lee Kunzman	Jamieson Racing Team	Jamieson Racing, In.	Penske PC-7/Cosworth
48	Mike Mosley	All American Racers Eagle	All American Racers, Inc.	Eagle/Chevy V-8*
48T	Mike Mosley	All American Racers Eagle	All American Racers, Inc.	Eagle/Chevy V-8*
49	Chip Mead	Jamieson Racing Team	Jamieson Racing, Inc.	Eagle/Cosworth
50	Bobby Unser	Schlitz Gusto	Garza Racing	March/Cosworth
52	Hector Rebaque	Carta Blanca	Forsythe Racing, Inc.	March/Cosworth
53	Danny Sullivan	Forsythe-Brown Racing	Forsythe Racing, Inc.	March/Cosworth
55	Josele Garza	Schlitz Gusto	Garza Racing	March/Cosworth
56	Tom Bigelow	Genesee Beer Wagon	Gohr Distributing Co., Inc.	PC-7/Chevy V-8*
57	Salt Walther		Des Cognets Nicholas Andrews	Phoenix/Cosworth
58	Joe Saldana	Genesee Beer Wagon	Gohr Distributor Co., Inc.	PC-7/Chevy V-8*
59	Billy Engelhart	Beaudoin Racing	Beaudoin Racing, Inc.	McLaren/Cosworth
60		STP Oil Treatment Spl.	STP-Patrick Racing Team, Inc.	Wildcat 8B/Cosworth
61	Tim Richmond	Mach I Racing	Mach I Racing	Penske PC-7/Cosworth
62	Tim Richmond	Mach I Racing	Mach I Racing	Penske PC-7/Cosworth
63	Ken Hamilton	Eagle Aircraft Flyer	Ken Hamilton	DW2/Chevy V-8*
64		Jet Engineering Eagle	Jet Engineering, Inc.	Eagle/Chevy V-8*
66	Pete Halsmer	Colonial Bread, Payless Markets, Arciero Eagle	Aciero Racing	Eagle/Chevy V-8
67	Teddy Pilette		Mergard's 20th Century Enterprises,	McLaren M-24/Chevy V-8*
67T	Teddy Pilette		Mergard's 20th Century Enterprises,	Penske PC-7/Cosworth
68	Michael Chandler	Freeman/Gurney Eagle	Bill Freeman Racing, Inc.	Eagle/Chevy V-8
69			Hoffman Auto Racing	March/Cosworth
70			Longhorn Racing, Inc.	Longhorn LR-02B/Cosworth
70T			Longhorn Racing, Inc.	Longhorn LR-03/Cosworth
71	Dean Vetrock	Vetco Racing/Larrie Ervin	Vetco Machine, Inc.	Lightning/Chevy V-8*
72	Roger Rager	Indiana Coal Spl.	Rhoades Racing, Inc.	Wildcat/Cosworth
73	Ray Lipper	Center Line	Center Line Racing Wheels	Eagle/Chevy V-8*
74	Neil Bonnett	Hodgdon Racing	National Engineering Co./ Warner Hodgdon Racing	McLaren/Cosworth
75	Dennis Firestone	B.C.V. Racing	B.C.V. Racing, Inc.	Eagle/Milodon V-8*
77	Tom Frantz	Burger King "Phantom"	Frantz Racing	"Phantom"/Chevy V-8*
78	Larry Rice		Lindsey Hopkins	Lightning/Cosworth
79	Bob Harkey	C & H Racing, Inc.	C & H. Racing, Inc.	Parnelli/Cosworth
80	Tom Gloy	Machinists Union Racing Team	International Association of Machinists and Aerospace Workers	Penske PC-7/Cosworth
82	Sammy Swindell	Jet Engineering Eagle	Jet Engineering, Inc.	Eagle/Chevy V-8
83			Vern Schuppan, Inc.	March/Cosworth
84	George Snider	Valvoline-Gilmore	A. J. Foyt Enterprise	March/Cosworth
86	Al Loquasto	Empress Traveler Eagle	George T. Smith	Eagle/Drake Offy
87	Tom Grunnah	Larlin Racing	Larry W. Beadling	Penske PC-9/Cosworth
88	Billy Scott	Frito-Lay/Timberwood Racer	Timberwood Racers	Lightning/Donovan V-8*
89	Phil Krueger		Joe Hunt	Hunt-Penske/Chevy V-8*
90	Gary Irvin	Swingler (S-2) Chevy	Gary Irvin	Swingler/Chevy V-8*
91	Don Whittington	Whittington Brothers Racing, Inc.	Whittington Brothers, Inc.	March/Cosworth
92	Jan Sneva		P.W.S.Racing, Inc.	Penske PC-7/Drake Offy
93	Steve Chassey		P.W.S.Racing, Inc.	Duke/Cosworth
94	Bill Whittington	Whittington Brothers Racing, Inc.	Whittington Brothers, Inc.	March/Cosworth
95	Dale Whittington	Whittington Brothers Racing, Inc.	Whittington Brothers, Inc.	March/Cosworth
98	Jimmy McElreath	Giuffre Bros. Crane	Agajanian-King Racing	King/Chevy V-8*
98T	Jimmy McElreath		Agajanian-King Racing	King/Chevy V-8*
99	Vern Schuppan	Kraco Car Stereo Spl.	Kraco Enterprises, Inc.	PC-9B/Cosworth
#			Penske Cars, Ltd.	Penske PC-10/Cosworth

*Normally aspirated (all other cars are turbocharged.)
#This car had not been assigned a number at press time.

THE FIELD

By Jep Cadou

GORDON JOHNCOCK 1st

Indianapolis Motor Speedway Photos

Gordon Johncock

If it weren't for mechanical failures in past years, Gordon Johncock might well have become a four-time winner of the Indianapolis 500 in 1982 instead of just a two-time winner. The little guy with the big foot found himself outside of and dead abreast of favorite Rick Mears with one lap to go. Many a lesser driver would have conceded that first corner — and the race to Mears. Not the game and highly competitive Gordy. He legged it into the corner, beat Mears to it and hung on for the closest victory in Indianapolis history — by a mere 16/100ths of a second.

Gordy seems to have a whole new attitude in 1982. He is super-competitive and aggressive this trip and he is getting the best out of some excellent equipment provided by the Patrick Racing Team which carries the STP colors on the Indy circuit. He always has been a feared competitor but this season, he seems to have renewed vigor and determination at the ripe age of 45. It is as if he were getting something of a second wind in his racing career that dates back to 1955.

Johncock's Speedway victories seemingly must always be tinged with tragedy. When he won his first in 1973, the fatal injury of teammate Swede Savage and death of crewman Armando Teran in the race took most of the joy out of it. This year, shortly after the conclusion of the Victory Banquet, Gordy got word of the death of his mother. Maybe, No. 3 for Johncock will have no discordant notes.

This was the 18th consecutive year that Gordy has made the 500 starting field, no mean achievement in itself.

In addition to his victories, he was fifth in his rookie year of 1965, fourth in 1966, fourth in 1974, third in 1976, third in 1978, sixth in 1979, fourth in 1980 and ninth in 1981 — a total of 10 top-10 finishes in 19 tries.

Johncock got his start in stock cars, then graduated to Super-modifieds and USAC Sprint cars, where he made his mark including setting a world record at Winchester, IN. His performance gained him Championship car rides and he took full advantage of the opportunity.

CAR
Wildcat PR8B04/Cosworth

CHIEF MECHANIC
George Huening

SPONSOR
STP Oil Treatment

STATISTICS OF CAR
A new Wildcat in which Gordy outdistanced Rick Mears by .16 seconds to win his first "500" since 1973. He had qualified at 201.884 to start 5th.

[97]

2nd *RICK MEARS*

Rick Mears

Rick Mears proved in 1982 that he is a gracious loser as well as a very good winner. A lesser driver might have bad-mouthed Gordon Johncock for his last-lap driving performance or cried that he should have been the victor instead of Gordon. Not Rick Mears. He exhibited plenty of class by praising Johncock's last-ditch effort and bearing no malice to the man who nipped him in the closest finish in Indianapolis history.

Mears had proved to be an excellent winner in 1979, making friends for the sport wherever he went after achieving a rare sophomore-year victory in one of Roger Penske's excellent race cars. Mears started the 1982 season like a house afire, setting new track records and winning races at Phoenix and Atlanta. When practice time began at Indy, Mears was something of a prohibitive favorite.

Somehow, the STP team caught up with the Penske outfit by race day, but the runnerup effort certainly did nothing to dim the lustre of Mears' ability. He got a terribly bad break during a late pit stop when another and slower car pulled directly into his path as he came in for a pit stop and Rick nudged it with a front wing, slowing down his entrance to his pits considerably.

Even so, his 1982 showing was a great improvement over 1981 when Mears finished 30th and suffered painful facial burns during a flash fire in the pits that erupted after he came in leading the race.

Mears has something of a unique background among Indianapolis drivers in that he is primarily a product of off-road racing, not exactly a common spawning ground for Championship talent. He got his start racing Sprint Buggies at Ascot in Los Angeles, then branched into off-road racing where he impressed former Indianapolis 500 winner Parnelli Jones by beating him. Acquaintances with Bobby Unser and Bill Simpson led to eventual Indy-car rides and he hooked up with Penske in 1978, putting his car on the front row that year and sharing Rookie-of-the-Year honors. He swept the pole and the race in 1979, ran fifth in 1980.

CAR

Penske PC-10-02/Ford

CHIEF MECHANIC

Peter Parrott

SPONSOR

The Gould Charge

STATISTICS OF CAR

The latest in the fine line of Roger Penske's machines. New this year, Rick set qualifying records for 1-lap of 207.039 and a 4-lap mark of 207.004. He started on the pole and finished second trailing Gordon Johncock across the finish line by seconds.

Pancho Carter

Pancho Carter's third-place finish in the 1982 Indianapolis 500 was his best in nine races at the Speedway. And, if they were going to give some kind of prize for getting the most out of a relatively low-budget operation, it would probably go to Pancho and his chief mechanic, Johnny Capels. Carter was in the thick of the action all the way this year and he finished just one lap behind Gordon Johncock and Rick Mears.

One of the best of the crop of second-generation drivers, Pancho is the son of longtime Indianapolis driver and former USAC chieftain Duane Carter and his former wife, Arza. He also is one of the last of the big-time drivers to get to the Championship cars through the time-honored route of excelling in midgets and sprint cars.

Pancho has been driving race cars since he was 4 years old, having started in Quarter Midgets at that age along with his half-brother, Johnny Parsons.

A graduate of Long Beach State College in California, Pancho won the USAC Midget championship in 1972 while commuting between college classes and the race tracks. He proceeded to win USAC Sprint crowns in 1974 and 1976 and then added the Dirt Championship in 1978 in a sterling comeback effort.

Pancho was critically injured in a testing mishap at Phoenix International Raceway in 1977 caused by a mechanical failure. He still walks with a decided limp as a result of the accident. But, he came back to win the first two Sprint races in which he participated after the accident and then added the dirt crown.

Carter was Rookie-of-the-Year in his initial Indianapolis 500 appearance of 1974 when he finished seventh. He was fourth in 1975 and fifth in 1976 before running into a string of mechanical failures which ousted him in 1977-79. In 1980, Carter would have been the runnerup except for a controversial one-lap penalty he suffered for passing the pace car under the yellow light. Pancho thought he had been waved around it. In 1981, he placed 28, lasting only 63 laps before a mechanical failure.

Carter scored his biggest victory when he won the inaugural Michigan 500 in 1981.

CAR
March 82C/Cosworth

CHIEF MECHANIC
Johnny Capels

SPONSOR
Alex Foods Special

STATISTICS OF CAR
A new car from England. Pancho qualified it with a good average of 198.950 to start 10th. He finished third, completing 199 laps.

4th TOM SNEVA

Tom Sneva

The only other driver who showed he could really race for position with Gordon Johncock and Rick Mears in the 1982 Indianapolis 500 was Tom Sneva, the former school principal and coach who is among the most articulate drivers in Speedway history. Sneva talks with his foot as well as his mouth and is now almost universally recognized as the best driver who has never yet tasted victory at Indianapolis.

Is Sneva doomed to play the Rex Mays-Ted Horn type of role and be close many times but never drive into Victory Lane?

His many friends certainly are hoping the answer is in the negative and that he will bust through one of these days and take the checker in first place at the end of 200 laps. But, who knows? His record now is shaping up much like that of Mays or Horn.

When he is still in the race in competitive equipment, Sneva is always a factor to be reckoned with. But, something always seems to go wrong. This year, it was a balky engine only a few laps from the finish which sidelined him.

Sneva also saw his one-lap and four-lap qualifying records wiped out in time trials.

But, the Bignotti-Cotter team for which Tom is now the mainstay appears to be gaining ground and there could well be an Indianapolis victory in Tom's future.

Sneva was fortunate enough to acquire rear-engine pavement experience early in his career, driving Supermodifieds on the CAMRA circuit in the Northwest and then moving up to the USAC Sprints at a time where rear-engine sprinters were still allowed. In fact, Sneva's striking success in the rears was a

prime reason for their subsequent banning by USAC.

Moving up to Championship cars, Sneva was a pronounced success after a somewhat rocky beginning. He was the fastest rookie qualifier for the 1974 Indianapolis 500 and has moved up from eighth to fourth at the at the 20 lap mark when he ran into transmission troubles, ultimately placing 20th. After being eliminated in a spectacular second-turn accident in 1975 and placing sixth in 1976, Tom finished second three out of the next four years, broken only by the 1979 race in which he crashed. In 1981 he placed 25th, with clutch trouble eliminating him after 96 laps.

CAR
March 82C/Cosworth

CHIEF MECHANIC
George Bignotti

SPONSOR
Texaco Star

STATISTICS OF CAR
One of the new Marchs this year. Tom qualified with a 201.027. He started the race in 7th and was black flagged on the 197 in 4th place when a engine blew.

Al Unser

There were many drivers in the 500 field who would have been glad to settle for fifth place. Al Unser is definitely not one of them. Al Unser is a winner if there ever was one, and even second place would not be satisfying to the younger of the Unser brothers.

Al is the only man in auto racing history to have captured the Triple Crown of Auto Racing. He did it in 1978, sweeping the 500-mile races at

Indianapolis, Pocono, PA., and Ontario, CA., a feat that will stand unequaled forever, since Ontario is now closed. That was Al's third Indianapolis victory. The other came in 1970 and 1971.

Many people in auto racing have second-guessed Al's decision to leave Jim Hall's Pennzoil Chaparral team to switch to the Bobby Hillin Longhorn outfit in 1980, particularly since Johnny Rutherford took over the Pennzoil ride and went on to win the Indianapolis 500 and both the USAC and CART driving championships that year.

Al has disregarded their jibes and gone about his business in his usual quiet and determined manner, trying to bring victory to the Hillin stable. So far, it has been a losing struggle but one always must realize that Al is a winner by nature and that some day, when and if the mechanical problems are solved, Al is likely to be in Victory Lane to tie A. J. Foyt at four triumphs each.

To be downright honest about it, Al was never really a factor in this year's 500 scene. He was not among the top practice runners and qualified in the sixth row, an unusually far-back starting spot for Al. And, he was never among the race-day leaders, finishing three laps behind.

Al got his start driving Modifieds in

the Albuquerque area and then joined in the family tradition of running in the annual Pike's Peak Hill Climb with considerable success. He moved up to USAC Sprint cars and then got a Speedway ride in an A. J. Foyt backup car in 1965, finishing ninth. In 1966, he was dueling with Gordon Johncock for the lead when he spun into the inside wall on the main straight. He was second to Foyt in 1967, crashed in 1968. He was one of the pre-race favorites in 1969 but broke a leg in a motorcycle accident on the washed-out opening qualifying day, missing the show. Al was second in 1972, seventh in 1976 and third in 1977 before scoring his third victory in 1978.

CAR

Longhorn LR-03/Cosworth

CHIEF MECHANIC

Ray Kuehlthau

SPONSOR

Longhorn Racing

STATISTICS OF CAR

A new car from Texas which qualified at 195.567. It started 16th and was flagged at 197 laps to finish 5th.

6th DON WHITTINGTON

Don Whittington

Don Whittington, along with his two brothers who made Indianapolis 500 history by becoming the first three-brother group ever to make the field, was under close guard by Indiana State Police plainclothesmen because of a death threat as he did a cool job of driving to sixth place in this year's race.

A man left for dead in Alligator Alley in Florida told police the hit-man said he was next going to Indianapolis to "get" the Whittingtons; there was no explanation of the motive.

Whatever the pressure on him, Whittington gave the lie to critics who had predicted the Whittingtons would never finish a race and had made bad jokes about the brothers every year "coming to Indianapolis, crashing and going home."

True, Don had crashed in Turn-2 in the 1981 race and brother Bill had wrecked along with Dick Ferguson in Turn-1 in 1980. And, Bill crashed there again in practice this year.

The Whittingtons made some racing history by being the first team to bring the new March chassis to Indianapolis in 1981 and they quickly made believers out of some other racing teams by posting fast practice and qualifying speeds. So great was the swing to the brand of chassis which resulted that a majority of this year's field — 17 cars — were Marchs.

Don didn't even start racing until 1978, running his first event at Sebring, FL. in March, driving a Porsche in IMSA competition. By the end of the season, Don finished fourth in points and he and brother Bill purchased the Road Atlanta road racing course.

In 1979, Don won the World Challenge for Endurance Drivers and co-drove to victories in the LeMans 24-Hour event, as well as the 6-hour races at Riverside, CA. and Watkins Glen, NY. and the El Salvador 1000.

After beginning the 1980 IMSA season by setting a new qualifying record at the 24 Hours of Daytona, and finishing third at Sebring with brothers Bill and Dale, Don competed in six NASCAR races. He qualified for his first Indianapolis 500 in 1980 starting 18th and making a record 20 pit stops en route to a 13th place finish. In 1981, Don started 26th at Indianapolis and crashed coming out of Turn-2 after 32 laps.

CAR
March 81C/Cosworth

CHIEF MECHANIC
Keith Layton

SPONSOR
The Simonize Finish

STATISTICS OF CAR
A second year March driven in '81 by brother Bill. Qualified 8th (200.725) and finished 6th being flagged after 196 laps.

JIM HICKMAN 7th

Jim Hickman

Jim Hickman took the AFNB Rookie-of-the-Year Award with a consistent if not spectacular drive to seventh place in the 1982 Indianapolis 500. Hickman is yet another graduate of SCCA road racing to make his mark on the Indianapolis scene.

A former Navy pilot, Hickman operates the largest Datsun agency in the Southeastern United States at Atlanta and also is a rancher with extensive holdings in Oklahoma. Hickman also is a business manager, financial planner and public relations executive when he isn't racing.

Hickman holds SCCA track records at Watkins Glen, NY., Savannah, GA., Daytona Beach, FL. and Road Atlanta, GA. in Formula C cars. He was SCCA's Formula C National Champion in 1981.

Born in Panama, OK., Jim attended high school there and also studied at Oklahoma State University. He drove his first race in 1972 at Lakeland, FL. in a Formula Ford.

In 1982, Jim also made several starts in Supervee racing in the Mini-Indy series, finishing in the top 10 three times. He was runnerup for the Formula Ford championship of SCCA in 1980, with 11 finishes in the to 10 during 17 events.

Hickman credits a chance conversation on a commercial airplane en route to a Supervee race where Championship cars also were running with landing him his ride with the Rattlesnake Racing team.

Hickman qualified his Stroh's March at 196.217 on the second weekend of time trials to earn the outside starting spot in the Eighth row. He drove a steady and conservative race, moving into the top 10 for the first time at the 400-mile mark and finally finishing 11 laps behind winner Gordon Johncock. Hickman exhibited good promise during the USAC rookie orientation period in April and was marked down as a driver to watch.

CAR
March 82C/Cosworth

CHIEF MECHANIC
Danny Jones

SPONSOR
Stroh's March

STATISTICS OF CAR
Jim Hickman received Rookie-of-the-Year honors for his ride in this new March. He qualified at 196.217, started 24th and was flagged in 7th place after completing 189 laps.

[103]

Johnny Rutherford

Although Johnny Rutherford moved up from 32nd finishing position in 1982 to eighth this year, he was obviously not a very happy man this May. It was plain that John realized that time had obsoleted his Pennzoil Chaparral, which was clearly the boss car on the race track only two years before. The Penskes and the Patricks had caught up and gone around the Jim Hall Chaparral.

One of the handful of three-time winners of the race, Johnny was still smiling and pleasant to all at the Speedway, but it seemed he was having to make some extra effort to be such a good front man this time because things weren't going well in the Chaparral camp.

Rutherford qualified way back — for him — in the fourth row, outside, at 197.066. He had moved into 10th place by the 10-lap mark and was up to eighth at 40 laps, seventh at 70 laps, sixth at 100 laps and fifth at 140 laps before late engine problems put him out at 187 laps.

Johnny still has winning a fourth Indianapolis 500 as his goal and has been doing some strong lobbying in the Chaparral outfit to get him a newly-designed car for the 1983 running. If it is as much of an advance as Hall came up with when he brought his ground-effects Chaparral to the Speedway, his 1979 with Al Unser as the driver, it is bound to be successful and likely to carry "J.R." to #4.

Rutherford is a graduate of the USAC midget and sprint-car ranks. He won the USAC National Sprint title in 1965 by a 2.5-point margin in an epic struggle with Greg Weld. The next year, Johnny broke both arms in a spectacular flip at Eldora Speedway, Rossburg, OH.

Rutherford failed to finish his first 10 Indianapolis 500's. But when he finally finished one, 1974, he won it, driving for Team McLaren. He was second to Bobby Unser in 1975, but came back strong to post Victory No. 2 in 1976, again for McLaren. When McLaren quit racing after the 1979 season, Rutherford suddenly found himself high and dry. But Hall had just lost Unser to Bobby Hillin, a fellow Midland, TX. resident, and a phone call hooked up Hall and Rutherford. They were rewarded with victory in the 1980 500.

CAR
'79 Chaparral/Cosworth

CHIEF MECHANIC
Tony Dowe

SPONSOR
Pennzoil Chaparral

STATISTICS OF CAR
The bloom was off this Jim Hall car. Al Unser ran 22nd, retiring with oil seal trouble in '79. Rutherford only practiced with it in '80; and this year it started 12th; (197.066) broke water line, ran 187 laps and finished 8th.

Herm Johnson

Herm was the hero for stock-block fans at Indianapolis in 1982, pacing the Chevies in practice most days and also qualifying nicely at 195.929 mph and finishing the race "first in class" in ninth position.

Johnson also is a lesson in persistence. This was his third year at Indianapolis but also was the first time he had made the race. Herm first came here in 1980 and passed his driver's test but was unable to get up to qualifying speed and made no attempt. He ran eight Championship races that year with his best finish being an eighth place at Phoenix. In his only start that year in the Robert Bosch-Volkswagen Cup Series, Herm won the race at Watkins Glen, NY.

In 1981, Johnson qualified for the 500 at a speed of 185.874 but was bumped from the starting lineup by the final qualifier and became first alternate.

The blond-haired driver, a resident of Eau Clair, WI., lost his father and #1 fan by death shortly before this year's race.

Johnson gained most of his racing experience from Supervee competition. In 1977, he shared the USAC Mini-Indy title with Tom Bagley, winning the final race of the year at Phoenix.

In 1978, Herm finished fourth in the Mini-Indy series, scoring seven finishes in the top 10. During the 1979 season, Herm ran only two Mini-Indy races but also drove his first Championship event, finishing eighth in the Milwaukee 200.

Johnson ran nine CART races during the 1981 season, with his best finish being a seventh in the Riverside, CA., 500-kilometer event. His car caught fire during a pit stop in the 1981 Michigan 500 and the ensuing blaze caused the race to be red-flagged with nearly an hour's delay before the restart.

CAR
Eagle 8104/Chevy V-8 (n.a.)

CHIEF MECHANIC
Dan Cota

SPONSOR
Menard Cashway Lumber

STATISTICS OF CAR
A brand new Eagle which Herm qualified at 195.929. It started 14th; still running on the 186th lap; flagged in 9th.

[105]

10th HOWDY HOLMES

Howdy Holmes

Howdy Holmes, the jockey-sized driver who won Rookie-of-the Year honors in 1979 when he was the only neophyte to make the race, returned to the starting field for the first time in three years and drove to a trouble-plagued 10th-place finish, last car running.

Holmes had a new March/Cosworth owned by Doug Shierson and sponsored by the Domino's Pizza people and made the race with an opening-day qualifying average of 194.468 which ultimately proved to be the second lowest speed in the starting field.

A resident of Ann Arbor, MI. and graduate of Eastern Michigan University, Holmes owns his own advertising and marketing consulting firm.

He started driving Formula Fords in 1971. In 1972, Howdy was the Sports Car Club of America Central Division champion in Formula Supervee. Repeating that championship in 1973, Howdy set five official track records.

Holmes drove in the Canadian Player's Formula Atlantic Series in 1974 and won Rookie-of-the-Year honors in that competition.

After competing in Formula Atlantic and Supervees in 1975 and 1976, Howdy finished in third place behind Tom Bagley and Herm Johnson, who tied for first, in the 1977 USAC Mini-Indy Series. In 1978, he was the champion of the Labatt's North American Formula Atlantic championship.

As the only first-year man to make the 1979 Indianapolis starting field, Holmes was a virtual cinch for rookie of the year honors in his Armstrong Mould/Jiffy Mix Special. But he showed his mettle by moving from a 13th place start to a seventh-place finish, being flagged after 195 laps.

Holmes made three qualifying attempts at the 1980 Indianapolis 500. He waved off his first after three laps, came in after a first-lap speed in the 184 range on his second, then hit the wall at the end of the backstretch on his third try. He ran five Championship races, with his best finish an eighth place at Pocono. The year 1981 was something of a blank for Howdy. He didn't make a qualifying attempt at Indianapolis — he didn't have a ride — and did not start a Championship race. But he came back strongly into the picture this time.

CAR
March 82C/Cosworth

CHIEF MECHANIC
Dennis Swan

SPONSOR
Domino's Pizza/Team Shireson

STATISTICS OF CAR
A new March qualified by Howdy at 194.468 to start 18th. It was the last car running when it was flagged in 10th after 186 laps.

BOBBY RAHAL 11th

Bobby Rahal

A quiet and modest driver who came here with first-class equipment and shunned the limelight, Bobby Rahal made friends wherever he went during May and acquitted himself well in qualifying and the 500-Mile Race. He was running well in qualifying and the 500-Mile Race. He was running well in sixth position toward the end of the race but an engine problem eliminated him after 174 laps, pushing him back to an 11th place ranking.

A long-time competitor on the international road racing scene, Bobby had good financial backing coming to Indianapolis from Jim Trueman and the Red Roof Inns group and had a new March/Cosworth in which to race. He qualified on opening day of time trials at 194.700 for the 17th starting spot and drove consistently during the race.

Born in Medina, OH., Rahal was graduated from Denison College in Granville, OH. He started driving at Wentzville, MO. in a Lotus in 1973. He has been driving in SCCA competition since 1974 and in IMSA since 1976. Rahal has won more than 30 SCCA and Formula Atlantic races in the past eight years and also holds over 40 lap records.

Rahal won the SCCA Bs/n championship and was American Formula Atlantic champion and winner of the SCCA President's Cup in 1975. He was runnerup in the Labatt's Formula Atlantic series in 1977. In 1978, Rahal raced in both the Formula One Grand Prix circuit and the European Formula III series.

Bobby raced in the Can-Am series in 1979, winning the Laguna Seca, CA. race and the Lumbermen's 500 and finishing fifth in the point standings. He also found time that year to compete in the European Formula II series.

Rahal again was fifth in the 1980 Can-Am standings and also competed in the IMSA-GT series. He won the Daytona 24-Hour race in 1981 in a Porsche 935 and sat on the pole for the Daytona race this year. Also in 1981, he was third in the World Endurance Drivers' Championship and fourth in the IMSA-GT series.

CAR
March 82C/Cosworth

CHIEF MECHANIC
S. G. Horne

SPONSOR
Red Roof Inns

STATISTICS OF CAR
A new car, Bobby qualified it at 194.700. In the race it started 17th and was out on the 174th lap with engine trouble, finishing 11th.

12th GARY BETTENHAUSEN

Gary Bettenhausen

The oldest son of the late Tony Bettenhausen, Gary is an outstanding product of USAC midget, sprint and stock car competition as well as the dirt championship circuit. He won USAC National titles on the sprint circuit twice (1969-71) and the dirt championship crown in 1980.

Gary started racing in Go Karts in 1961. He moved in USAC Stocks in 1963, making his debut in the Yankee 300 at Indianapolis Raceway Park.

After several years in the stocks, Gary started driving midgets and drove in 14 midget races in 1966 as well as all 17 races on the stock car circuit, where he finished 10th in points. He also drove his first Championship race that year, finishing 19th in the Phoenix 200. Bettenhausen concentrated on the Midgets in 1967, winning five of the 36 features he ran and placing third in point standings.

Gary got his first Indianapolis ride in 1968. He was running ninth at the 43-lap mark when he ran over some debris from Al Unser's wrecked car and was eliminated from the event.

Gary drove for the Thermo King team of Fred Gerhardt his first four years at Indianapolis, with his best finish being a 10th place in 1971. He switched to the Penske team for 1972 to drive a Sunoco McLaren and was in clear command when ignition problems slowed him and finally put him out of the race after 182 laps, allowing the victory to go to his teammate, the late Mark Donohue. Finishing fifth in 1973, Gary then was dogged by persistent mechanical failures which put him out of every race through 1978. He missed the 1979 runing. His career had received a marked setback when he lost much of the use of his left arm in an accident at Syracuse, NY. in 1975. But he came back gamely. In 1980,

Gary came up with one of the great drives in Indianapolis history to move from 32nd starting position to a third-place finish nosing out Gordon Johncock.

In the race, Gary exhibited his usual dogged determination with a car that did not seem to be handling very well until he went out after 158 laps with engine problems.

CAR
Lightning (Dave Klym)/Cosworth

CHIEF MECHANIC
Chuck Bockman

SPONSOR
Kraco Special

STATISTICS OF CAR
Prepared by Gary, his twin sons and their young friend. The car was driven in 1980 by Janet Guthrie, who failed to qualify. Gary started 11th in '81 and threw a rod on the 69th lap finishing 26th. This year he qualified at 195.673, starting 31st. He finished 12th after blowing an engine on the 158th lap.

Hector Rebaque

There were a lot of people among the close students of the Indianapolis scene who thought that former Grand Prix driver Hector Rebaque should have followed in Josele Garza's footsteps and been the second consecutive Mexican driver to be selected Indianapolis 500 Rookie-of-the-Year. It is certainly no discredit to Jim Hickman, who did win the rookie accolade, to report that Rebaque really did an outstanding job. After

qualifying at 195.684 on opening day in his Carta Blanca March/Cosworth, Rebaque moved steadily up in the field from his 15th starting spot on race day.

He was in 10th place after 100 miles, sixth at 200 miles, fifth at 300 miles and still in the top 10 despite a two-lap penalty for passing under the yellow, when a flash fire in the pits eliminated him at the 150-lap mark.

He moved up to GT cars in 1973 and in 1974 and 1975 competed in Formula Ford events in both the United States and England. In 1976, Hector raced Formula Atlantic cars in the U.S. In 1977, he drove in Formula I for Lord Hesketh's team and also raced the Formula II circuit in Europe.

After driving in Formula I with Rebaque Racing in 1978 and 1979, he got a ride with the highly-touted Brabham team in 1980 and 1981, finishing in 10th place in the World Championship of Drivers the latter year.

When he isn't racing, Rebaque is in the construction business. He enjoys water sports as a hobby. The Garvin Brown-Forsythe Brothers team which brought Rebaque to the Speedway performed the difficult feat of getting two rookies into the race, Hector and his teammate, Danny Sullivan.

CAR
March 82C/Cosworth

CHIEF MECHANIC
Hywel Absalom

SPONSOR
Carta Blanca

STATISTICS OF CAR
The young Formula I graduate turned a 195.684 average to qualify this new March for a 15th starting slot. A fire in the pits and clutch trouble retired the car on the 150th lap in 13th position.

14th *DANNY SULLIVAN*

Danny Sullivan

A handsome young man from Louisville, KY., who is still single, Danny Sullivan made feminine hearts flutter wherever he went during Maytime in Indianapolis. He also did a very workmanlike job of making the field for his first Indianapolis 500 and running well until an accident sidelined him after 149 laps, placing him 14th in the final standings. Sullivan was uninjured and his countenance unmarred when he spun in the fourth turn and hit the wall. "I don't know what happened," Sullivan said, "Maybe I just made a mistake. The car got away from me in a hurry."

After attending the Kentucky Military Institute and the University of Kentucky, Danny went overseas to launch his racing career, driving a Formula Ford at his first race in England in 1972. He competed in England and Europe in Formula III events from 1973 to 1976, taking runnerup honors in the 1974 British Formula II championship and placing fourth in the European Championship in 1975. In the latter season, Danny had five victories, four pole positions and five lap records.

In 1976, Danny moved up to Formula II. He also took up endurance racing in 1977. In 1978, he competed in the North American Formula Atlantic Series, placing 8th, and also was fourth in the New Zealand championship.

After concentrating on endurance racing in 1979, Sullivan competed in SCCA Can-Am and Formula Atlantic races in 1980, finishing sixth in the Can-Am point standings. He drove from 20th starting spot to a third-place finish in the 1980 Montreal Formula Atlantic race.

Danny scored an outstanding victory in the final Can-Am race of 1981 at Caesars Palace in Las Vegas after he had led four previous Can-Ams that season. The victory enabled Danny to finish fourth in the 1981 Can-Am point standing and won him a series ride for 1982 with the vaunted Paul Newman/Budweiser team. He also was 15th in points in the North American Formula Atlantic series with a third place at Long Beach, CA. as his best finish.

CAR
March 82C/Cosworth

CHIEF MECHANIC
Hywel Absalom

SPONSOR
Forsythe-Brown Racing

STATISTICS OF CAR
Apparently the first of this year's shipment of Marchs did rookie Danny Sullivan in good stead as he qualified it at 196.292. He started 13th and finished 14th, dropping out on the 148th lap when the car hit the wall.

Chip Ganassi

Chip Ganassi, still another graduate of the road racing ranks, was the fastest rookie qualifier for the 1982 Indianapolis 500, winning the American Dairy Association Award and being guest of honor at a luncheon shortly before the race. He also was one of the younger drivers in the race, celebrating his 24th birthday only six days before race day and being graduated from Duquesne University also during the pre-race period.

Chip began racing Formula Fords at Lime Rock, CT., in 1977. A 1978 graduate of the Bob Bondurant School, he continued in Formula Ford competition in 1979 and 1980, scoring five first-place finishes and three seconds and winning the Northeast Division SCCA championship.

In 1981, Chip competed in the Robert Bosch/Volkswagen Supervee Series, leading two races and finishing in sixth place in points. He had a third-place finish at Milwaukee and also other finishes of fourth, fifth, seventh and eighth.

Ganassi made his Championship debut at Phoenix in October, 1981, logging some 150 test laps but failing to qualify for the race because of a timing-gear failure.

After looking good in the USAC Rooke Orientation Program in April at the Speedway, Ganassi qualified his Jack Rhoades-owned First Commercial Corporation Wildcat/Cosworth at a surprisingly fast 197.704 miles per hour on the opening day of time trials. That earned him 11th starting spot.

Engine problems eliminated him from the race at 147 laps.

Ganassi enjoys skiing and snowmobiling in the off season.

CAR
Wildcat VIII/Cosworth

CHIEF MECHANIC
Mark Bridges

SPONSOR
First Commercial Corp.

STATISTICS OF CAR
Originally built for Mario Andretti but qualified by Wally Dallenbach in 1981 while Mario was Grand Prix racing. It started 32nd but finished 2nd. Chip qualified it at 197.704 and after starting 11th it finished 15th; retiring on the 147th lap with engine trouble.

16th *BILL WHITTINGTON*

Bill Whittington

Bill Whittington had to sweat out repairs to his already-qualified #94 Whittington Brothers/Warner Hodgdon March/Cosworth after he crashed in a practice run on the final qualifying day, to say nothing of the aforementioned death threat against the Whittington brothers. But, the car was ready in time for the final practice day on the Thursday before the race and State Police plainclothesmen guarded him along with his brothers

on race day so things went reasonably well for the middle Whittington brother. He didn't last as long as he had in the 1981 race before engine problems again kayoed him, 121 laps this year compared to 146 last. But the attrition was greater this time so he placed 16th, compared to 21st in 1981.

Since they have usually run as a team, Bill's career has closely paralleled that of older brother Don. Their outstanding accomplishment was victory in the 1979 LeMans (France) 24-Hour race.

Bill began racing in 1978. He finished second in the Camel GT series during his first year, including a victory in the finale at Daytona Beach, FL.

In addition to the LeMans victory, in 1979 he co-drove with Don to win in 6-hour events at Watkins Glen, NY, Daytona and the El Salvador 1,000. He ended the season third in the World Challenge for Endurance Drivers and seventh in the IMSA GT series.

Bill's first Championship car start came in the 1979 Ontario (CA.) 500, where he finished 12th.

Qualifying for his first Indianapolis 500 in 1980, Bill was involved in a first-turn crash with Dick Ferguson on the 10th lap and suffered a broken left leg, placing 30th. That sidelined

him for most of the season.

Bill had a highly unusual experience at Indianapolis in 1981. He originally qualified at 184.833, was bumped by Roger Mears, then got in his backup car and qualified at 197.098 — 13 miles an hour faster and quick enough to have made the outside of the front row had it been turned on the opening qualifying day! He started 27th and placed 21st. Bill also drove in eight IMSA-GT events in 1981, finishing third at Sebring, Mosport and Daytona Beach.

He ran as high as ninth in this year's race before a two-lap penalty was assessed against him for passing under the yellow light.

CAR

March 81C/Cosworth

CHIEF MECHANIC

Jerry Eisert

SPONSOR

Whittington/Warner Hodgdon

STATISTICS OF CAR

A never-run '81 March. Qualifying speed was 201.658 which gave it 6th starting spot. Broke its header and retired on the 121st lap with 16th place.

Michael Chandler

A Speedway sophomore, Mike Chandler was the fastest of the stock-block qualifiers for the 1982 Indianapolis 500 and did a good job on race day of convincing Dan Gurney and other assorted onlookers that he is an excellent race driver. His experiences included racing winner, Gordon Johncock, closely, lap after lap, although he was a lap down to the ultimate victor at the time.

Starting 22nd, Chandler worked his way into the top 10 by the 150-mile mark and had run as high as ninth before gearbox problems eliminated him at the 104-lap mark.

Although the fact that he is the son of Otis Chandler, publisher of the Los Angeles Times has doubtless opened a few doors for Mike, those who conclude automatically that Mike has had a doting father around to buy him race cars are wrong. Mike has had his ups and downs and has done most of it on his own.

Born in Los Angeles, Mike attended Orange Coast College. He drove his first race in 1978 in a Supervee at Riverside, CA.

Chandler had an outstanding season in USAC Mini-Indy competition in 1979, winning races at Michigan, Texas World Speedway and Ontario. He also set the course record at TWS with a speed of 156.372. Mike finished second in the series point standings and was selected as USAC's Mini—Indy Rookie-of-the-Year.

In 1980, Mike finished fifth in the Robert Bosch Supervee standings and drove his first Championship race in the Ontario 500, finishing 14th. He also drove to fourth place in the 6-hour Grand Prix of Endurance at Riverside, CA.

Mike passed his rookie driver's test at Indianapolis in 1981 and qualified for his first Indianapolis 500 at a speed of 187.568 in a Warner Hodgdon National Engineering Eagle. He was flagged in 12th place after 192 laps of the race. He drove in three CART races in 1981 with his best finish a fourth place at Riverside, CA.

Chandler enjoys riding dirt bikes and skiing when he isn't racing.

CAR

Eagle 8113/Chevy V-8 (n.a.)

CHIEF MECHANIC

Steve Frase

SPONSOR

Freeman/Gurney Eagle

STATISTICS OF CAR

A new car with a new record. The fastest normally aspirated Chevy ever! 198.042 was the speed; it started 22nd. Transmission broke on 104th lap. Mike was 17th.

18th TOM BIGELOW

Tom Bigelow

Tom Bigelow had a big decision to make in order to get into the 1982 Indianapolis 500-Mile Race and he paid a huge price in order to get the job done. But his many enthusiastic followers will certainly understand that Tom was willing to pay almost any price to get into the race.

The situation developed because Tom was obviously going nowhere in the #56 Genesee Beer Wagon Penske/Chevy in which he was entered for car owner, Dick Hammond and Chief mechanic Galen Fox. He had been unable to get any more speed than the high 180's out of it.

So, the Hall brothers, old friends, approached Tom with the idea of buying the #73 Eagle/Chevy from Ray Lipper of Center Line Wheels for Tom and having him put it in the race. The catch was that Hammond and Fox weren't ready to throw in the towel yet. And, they were the fellows for whom Tom drove USAC Silver Crown and Sprint cars.

What to do? To take the Halls' offer and risk the almost certain loss of excellent rides in two other circuits which are his bread-and-butter? Or to stay hitched and miss the race?

Tom chose the former course of action and qualified for the last row at 194.784 in the renamed H.B.K. Racing Eagle/Chevy which was renumbered #27 through the cooperation of entrant Rolla Vollstedt, from whom the Halls acquired the necessary entry.

Bigelow is renowned for the size and enthusiasm of his fan club, which ranks among the largest of any racing driver in the world.

He is the all-time winningest driver in USAC Sprint car history with a total of 52 victories at this writing.

Bigelow started racing way back in 1957 with the Badger Midget Racing Association at Rockford, IL. He joined IMCA in 1965 and finished fourth in Sprint points and third in Midget points.

Bigelow joined USAC in 1967 and scored one of his major victories by winning the Houston Astrodome Midget Championship in 1969. He made his Indianapolis debut in 1974, finishing 12th. His best Indy finish was sixth in 1977 and he was eighth in 1980.

CAR
Eagle 8103/Chevy V-8 (n.a.)

CHIEF MECHANIC
Martin Clifton

SPONSOR
H.B.K. Racing

STATISTICS OF CAR
The Gurney Eagle was Mike Mosley's ride in '81. This year Tom's friends, the Hall Bros., bought it from Ray Lipper. Tom, with little practice, qualified it at 194.784 on the last day. Starting 31st it lost oil pressure and dropped out on the 96th lap, finishing 18th.

A. J. Foyt

This was the silver anniversary year for A..J Foyt at Indianapolis and many of his supporters were wearing simulated orange sheriff's badges that read "25-5". That, of course, meant that Foyt would win his fifth Indianapolis 500 in his 25th consecutive year of participation.

While that didn't quite come about, Foyt did reward his many fans with a spectacular performance. After having to change steering arms because of damage inflicted to his Valvoline-Gilmore March by the pace lap accident, Foyt took off from his outside, front-row spot and led the first 22 laps of the race before making his first pit stop; he also led nine more laps later in the race.

Foyt was doused with fuel by his crew during a subsequent pit stop and then was sidelined after 95 laps with transmission trouble. When the car became stuck in third gear, A. J. took a hammer to the offending mechanical members and tried to fix it himself as the crowd roared in support. But to no avail and he was done for the day.

Any real listing of the accomplishments of A.J. Foyt in this size biography is, of course, strictly impossible. Suffice it to say that he is probably the greatest driver in the history of auto racing. And, the facts back up the statement. He has won in virtually every kind of race car from Midgets to endurance racing cars. And, he has victories in virtually all the big ones in racing . . . Indianapolis four times . . . Daytona . . . LeMans.

He leads all drivers in the following categories: miles run at Indianapolis, races won there, pole positions (tied with Rex Mays at four), races led (13), races started, points earned and money earned. In all Championship races, he is the leader in races won, money won and points earned. He has won the USAC national Driving Championship a record seven times.

Born in his present home town of Houston, TX., A. J. has been racing since 1953 when he started in midgets. He has raced at Indianapolis in four different decades. In addition to his four victories, he has two seconds, three thirds, a seventh and an eighth to show for his Indianapolis achievements.

CAR
March 82C/Cosworth

CHIEF MECHANIC
Jack Starne

SPONSOR
Valvoline-Gilmore

STATISTICS OF CAR
A new car in which A. J. qualified third at 203.332. The shift linkage broke and though A. J. tried to fix it with a hammer, the car retired on the 95th lap in 19th place.

Johnny Parsons

For most of the month of May, Johnny Parsons prowled the pit area looking for something to drive. Just when he was about to give it up, he found himself a ride — albeit one that two other drivers already had tried and given up on.

But Parsons tamed the Wysards' March/Cosworth to such an extent that he was able to put it into the race on the final weekend at a speed of nearly 196 miles an hour and then acquired some late sponsorship from Silhouette National Health Spas, Tombstone Pizza, and radio station WIFE.

Parsons was eliminated after 92 laps by a mechanical failure, which put him into a long sideways slide coming out of Turn-1, placing him in 20th spot.

The son of 1950 Indianapolis winner Johnnie Parsons, Johnny started racing in Quarter Midgets when he was 12 years old. After winning 45 races, he moved into Go-Karts at 16 and then began running Three-Quarter and full Midgets at 18.

After competing in BCRA and URA sanctioned events on the West Coast, Parsons began running with USAC in 1968, competing in both midgets and sprint cars.

Parsons was entered in a car at Indianapolis as early as 1969, but was requested to get more experience before he would be permitted to take a driver's test. He finished seventh at Sacramento that year in his first Championship start. In 1970, Johnny ran in four Championship races and was fast qualifier at the Hoosier Hundred. He won a 100-lap midget race at San Jose, CA.

Parsons passed a driver's test at the Speedway in 1973 but made no qualifying attempt.

Parsons made the 1974 starting field in a Tassi Vatis car, but lasted only 18 laps before turbocharger trouble put him out. He made the field in every other race through 1980, finishing fifth in 1977 and 10th in 1978.

Johnny made three attempts to qualify at Indianapolis in 1981 but his speeds were too slow to make the field.

Parson's reputation is that of being one of the most talented of the second-generation drivers and many observers think that he has the talent to become an Indianapolis winner, if he ever gets the right kind of equipment.

CAR
March 82C/Cosworth

CHIEF MECHANIC
Lew Parks

SPONSOR
Silhouette/Tombstone Pizza/WIFE

STATISTICS OF CAR
A new car for a veteran driver. Johnny qualified at 195.929 for 26th starting spot and then broke a half-shaft on the 92nd lap to gain 20th.

George Snider

It may seem hard to understand that a 21st-position finish could mean a major driving championship, but that is what happened to George Snider on May 30.

The mere 15 points that "Ziggy" earned as a result of his finish were enough to keep him safely ahead of all of his rivals and give him the first USAC Gold Crown Championship. Snider took it in his characteristic stride, saying that since he isn't much of a talker, he probably would not be able to exploit the title to any great degree.

But, the championship is one that George will prize because it is emblematic of talent in various types of racing; on the dirt tracks as well as the super speedways. After A. J. Foyt decided to run only one car in the race, A. J. was instrumental in putting together the deal that resulted in Snider geting a late ride in the Bob Fletcher team backup car, re-christened the Cobre Tire Special.

Snider qualified the car handily, his 17th consecutive qualification for the 500, but the car quit on him after 87 laps and he had to be towed in off the course.

George has been driving race cars for more than 20 years, having started in Modifieds at Fresno, CA. in 1961. At his best on the dirt, Snider was USAC's first Dirt Car Champion back in 1971.

Snider made his Speedway debut in 1965, lasting 64 laps before rear end failure put him out. His only top-10 finishes in a career plagued with mechanical failures were in eighth place in both 1975 and 1978.

He had the distinction of starting the 1979 race in 35th — yes, that's right — 35th place after making the field during an extraordinary special qualification period on the morning before the race, which was the result of the great waste-gate gimmicking controversy. But his race lasted only seven laps before a bent valve put him out.

George qualified a Valvoline-Gilmore Special for the 1981 race but the car was sold out from under him and driven in the race by Tim Richmond.

CAR
March 82C/Cosworth

CHIEF MECHANIC
Derek Mower

SPONSOR
Cobre Tire

STATISTICS OF CAR
A new March fell to "Ziggy" Snider thanks to the help of A. J. Foyt and he qualified it at 195.493 Started 26th; finished 21st after losing transmission on 87th lap.

22nd DANNY ONGAIS

Danny Ongais

Danny Ongais, one of the all-time hard chargers and always a favorite of the fans, wound up his race against the wall for the second staight year. But the outcome was a lot happier this time, when he was unhurt in a second-turn crash after 62 laps, than in 1981, when he was critically hurt in a third-turn accident. Again, it was a mechanical failure, a wheel bearing, that put Danny into the concrete.

Born in Hawaii, Danny started racing motorcycles there at the age of 17 in 1957. He was Hawaiian Motorcycle Champion in 1960 and also raced motorcycles in Europe. He started racing sports cars in 1960 and then became active in drag racing. He won the national championship in AA Gas dragsters in 1963 and 1964 and the AA Fuel dragster title in 1965. Part of an American team that went to Europe in 1965, he was the first driver to exceed 200 miles an hour on an European drag strip.

Ongais went to work for Goodyear in 1967 and was part of the crew servicing the USAC Championship cars. Listed as the driver of a car entered by Mickey Thompson in the 1969 Indianapolis race. Ongais was denied permission to take a driver's test and requested to get more experience.

Running in SCCA amateur road racing in 1974, Danny won 12 races in 15 starts. He ran the Formula 5000 series in 1975 and 1976, finishing fifth the latter year. Making his first USAC Championship start, he ran 28th in the California 500.

Ongais qualified for his first Indianapolis 500 in 1977, winning seventh starting spot. Engine problems put him out after 90 laps. He had the fastest lap of the race, his 42nd, at a speed of 192.678. He scored his first Championship victory in the Michigan 200 in 1977 and was 12th in the point standings. He also participated in the IMSA Camel GT series, driving a Porsche 934 to victory at Laguna Seca and Brainard. In 1978, Danny led all the 17 Championship races he started, winning at Ontario, Texas, Mosport, Milwaukee and Michigan and finishing eighth in the point standings.

He was fourth at Indianapolis in 1979 and seventh in 1980 before ending the next two years with crashes.

CAR
Interscope -03/Cosworth

CHIEF MECHANIC
Phil Casey

SPONSOR
Interscope Racing

STATISTICS OF CAR
The new "Batmobile" was qualified by Danny at 199.148. Starting 9th he was involved in an accident on the 62nd lap, also involving Jerry Sneva and Chet Fillip. He was awarded 22nd place.

[118]

Jerry Sneva

Jerry Sneva had the misfortune to be in the right place at the wrong time and the experience ended his 1982 500-Mile Race. In the aftermath of Danny Ongais's crash, Sneva and Chet Fillip tangled and Jerry was on the sidelines for another year.

Younger brother of the more well-known Tom Sneva, Jerry is well-liked and popular among the racing fraternity as well. "Giles" is an enthusiastic golfer and often can be found on the Speedway links during May when he isn't driving.

Jerry played high school football, basketball and hockey and finished three years at Eastern Washington State College.

He started racing modified stock cars at the Spokane, WA. fairgrounds in 1968. he moved up to the Canadian-American modified Racing Association (CAMRA) in 1971 and won Rookie-of-the-Year honors. He won the CAMRA title in 1974 after finishing fourth in 1972 and second in 1973. In his championship year, he won 30 races in 37 starts to take the title by the largest margin ever.

Jerry passed a driver's test at Indianapolis in 1975 but made no attempt to qualify. Returning to the Northwest, he was third in the CAMRA standings. Sneva was unable to find an Indianapolis ride in 1976.

Jerry won the Rookie-of-the-Year award at Indianapolis in 1977, qualifiying for 16th starting position and moving up to 10th in the race, for his best-ever Indianapolis finish up to the present.

Mechanical mishaps put Sneva out of the race in 1978 after only 18 laps and in 1979 after only 16 circuits.

Jerry had the distinct pleasure of out-qualifying his more famous brother in 1980, winning fifth starting spot. But he hit the wall in the first turn after 130 laps.

Jerry's qualification run in 1981 was fast enough to make the race but his car was disqualified by race officials on the grounds the crew had tampered with the waste-gate affecting turbocharger boost pressure. He drove in the Pocono 500 and finished 25th.

CAR
March 81C/Cosworth

CHIEF MECHANIC
Paul Diatlovich

SPONSOR
The Great American Spirit

STATISTICS OF CAR
Brother Tom's No. 2 from last year, Jerry qualified it at 195.270 to start 28th and finish 23rd. It was wrecked on the 61st lap, when it tangled with Chet Fillip.

24th CHET FILLIP

Chet Fillip

It was like a dream come true for Chet Fillip of Ozona, TX., finding himself in a garage next to his idol, A. J. Foyt of Houston, TX., in Gasoline Alley at Indianapolis.

Fillip was the first bearded driver to run in the Indianapolis 500 since Doc MacKenzie ran his final race in 1936. A modest and humble fellow, Chet made friends easily wherever he went during May. It was something of a surprise to many followers of the sport when he made the starting field at 194.879 in the final weekend of time trials, in view of Fillips's limited experience.

Fillip was unlucky enough to be right behind Danny Ongais when Danny hit the wall and the resulting tangle between Fillip's car and that of Jerry Sneva eliminated both machines.

Chet was a member of the National Honor Society at Central High School in San Agelo, TX, where he graduated in 1975. He also attended Angelo State and Texas Tech Universities.

Chet was reared in a racing family. Five members of his family run an automotive warehouse and his father, Marvin Fillip, has been racing actively for 15 years and gave Chet his start in racing with financial backing and advice.

Fillip moved from Soap Box Derby cars and go-karts to stock car racing at the age of 16, starting with a 1956 Chevy which he built with the help of his father. He won two main events with the Chevy during his first season. Moving up to Supermodifieds, Chet won two main events and placed second twice in the first four races of his 1976 season. Driving a Chevelle that year, Chet ran fourth in his first super-speedway race at Texas World Speedway.

Driving a rear-engine, winged Supermodified in 1977, Fillip set a track record on the 3/8-mile track at Kalamozoo, MI. and had a 50-lap victory at Owosso, MI.

In 1979, Fillip took a new model rear-engine car to the Northeast to race and in 1980 ran dirt sprint cars in the Midwest, stock cars on asphalt and dirt in Texas and asphalt Supermodifieds in Jackson, MS.

CAR
Eagle/Cosworth

CHIEF MECHANIC
Bill Hite

SPONSOR
Circle Bar Truck Corral

STATISTICS OF CAR
It was an '81 Eagle which had never run before, that Chet Fillip qualified at 194.879. He started 29th; finished 24th, when he got mixed up with the Sneva-Ongais tangle on 60th lap. Car suffered body damage.

Pete Halsmer

Pete Halsmer had an uphill struggle all month to make the Indianapolis 500 starting field for the second straight year, plagued by constantly-recurring engine problems with his turbocharged Chevy. But he finally qualified the Colonial Bread/Pay Less markets Eagle/Chevy for the middle of the back row and was a joyful participant in the Indianapolis Press Club's traditional "Eleventh Row Society" festivities.

Transmission troubles sidelined Pete after only 38 laps on race day, relegating him to 25th position.

Born in Lafayette, IN., where his father operates an airport and flying service, Halsmer was graduated from Purdue University in 1967 with a degree in Industrial Education.

Pete started racing in Formula Vees in 1970. He later moved up into Formula Fords and drove a Brabham in Formula B competition on the West Coast, winning five of his last nine races.

Pete became a professional race driver in 1978 finishing 12th in the USAC Mini-Indy series. He moved up to fourth in the Mini-Indy points in 1979 and the following season, he ran the entire series except for the opener at Charlotte, NC., scored a victory at Ontario, CA. and again was fourth in the point standings.

Pete made his first Championship start in the 1980 Ontario (CA.) 200, finishing 20th; he was sixth at Phoenix in his only other Championship start.

Halsmer qualified for the 1980 Indianapolis 500 at a speed of 181.351 but' was bumped from the starting lineup.

Halsmer qualified for the 24th starting spot for his first Indianapolis 500 in 1981. He finished in exactly the same spot, crashing after 123 laps in Turn-3.

Pete had his best year in the Supervees in 1981, winning three of the Robert Bosch/Volkswagen Series races and finishing second in the season point standings. This season, Pete is acting as manager for the Frank Arciero team on the Supervee circuit.

CAR
Eagle 8111/Chevy V-8 (t.c.)

CHIEF MECHANIC
Chuck Looper

SPONSOR
Colonial Bread/Payless Markets/Arciero Eagle

STATISTICS OF CAR
A new car which ran 194.595 in qualifications. Started 32nd; finished 25th. Out on 38th lap with a broken gear box.

26th *TONY BETTENHAUSEN*

Tony Bettenhausen

Tony Bettenhausen had a May that is the kind you like to forget. It was plagued with mechanical failures to his Provimi Veal McLaren/Cosworth which caused him to crash twice, once in practice and once on race day. The latter accident, on the main straightaway after 37 laps, left Tony with nothing more than a bad case of "racetrack rheumatism" but he was out of the race, placing 26th.

The son and namesake of the great Tony Bettenhausen, two-time National Driving champion who died at the Speedway in 1961 while test-hopping a car for buddy Paul Russo, Tony has been something of a pleasant surprise to his many friends. He has achieved much more success in Championship cars than he ever realized in midgets or stock cars. He always has liked the big superspeedways more than the quarter or half-mile dirt tracks.

Tony started in Late Model Sportsman stock cars in Houston, TX. in 1969. He moved up to NASCAR Late Model stocks in 1972, competing in 78 features and finishing second in the national point standings. Running both NASCAR and USAC Late Model stocks in 1973, Tony had a best finish of seventh in the USAC 500-miler at Pocono, PA.

Tony ran the Winston Cup Grand National series in 1974 and finished sixth in the ARCA Daytona 200 and qualified for the Daytona 500.

Joining USAC in 1975, Tony competed in the midget, sprint and stock divisions, winning a 50-lap midget race at Jackson, MS.

Tony started his first USAC Championship race at Texas World Speedway in 1979 and finished ninth. He also was ninth at Milwaukee 150, 13th at Pocono and in the second Texas 200 and 15th in the Milwaukee 200. He finished 17th in points and was selected as the USAC Championship Division Rookie-of-the-Year.

Bettenhausen qualified for the 1980 Indianapolis 500 with a speed of 176.410 but was bumped by a faster car. He was 32nd at Pocono in his only Championship start.

Tony made the starting field for his first Indianapolis 500 in 1981 with a speed of 187.013 and drove steadily to a seventh-place finish. He was named "Most Improved CART Driver" for his sixth-place finish in the points. His second place in the Michigan 500 was his best finish.

CAR

March 82C/Cosworth

CHIEF MECHANIC

Bobby Hatch

SPONSOR

Provimi Veal

STATISTICS OF CAR

Yet another new March in which "ToTo" qualified at 195.429. He started 27th but on the 37th lap a half-shaft broke and he hit the front-stretch wall. He was credited with 26th position.

Dennis Firestone

Dennis Firestone is still another product of the Mini-Indy competition in Supervees who has gone on to become an Indianapolis 500 fixture. He made the field for the race for the third straight year, doing an excellent qualifying job on the first Sunday in the Milodon stock-block-engined B.C.V. Racing Eagle.

Rear-end problems put Firestone out of action after 37 laps, placing him 27th.

It comes as a surprise to many racing fans to discover that Dennis is not a scion of the Firestone tire family. He is a professional racer who had made it on his own.

Born in Australia, Dennis attended San Jose State College in California. He works as the president of a trucking company when not racing.

Dennis started racing in a Formula Ford at Riverside Raceway in late 1971. He won the 1974 and 1976 South Pacific Formula Ford championships and the 1976 National Formula Ford Championship. In 1976 and 1977, he won 23 straight National or Pro races in Formula Ford and Formula Atlantic and captured the Kimberly Cup as the SCCA's most outstanding driver and the Bert Hawthorne Trophy as the nation's top Formula Ford driver.

Dennis moved into the USAC Mini-Indy Series in 1978 and placed second in the points. He was named the series Rookie-of-the-Year. Firestone won the 1979 Mini-Indy Championship, scoring five victories and three seconds in eight races. He drove his first Championship race at the 1979 Ontario 500.

Firestone made the Indianapolis 500 first in 1980 with a qualifying speed of 183.702 miles per hour. His car was eliminated after 137 laps by ring and pinion gear trouble, placing

him in 16th position.

In 1981, Firestone qualified his own car at a speed of 185.701 but was bumped by Scott Brayton. He then got into a Patrick team backup car which was acquired for him by car owner Jack Rhoades and qualified it at 187.784 to get back into the field, starting 28th Engine failure put him out after 193 laps, placing him 10th.

CAR
Eagle 8106/Milodon Chevy (N.A.)

CHIEF MECHANIC
John Buttera

SPONSOR
B.C.V. Racing

STATISTICS OF CAR
Another new Eagle. Dennis qualified for 21st starting spot with a 197.217 but only lasted 37 laps. It was given 27th place. The ring gear failed.

28th GEOFF BRABHAM

Geoff Brabham

Geoff Brabham's 1982 Indianapolis 500 was all too short for the Australian native who is the son of Sir Jack Brabham, the three-time World Grand Prix champion who brought the rear-engine revolution to Indianapolis.

Geoff lasted only 12 laps before engine failure put his Pentax Super on the sidelines. He had some problems qualifying, too. His first attempt never got the green flag due to a crew mixup and his second presentation ended in a mechanical failure. But he made it the third time he came to the line, qualifying at 198.906 to pace the first-Sunday qualifiers.

Geoff began racing in Formula Fords in Australia in 1973. In 1974, he won four Formula Ford races. Moving up to the Formula II series in 1975, Brabham won six races and was Australian Formula II champion.

From 1976 to 1978, Brabham competed in the Formula III series. He moved up to the USAC Mini-Indy series in late '78 and won the fall race at Trenton. In 1979, Geoff was the SCCA Gold Cup Supervee champion, winning five events. He also was selected as the SCCA Pro Rookie-of-the-Year for 1979.

Driving the SCCA Can-Am series in 1980, Geoff won the Atlanta race. He won the Long Beach, CA. Formula Atlantic race in the spring of 1981 and then finished ninth at Phoenix in his first Championship race.

Brabham passed his rookie test at Indianapolis in 1981, driving for the Psachie-Garza Esso team, and qualified for the 15th starting spot at 187.990 miles per hour.

Brabham was flagged in fifth place after 197 laps. He finished second to A. J. Foyt in the Pocono 500 last year. Brabham went on to win the 1981 Can-Am driving championship, producing victories at Road American and Edmonton. He also finished 13th in the North American Formula Atlantic Series.

CAR
March 82C/Cosworth

CHIEF MECHANIC
George Bignotti

SPONSOR
Pentax Super

STATISTICS OF CAR
A new March in which Australian Geoff Brabham qualified at 198.906 to start 20th. He lost an engine on the 12th lap and finished 28th.

[124]

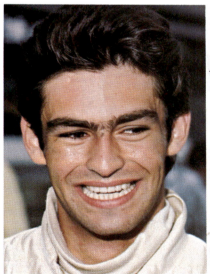

Josele Garza

This handsome young man from Mexico who had such an effortless month, seemingly at least, when he won Rookie-of-the-Year honors at Indianapolis in 1981, saw the other side of the coin this year. He had all kinds of problems getting his Schlitz Gusto March/Cosworth to handle well enough to get to qualifiying speed. His team manager, Bobby Unser, finally put on his familiar blue driving uniform, got in the car and got it sorted well enough for Jose to make the field — barely. He started in 33rd and last position, a marked contrast to his sixth-place start of 1981. And he lasted only one lap before his engine blew going into the first turn. That gave him 29th place.

Born in Mexico City, Garza still retains his residence there. He attended Anahuac University in his native land. During the off season, Josele works in business administration.

He started racing Go-Karts in Mexico City in 1976 and 1978, won a Kart race at Izcali, Mexico. He moved up the Formula Fords and IMSA-GT cars in 1979.

Moving into the Mini-Indy Series for the Robert Bosch/VW Cup in 1980, Garza ran every race and won the 100-miler at Pocono, PA. He also had two seconds at St. Paul, MN. and was runnerup for the series championship.

Josele made his first Championship start in the 1981 Phoenix 150, turning in the ninth fastest qualifying time. He crashed on the second lap of the race, placing 21st.

Garza passed his rookie test easily at Indianapolis in 1981 and his 195.101 qualifying was good for the outside starting spot in the second row.

Josele did an excellent job during the race, leading 13 laps and running with the leaders most of the event. He was eliminated after 138 laps when a mechanical failure caused him to hit the third-turn wall. He was selected as the AFNB Rookie-of-the-Year for his performance. A sixth-place finish in the Phoenix finale was Josele's best in the 11 CART races he ran during the year.

CAR

March 82C/Cosworth

CHIEF MECHANIC

Ron Dawes

SPONSOR

Schlitz Gusto

STATISTICS OF CAR

Bobby Unser was the Team Manager for the new March. Plagued by trouble most of the month, Josele finally qualified at 194.500 to start last. The car lasted only 1 lap before blowing its engine. It was credited with 29th place.

[125]

30th KEVIN COGAN

Kevin Cogan

This quiet, polite blond lad would have seemed probably the least likely of the 33 drivers in the starting field to be the storm center of just about the only controversy growing out of the 1982 Indianapolis 500. But that's the way it turned out. The sudden move to the right of Cogan's #4 Norton Spirit Penske/Ford into the side of A. J. Foyt and then back across the track, collecting Mario Andretti's car in the process, took Cogan and

Andretti both out of the race before it had begun, damaged Foyt's car to the extent a steering arm had to be replaced before the re-start and delayed the race for nearly an hour. Cogan was the target of bitter accusations from both Andretti and Foyt, who seemed to forget they were once young drivers who had their share of accidents.

Cogan said that the quick move was the result of a mechanical failure, of a constant velocity joint in his right rear. Others expressed grave doubt. But, whatever the truth, Cogan certainly didn't mean to cause the pre-green flag accident.

Cogan had been one of the two top runners in practice, along with teammate Rick Mears, and had qualified the team's backup car well at more than 204 miles per hour after blowing an engine on his primary car on "pole day." In only his sophomore year, he was well regarded and given a chance for victory. So, he was as disappointed as anyone.

A resident of Redondo Beach, CA., Cogan attended El Camino College in Torrance, CA. He holds a private pilot's license and flies his own plane.

Starting in Go-Karts in 1972, Cogan was the U.S. Western Division champion in two classes. He moved up to Formula Fords in 1975 and the next year won two races in six starts.

Cogan finished eighth in the Formula Atlantic series in 1977. He also won the National Championship Formula B race at Atlanta, GA., one of six victories in seven starts. He won three Formula Atlantic races in 1979.

Cogan qualified for the 1981 Indianplis 500 at 189.444 to earn 12th starting spot. He drove a steady race to finish fourth, despite losing a wheel at one point and having to come into the pits on three wheels.

CAR

Penske PC10-02/Ford

CHIEF MECHANIC

Bob Sprow

SPONSOR

Norton Spirit Penske PC-10

STATISTICS OF CAR

A brand new car from the Penske stable. Kevin qualified at 204.082 to break Tom Sneva's one and four lap records. He started second; but was involved in the pace lap accident; finished 30th.

Mario Andretti

The 1982 Indianapolis 500 represents frustration piled upon frustration for Mario Andretti, one of the all-time fan favorites. The little champion from Nazareth, PA., who had given up his Grand Prix ride to concentrate entirely on Indy-car racing, was one of the pre-race favorites after qualifying for the inside of the second row at 203.172. But he never even got to take the green flag due to the first lap accident which wiped out his #40

STP Oil Treatment Wildcat/Cosworth. Coming on top of the Appeals Board reversal of his 1981 "victory," it is little wonder that Andretti was an angered and embittered man over what transpired on the track just before the start/finish line this year.

Although he has only a single victory in 1969 to show for his 17 Indianapolis races, Mario has always been a factor as long as he is running and is one of the most feared and respected drivers in the trade.

Andretti is only the second American ever to have won the World Grand Prix championship. He did it in 1978, driving for the John Player Team Lotus. But even that triumph was tinged with tragedy when his teammate and close friend, Ronnie Peterson, was killed in the Italian Grand Prix where Mario clinched the title.

Born in Trieste, Italy, Mario started his racing career over there in Formula Junior cars in 1953 when he was only 13 years old. After his family moved to Pennsylvania, he started driving modified stock cars in 1958 and won more than 20 races in the next three years.

Joining USAC in 1964, Mario finished third in the Sprint points, winning the Joe James-Pat O'Connor Memorial 100-lapper at Salem, IN. In 1965, in addition to making the

Indianapolis 500 starting field for the first time, finishing third and winning Rookie-of-the-Year honors, Mario went on to win the first of his three USAC National Driving Championships.

Mario didn't finish another Indianapolis race until his 1969 victory, although he did win the pole position in both 1966 and 1967. His only top-10 finishes since his triumph were sixth in 1970, eighth in 1972, eighth in 1976 and runnerup — finally — in 1981.

CAR
Wildcat 8B-PR8B-003/Cosworth

CHIEF MECHANIC
Ron Baddeley

SPONSOR
STP Oil Treatment

STATISTICS OF CAR
Mario was visibly unhappy when the new car he had qualified for 4th starting spot at 203.172 was wrecked when Mario hit Kevin Cogan coming down for the start. Although he completed no laps Mario, was given 31st position.

Roger Mears

Probably already thoroughly tired of being known primarily as "Rick Mears' older brother," Roger Mears was deprived of a chance to make a good showing in his rookie year at the Indianapolis 500 through no fault of his own. As a secondary effect of the Cogan-Foyt-Andretti tangle at the front of the pack, Mears was "run over" by Dale Whittington back in the ranks and sidelined before ever getting the green flag. To say that

Roger was unhappy with Whittington's apparent failure to realize what was transpiring is to put it very mildly.

Roger got a good break when the Machinist Union Racing Team picked him as their "A" driver for 1982 and he responded by putting their Penske/Cosworth in the starting lineup at 194.154. Roger had some anxious moments during the final Sunday of qualifying as he "rode the bubble" for about four hours, but nobody was able to bump him from the starting field.

Roger is a lesson in perseverance. He had been trying to make the starting field for the 500 since 1978 when he passed his rookie test. But this is the first time he was able to crack the lineup.

He started racing in Go Karts when he was 13 years old, then moved up to motorcycles and stock cars. In 1972, Roger won the Mini-Stock championship in his home town of Bakersfield, CA. Roger and brother Rick then moved into off-road racing and drove sprint buggies at Ascot Speedway in Gardena, CA. Roger won the 1973 Ascot World Championship.

Roger won the 1978 SCORE Off-Road world championship and won many other honors in off-road racing, sometimes competing as a teammate of brother Rick.

Roger finished sixth in the California 500 at Ontario, CA in 1978. In 1979 at the Ontario 500, driving for the Patrick Racing team, Roger charged from 17th starting spot to sixth before engine failure put him out.

Roger had a ride with the Grant King team at the 1980 Indianapolis 500 but did not get up to qualifying speed. He qualified for the 1981 Indianapolis race at a speed of 184.890 but was bumped from the starting field.

CAR

Penske PC9B/Cosworth

CHIEF MECHANIC

Chuck Swearengin

SPONSOR

Machinist's Union Racing Team

STATISTICS OF CAR

Was run over by Dale Whittington on the pace lap after Mears had qualified it at 194.154 to start 19th. The new car completed no laps and was given 32nd place.

Dale Whittington

Dale Whittington made history when he qualified for the 1982 Indianapolis 500 at a speed of 197.694. It was the first time that three full brothers ever have qualified for an Indianapolis classic in the same field. Whittington, the younger, made a whirlwind entrance into the Indianapolis ranks — and a whirlwind departure from competition.

Dale was never on the track until less than a week before he qualified.

After brothers Don and Bill Whittington both got into the field, they switched their attention to getting Dale in. They ushered him through his driver's test, then worked him up at the rate of 2 or 3 miles an hour per day until he was ready to qualify. Unfortunately, Dale failed to notice all the tangle going on up ahead at the start and ran over Roger Mears car, ending the day for both of them.

Born in Farmington, New Mexico, Dale attended high school in Fort Lauderdale, FL. He is involved in the mobile home sales phase of his family's business. At 22, he is the youngest of the brothers and also was the youngest man in the 500 starting field.

Dale attended the Bob Bondurant Driving School in 1978. In September of that year, he drove his first race at Road Atlanta, an IMSA event. In 1979, Dale competed in all the endurance races of IMSA along with his brothers, including LeMans, Sebring and Daytona. He also competed in four Mini-Indy races, finishing third at St. Paul, MN. and fourth at Texas World Speedway; he was 14th in the series point standings.

Dale again took part in all the IMSA endurance events during the 1980 season.

In 1981, Dale ran 69 practice laps at the Speedway during the USAC Rookie Orientation Program but never got on the track during May, although he was listed as driver of one of the team's three cars, which never was ready to race.

Dale ran four races in 1981 in the IMSA-GT series, his best finish being a fifth at Road Atlanta.

CAR
March 82C/Cosworth

CHIEF MECHANIC
Keith Leighton

SPONSOR
Whittington/Warner Hodgdon

STATISTICS OF CAR
The team's newest March went to the youngest brother. Dale qualified it at 197.694. He started 23 but ran over Roger Mears on the false start and completed no laps. He was credited with 33rd.

What Makes Roger Run?

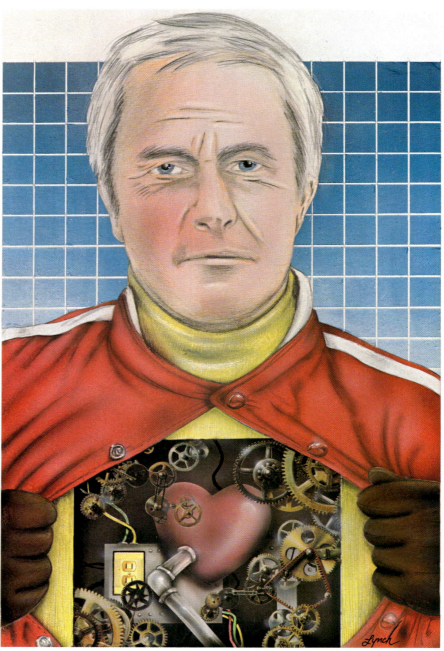

Roger Penske

by Dave Woolford

Roger Penske is a man possessed by success.

His exploits as a race car owner and an entrepreneur are all but unequaled.

Penske's energy should be measured in revolutions per minute. His success is gauged in winning, whether it be on the race track or on the bottom line of a financial statement, which he refers to as, "The Bottom Line."

It's that way now and it was that way 33 years ago when Roger, a lad of 12, attended Culver Military academy, Culver, Ind., during the summer.

He called home to Shaker Heights, O., one day to tell his mother he was interested in joining the Drum and Bugle

Corps. Just as she was wrapping an old, borrowed bugle to send to Roger, he called home again and said, "Mom, I'm drummer number 21."

Young Penske became the drum major soon afterward.

"Everything was a challenge to him. It still is, Martha Penske says of Roger, the oldest of her two sons. "His late father always said work didn't hurt anyone. Roger learned that."

Roger also learned in later life that one can parlay the old work ethic as it applies to auto racing and carry it into business and never the twain shall part.

Penske is an extension of his own elaborate, precise, finely tuned and immaculate machinery.

One of his mottos is, "Show me a good

loser and I'll show you a loser." Another is "Effort equals results," and Penske's results have been unequaled, especially over the last few years on the Indy car circuit.

Since forming his first racing team in 1966 Penske has won over 30 Indy-car races, six NASCAR Grand National stock car races, two United States Auto Club (USAC) stock car races, two Canadian-American Challenge Cup championships, three Trans-American titles, the 24 hours of Daytona, two U.S. road racing championships, and the 1976 Austrian Grand Prix Formula One race.

The Penske Racing Team has won an unprecedented four Indy car series championships. His cars have won the Indianapolis 500 three times with drivers

Mark Donohue, Rick Mears, and Bobby Unser.

Penske's race team hallmarks have always been immaculately prepared cars, spotlessly attired crews, and concentration on seemingly minor details that border on the obsession.

He considers every imaginable contingency, and he drills his crew to Prussian precision. Mere super-human dedication to detail won't win races, but it helps cut the many variables in the sport to a minimum.

"Racing is something I always liked as a hobby, but we run it strictly as a business," Penske says. "If I learned one thing in racing, it's that they don't wait for you. They've never held a race for us and they're never going to. In our business we try to teach our people that you make it happen; you don't wait for it.

"The racing business is something that puts incentive into everything we do in business. It taught me that when somebody says 'No' to me, it just turns me on, because in racing every sign you ever see says 'No' and I've got to turn it around so that it says 'Yes.'"

Penske and racing were introduced at a beginning driver's school in Marlboro, Md., in 1958. Before his driving career ended six years later, at 27, he had won a number of amateur grand prix races.

His all-time high earnings were $34,000 in 1962, and at various times he was cited by the Los Angeles Times, Sports Illustrated, and the New York Times as Sports Car Driver of the Year.

Penske, a racer, was also a realist. His aim in life, upon graduation from Lehigh University with a degree in Industrial Management, was business.

"I was a good race driver and I knew that my future in the sport was as bright as I wanted it to be," Penske says. "But I also knew that I was a good businessman, and I wanted to prove just how good. I was torn between two loves."

Penske's men call him "Captain," as in Bligh, though with no rancor intended. After all, Roger wins.

"Roger always had a very wonderful way of choosing young men to work for him, and he wouldn't ask anyone to do anything he wouldn't do himself," Martha Penske states.

First it was the late Donohue, then Tom Sneva, followed by Mears, and Kevin Cogan, and of course the incomparable Bobby Unser and Mario Andretti. Penske pulled Donohue, Sneva, Mears, and Cogan out of nowhere to drive for him at Indy.

All four were chosen because Penske felt they had tremendous potential not only as drivers, but also for the abilities to test drive, to communicate with car sponsors, and to stay out of trouble on the race track.

"Roger is totally different from anyone I've ever driven for," Unser says. "He's willing and capable of gambling ... no, investing in a concept. It can be people, race cars, or his business.

"Take a person like Rick Mears. He was virtually an unknown. Everyone thought Roger took him because he could get Rick for nothing. No, that's not right.

"Mears was clean-living and he was a good image for the sponsors. Rick didn't wreck. He wasn't fast enough at the time Roger picked him (1978), but it turns out he was and no one knew that. Nobody was going to give him a ride. He was quiet and unassuming and he didn't have a racing career to look at in a short time period. He had been driving junk. Roger invested in him."

Mears won the 1979 Indy 500 and finished second by 16 hundredths of a second to Gordon Johncock this year.

"Roger has made my whole career," Mears says. "I would still be in the middle of the pack beating my brains out like a lot of other drivers are doing today if it weren't for Roger.

"He's very good about giving new drivers an opportunity. It's hard to find someone like that in this business today. Most car owners want a proven driver or a driver who will pay a lot of money for the ride."

Derrick Walker, a Scotsman, is general manager of the Penske racing shop, a single-level, windowless building of concrete block, not unlike others around it in an old Pennsylvania steel town called Reading.

The sign on the outside of the building says, "Penske Racing." It serves as the nerve center in regard to testing, development, and maintenance. It's one of four buildings on the complex identified by the U.S. Post Office as Penske Plaza. The other buildings on the 13-acre grounds include one of Penske' leasing outlets, a tire warehouse, Detroit Diesel Allison engine remanufacturing facility, and a three-story office building.

Walker sometimes feels Penske's presence even when Roger is not on the premises.

Penske's executive office is in Piscataway, N.J., but he's only a 45-minute ride in his private helicopter away from Reading and he checks in often. Penske also owns a Lear jet that he uses constantly to monitor his many business and racing interests.

"We have the best team on the circuit," Walker states matter-of-factly. "We have the best package on the lot and that makes the pressure even greater because we've got everything we need. We have no excuse. You can talk to the highest on high, but when Roger hits the shop he knows the temperature of things right away."

Penske also maintains a race car shop in Poole, Dorset, England that is an outgrowth of his Formula One racing.

There's a well worn axiom in auto racing that goes something like this: You invest a large fortune to make a small fortune.

Penske spends a large fortune — over $2 million annually — on his racing ventures, $1.6 million of which is generated from sponsorship programs, about $500,000 from prize money and another $250,000 from the sale of race cars, parts, etc.

Penske bristles when someone insinuates that he buys his way into the winner's circle.

"Our whole success in racing and business has been the ability to take people who have basically the same interests that I have, who want to get ahead, and to train them and motivate them and give them the decision-making capabilities," Penske says. "You want to make decisions at the lowest possible level. If every decision has to be made at the top you get bogged down. I must follow up and make sure people are responding. That's the key. Most of my people are results oriented. It's easy to look at the scorecard at the end of the game and know if you're ahead or behind."

Penske Racing, Inc., is set up as a separate subsidiary of the Penske Corp. and generates its own cash flow and pays its own bills. It's a break-even proposition at best.

Penske says the key thing is that he has set a goal and executes it in an arena where one is either on the top or the bottom. There's no plateau. If he does well he's very visible, and the same goes if he makes a mistake.

"The people who work for you understand how critical that is and it builds a great amount of morale within the company, plus it shows that you are capable of competing in a business which is highly technical and changes every minute," Penske states.

"The ruboff effect is that it reinforces what you're trying to sell and your relationship with your sponsors. Indy shows we do what we say.

"If I break even in my racing in a particular year my return is that I have a $2.1 million advertising and promotional budget for my companies with no investment."

Jim McGee discounts the amount of money Penske spends on racing. McGee was Penske's chief mechanic for six years before leaving at the end of the 1980 for personal reasons. He was later hired by Patrick Racing of Jackson, Mich.

"Money doesn't do it in racing," McGee said. "Everyone says it's money, money, money, but you have to have the organization and the people and Roger has that. Sure, you can buy a certain number of people, but there are some people who you can give all the money in

the world to and they won't find the right combination.

"One of the big secrets of Penske's success was Bobby Unser. You can have the best organization, but if you don't have the driver who's a leader and can do all of the testing and development you're doing it all in vain. Unser was a driving force behind Penske Racing. That Unser is tough."

But despite what McGee says, money is still one of the dominant aspects of auto racing and Penske was well aware of that even as an amateur road racer.

He showed up at a race in 1960 with advertising on the side of his race car.

"What's this, a traveling billboard, a high speed page out of the yellow pages?" angry race officials asked the brash young driver.

They quickly made Penske put tape over the advertising, but Roger made sure the tape fell off after a few laps.

When Penske turned this attention to business, his business began with racing as its medium for advertising and promotion. No one else in auto racing is as proficient as Penske in enlisting sponsors.

Penske looks for the nontypical racing companies with advertising budgets that are 3 to 4 percent of their total sales. He sells his program by explaining that it will be the basis of an employee morale program . . . a tie-in with the team . . . an exclusive base for customer entertainment.

"If I owned the New York Yankees I couldn't take 100 of my employees and have them set on the bench and go into the locker room," Penske says. "But I can take 5,000 to a race and they can feel that they're there and part of it."

Penske explains that the name on the side of the car and the picture in the

newspaper are only the most visible tips of the iceberg, that underneath are the tie-ins with promotion and product endorsement, the availability of drivers and crew for company functions.

Penske believes that his racing team has promotional and morale-building value not only for his sponsors but for the privately held Penske Corp.

The corporation (with 1981 sales of about $260 million, five times that of 1977) employs over 1,750 people at 57 facilities in 19 states. Penske oversees the entire operation, aided by the heads of various subsidiary companies.

Penske, who forsees the corporation going public within the next few years, would rather be known as an entrepreneur than a race car owner, although his racing activities often overshadow those of Penske Corp. "We're still identified as a racing company," he says. "I want to be known as a key entity in the transportation and energy business."

The firm consists of three groups:

Energy and engines, which designs, fabricates, and assembles electrical generation systems used world wide for primary and emergency power; is the world's largst packager of mobile turbine gas generators, and distributes and services Detroit Diesel engines, Allison automatic transmissions, gas turbines, and associated replacement parts manufactured by General Motors Corp.

Transportation, which leases trucks and cars to many of America's top corporations, and operates the country's second largest Cadillac dealership in Downey, Calif.

Automotive Performance, which administers an automotive testing and development program for American Motors Corp. and conducts racing events

at its Michigan International Speedway located in Brooklyn, Mich.

Four major races are held at Michigan each year plus AMC testing programs. Penske says the track paid for itself after the first four years after he purchased it in 1973, primarily on the strength of its racing dates.

"The Michigan track has been extremely successful for us, and it emulates our company from a standpoint that it is well run, it's clean, it's as safe a a race track can be, and it has a lot of potential," he states.

Penske is totally consumed by his business and racing interests, a dual mode he's locked into by his own design.

Lemar Heydt, vice president and director of Penske Corp., draws this comparison:

"Reader's Digest has a section it calls, 'The Most Unforgetable Character I've Ever Met.' Roger would put any of them to shame. He could do every job in the company if he had to. He totally involves every person at every level. He makes everyone feel that what they're doing is going to make a difference."

Unser calls his former boss "Bullet proof."

"Roger asked me if something was worth trying and what he felt we could accomplish," Unser says. "If I said it was worth a try he backed me totally. Once he invests in you that's it. He doesn't ever want to be wrong himself. He's paranoid about ever being wrong."

Walker agrees that Penske is paranoid about failure, but says, "He's the ultimate competitor in business, racing, anything, and he's always under pressure to succeed. If a failure does occur he's the first to pick the team up. He'll find something good.

"Everything he touches turns to gold if he works at it and concentrates fully. It's probably the ultimate for him to succeed. He's obsessed or compelled by success. He cares about his image. It rubs off on the people who work for him. Sure, sometimes it can get very frustrating and it can almost drive you insane. You have to push with it over the crest. You can't take it as a personal affront."

Penske can rival Simon Legree. Sometimes he tends to carry his work ethic to the extreme.

"Roger will work twice as hard as you do," McGee states. "He sets an awful good example for his operation. You've got to give 100 per cent because he's always giving 120 per cent. Some people will kick back. He gets rid of them.

"When you work for Roger he's constantly intimidating you to see if you know what's going on. If you don't have the right answers and are not secure in what you're doing it could be hell. You have to have a lot of confidence in yourself and what you are doing.

"You get a little bullet proof about the

deal. After you've worked for him a while he knows not to keep poking you in the same area because he knows then that you know the situation and can handle it. He's a hell of a guy. We're both both very demanding, but you never buck heads if you're looking for the same results."

Penske exudes exactness even in his dress and extends it to his employees. He was once sought as a model for Vitalis. He was recently named in an international poll of best-dressed men.

"I've always been interested in the way our people look," Penske says. "That includes our salesmen, parts-countermen, and anyone who meets the public. I'm a firm believer in the proposition that sometimes the first impression is the only impression. If it's not good, you don't get another chance.

"Yes, it's tough being a perfectionist all the time. But I have a responsibility and I've set goals and standards for my people. They're looking to me. When you're a leader you have to be that way. That's the road I've taken.

"When you're visible you have to set an example. Of course, on the other side of the coin, if you're visible and are doing something that is detrimental it can have a tremendous impact on your organization, employees, and family.

As a boy, Roger shoveled snow and delivered newspapers, often winning prizes for attracting the most new customers.

Roger played offensive and defensive end on the football team and was on the swimming team of Shaker Heights High School.

He sang in the choir at Christ Episcopal Church, served as an acolyte, and never missed Sunday school.

He played football at Lehigh University, was active in student government, and was a member of the Air Force drill team.

Penske keeps his fingers on the pulse of everything he commands. He makes the best use of the three-hour east-west time difference of anyone in the country when traveling. He sometimes wishes there were eight days in the week instead of only seven.

That kind of schedule can also be trying to a man's family.

It probably served to terminate Penske's first marriage to the former Lisa Stouffer.

"That was the only thing in my life that was a failure," Penske once admitted. "We were married too young, and she never was attuned to what has to be with a man in business."

They had two sons, Roger, Jr., an aspiring race car driver, and Greg.

Penske and his present wife, Kathy, were married nearly 10 years ago. They have a daughter, Kathryn, and two sons, Mark and Jay.

"Roger's lifestyle was more glamorous and unsettled while mine was more settled," Kathy says. "I had little time to be with myself or Roger, and that was something that had to be weighed. His lifestyle is so established with his business and racing commitments. There are some wives who will say, 'If you love me you'll be home all of the time,' but that's not always the way it works.

"With small children it's hard to go anywhere. It's something I have to grow with and handle. I do very little socializing, and I spend a lot of time with the children. I have to exemplify a lot of personal things. I do have to travel a lot to see Roger and be with him.

"I feel very lucky. We lead a very stimulating and exciting life. We have a lot of luxurious living. I'd like to have more time with my husband. We have very little repetition in our lives. Sometimes I miss the repetition."

Roger admits that the social side of his life and his duties as a husband and father are "A tough one to handle."

"I don't have to say that people a lot smarter and a lot more successful than me have had trouble with that one," he adds. "I'm involved with my older boys, and we have a good relationship. It's a tough call. I should be home more at night."

Penske is a jogger, vacations in Vail, Colo., (where he owns a duplex), and plays a little golf. He admits that none of those activities really relax him and finally concludes that he's not a relaxing person.

Penske's true daily form of relaxation is planning his itinerary while driving from his home, located on a 20-acre plot on the banks of the Navesink River, near Red Bank, N.J., to his office.

"When I get up in the morning I've always said I don't have to look around for something to do," Penske says. "When I get up I'm ready to go. I hope I get up like that forever. If you're mentally motivated and you're in top shape physically you can live for a long time."

But Unser, who has observed his former boss from a unique point of view, sometimes sees Penske at ease on the edge of ecstasy,.

"Roger would rather see his race cars go fast than to chase the prettiest girls in the world . . . if he was single . . . eat the finest food, or drive the most luxurious cars," the veteran driver says.

"He gets off on watching those race cars so much you can't believe it. I'll bet a lot of husbands wish they could make their wives feel as happy as Roger is when he sees his race cars go fast."

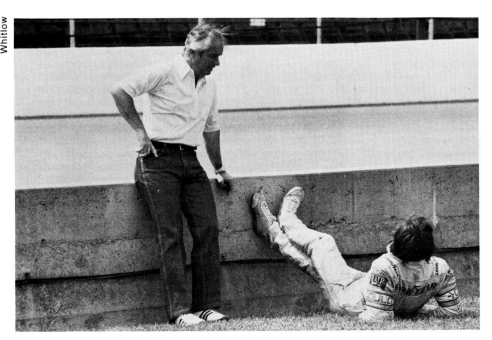

"You don't lie down on the job when you work for Penske", Roger might be saying to Mears.

Whitlow

Race Cars -

by Jack Fox

Want a race car . . . well, just pick a size. Wherever you look around Carmen Schroeder's you can find one. Full-sized Indy cars, sprints, TQ's and midgets . . . plus approximately 3500 models of the same beautifully displayed in glass cases.

That is what you find when you visit the Gordon Schroeder family. That's not all . . . there are perhaps a hundred Teddy bears guarding the collection and three black cats (and a nondescript one), a large dog and a turtle keeping watchful eyes on the Teddys.

The entire family is racing oriented. Gordon used to own the Spike Jones 16-cylinder Sampson which ran Indy in the late 30's and 40's. He still owns the chassis but that is now in the Hall of Fame museum, (although not accurately painted). His offer to repaint the car at his own expense has, apparently, fallen on deaf ears.

In the Schroeder "barn" is one of Gordon's prized possessions . . . the Spike Jones Sampson Midget. It is accurately restored and a beautiful example of a 1940's race car. Also under reconstruction at Schroeder's Burbank machine shop is the Blakely Oil Spl. which Bobby Ball and Jim Bryan drove at Indy in the 1950's. Ball's son located the remains of the chassis and Gordon has the restoration project well under way with Wayne Ewing doing the metal work. Unfortunately Wayne seems to have other unmentionable priorities and the car, which Gordon originally designed, still awaits completion. An old sprint car also awaits completion, likewise an antique Franklin.

The shop is the headquarters for Schroeder Steering. Most of the Midgets, Sprints and Champ cars use these units plus the Malibu Grand Prix cars. The Schroeder's eldest son, Gary, is the only member of the family to be bitten by the driving bug. He has been doing some fine TQ racing usually finishing up near the front. Alan, son No. 2, handles the fuel and tire truck at the TQ events. This leaves the mother, Carmen.

With the entire family involved in racing at one level or another she just couldn't be left out . . . and Carmen certainly wasn't. She manages the office for the steering company (Gary recently started purchasing it from Gordon and is really in charge), has been a member of the USAC technical committee, and has one of the finest model race car collections in existence.

At their home in the Hollywood Hills (Merv Griffin is a next-door neighbor) she has devoted a room for the small cars where they are displayed in wood and glass cabinets. Among the models are antique toys relating to auto racing, paintings, posters, pennants and other memorabilia dating back to the turn of the century. Speedway badges, trophies

The Schroeder family in their Burbank shop. Gary and Alan work on their TQ while Carmen supervises. Gordon, as usual, seems more interested in the championship car he is restoring.

Carmen inspects some of her 3500 model race cars in their glass cases.

Joe Henning Photos

BIG & SMALL

and the original steering wheel from Wilbur Shaw's Maserati are also on display.

The collection got its start when Grand Prix driver, Richie Ginther, gave Carmen a slush mold race car. Gordon had a little wooden race car with Indianapolis Motor Speedway printed on the side. That was all it took and Carmen started haunting swap meets, looking for others. Many models came from racing people. Sam and Alice Hanks, Johnnie Parsons, John Burgess, Jack Beckley, Joe Henning and Briggs Cunningham all have made contributions in the form of paintings, photos, trophies, jewelry, and programs, until the room has overflowed outward and upward, It would appear that sooner or later a garage will have to be incorporated into the den, relegating a Pantera to either the carport or the "barn." It will have company as a Ford GT-40 and the Sampson Midget are now in residence there.

The "barn", over which is Alan's apartment, is the scene each August of the famed Gilmore Roars Again party honoring those midget drivers who used to race at Gilmore Stadium between 1934 and 1950. The event, which lasts about twelve hours, is an annual affair for approximately 350, (including a ranch-style barbecue). Fortunately the Schroeders have 3 1/2 acres (shared with three horses) which handles the people although neighbor Griffin has contributed parking space a time or two. The Gilmore Party has its altruistic side as the money contributed for "Pit Passes" and proceeds from an auction, presided over by Freddy Agabashian and Bill Taylor, are banked in the name of injured driver, Billy Garrett.

For their friends not eligible for the Gilmore party, they have started hosting a chili cook-out in April. That keeps everyone happy (or should) except for the people who want to be invited to both. One good party deserves another.

Not content with the parties, the business, going racing, Western antiques, and a hundred other diversions Carmen has recently begun the study of geneology which occasionally takes her to Salt Lake City for a few days. This is just when things get slow at the office. Gordon may have partially retired, but NOT Carmen!

All in the family. The Schroeders with their favorite Midget. Carmen holds either Lucky, Trouble or Killer (who knows . . . they're all black.)

How about this for a family car . . . a GT-40!

[135]

Wysard Motor Company

Herb and Rose Wysard are certainly proponents of the saying, "When the going gets tough, the tough get going." Plagued by a series of events that saw their cars plastered along the retaining walls and all over the garage floor for the past couple of years, they dug deeper into their pocketbook and continued in their quest for a win at Indy. Talented veteran Johnny Parsons hooked up with the team late in the month and zipped the machine in the show with nary a bobble. Sponsors Silhouette Health Spa, Tombstone Pizza and Indy-based WIFE radio station were served well and couldn't have asked for a more dedicated team.

Provimi Veal

A couple of years back Indianapolis businessman Jack Rogers and Wayne Hillis sponsored young Tony Bettenhausen and set up a corporation to help upgrade his racing operation. Aat Groenevelt owner of the Provimi Veal company became involved with the team and has since elevated it to first-class status. A mid-month crash made it look doubtful the team would be competitive this year, but professional effort on the part of Chief Mechanic Bobby Hatch and crew put the team in the starting line-up. It appears as though the youngest of the Bettenhausen racing family might be the first to garner a win in the Indianapolis 500.

The Rookies

by Paul Scheuring

Take 15 American road-racers, 2 international imports, 11 drivers who cut their teeth on U.S. "Bull-rings," one ace stock-car driver, and a little London lady. Add them together, simmer in the Indiana May-time sunshine, and you have the 1982 Indy Rookie Class. It came out 30 drivers strong ... 4 more than in 1981 ... and left no form of racing untouched. It also spanned the globe, with the London Lady joined by a 2nd Mexican in as many years, and a Belgian with a legacy at Indianapolis. All chasing for the right to peel the stripes off the tails of their cars. Only 30% of the 1982 Freshman Class would be so lucky.

The Speedway and the United States Auto Club expanded their Rookie Orientation Program for its 2nd year of operation. Originally formed just for rookies who never had tried before, this year it would include ANY driver never to have qualified. That list, of course, included several drivers who had TRIED to qualify before. And it was no real surprise that the fastest of the 13 drivers who took advantage of the program, was one of this latter category. Ohioan Chip Mead, who wouldn't even BE a rookie anymore, if mechanical woes had not set in on the last day of quals in 1981, ran his Eagle to a speed of 186 miles an hour ... 4 miles an hour better than another "veteran rookie," Roger Mears. Rick's older brother had latched onto what seemed a sure thing: a PC9B Penske from the Machinists Union. But while officials knew these guys, along with 2nd-year-rookie Steve Chassey, and Gary Irvin, who tried this once before (1977), they knew others only by reputation, if at all. Defending World of Outlaws Sprint champ Sammy Swindell was sharing the Jet Engineering Eagle with team-mate Chassey. Can-Am aces Bobby Rahal and Danny Sullivan were part of a veritable wave of new big-buck teams: Rahal aboard an '82 March from Jim (Red Roof Inns and Mid-Ohio Raceway) Trueman, while Sullivan, along with Grand Prix veteran Hector Rebaque of Mexico, shared the one of Garvin Brown's new Marches that was ready. Brown, the Jack Daniels magnate, had spared no expense: his mechanic was '78-

winner Huey Absolom. But the driver the officials watched most closely, was the 2nd woman driver ever at Indy: Desire Wilson. This slip-of-a-girl arrived from London with Teddy Yip's Eagle, a pleasant demeanor, and the most impressive list of credentials any distaff pilot ever compiled ... including victory in a non-points Formula One race at Brands Hatch Racecourse in England ... a course managed, not coincidentally, by her husband Alan. Mechanical trouble precluded a full set of tests during the program ... a harbinger of what awaited her when they got down to the "for-real" business at hand. But there were others on hand ... Chip Ganassi and Jim Hickman, up from the Mini-Indy ranks ... unknown Rusty Schmidt (who shared his Vollstedt ride with Irvin for the R.O.P.) ... and a likeable Texan with a Lloyd Ruby-style drawl, Chet Fillip, who also provided the only incident of the April session when he tagged the fence off Turn 2 ... fortunately with minimal damage.

Finally came May, and many more rookies joined the graduates of April. But Steve Chassey, by now, had bade farewell to Jet Engineering, who replaced him with another USAC sprinter, Bob Frey. Unfortunately, they never did finish their 2nd car, so Sammy Swindell would remain a year away from his first 500. But he had company in that lot, from the registration-list of the Class of '82. Warner Hodgdon decided not to bring his 2 cars after all, so Neil Bonnett never got back to Indianapolis (he did pick up a pretty fair consolation prize by taking the NASCAR World 600 on May 30th). Tom Gloy's money never came through, for the 2nd Machinists Union car, so the Formula Atlantic hot-shot never showed. Rick Vogler's new car from A. J. Watson, was never completed. Another Formula Atlantic grad, Tom Grunnah, suffered the dubious fate of being this year's only rejection for lack of experience. And 47-year-old racing-wheel-maker Ray Lipper, faced with a similar fate after a tangle in the Phoenix champ-car opener, showed up only long enough to withdraw from the seat of his Eagle, and put it up for sale (eventually to a group from Indianapolis who made the show with Tom Bigelow).

Paul Scheuring is not only a fine sports editor of WIFE but a good vocalist as his rendition of "New York, New York" at the Monroe banquet attests.

A little arithmetic shows a count, then, of 24 tyros for Indy-82. Some had easier paths to veterancy than others. Roger Mears, Chip Mead, Steve Chassey, Herm Johnson and Phil Caliva, all were deemed of sufficient experience to require no test at all, and were cleared to go fast right away. For some of the rest of the Class of '82, the test was a mere formality, quickly dispensed-with. The 4 in that class seemed to be the Forsythe-Brown team of Sullivan and Rebaque, and Rahal, and Ganassi, whose Jack Rhoads Wildcat had long-time Johncock groom Mark Bridges on wrench. Jim Hickman, who was Chassey's team-mate aboard a Rattlesnake Racing Stroh's March, quietly eased through his first exam, as well.

Others in the freshman crop, were having a bit harder go of it. Ken Hamilton, the 2nd-year rookie from Boise, Idaho, had what may well have been the strangest-looking car since Granatelli's "pregnant flounder:" the Eagle Aircraft Flyer had been designed by an aircraft designer, and quickly drew the nickname "crop-duster" from pit-side wags. It may have been the longest car ever run at Indy; it looked like it. Sadly, the effort was doomed to disappointment, when the car, after 2 slides while trying to get Hamilton through his refresher, was withdrawn. But Hamilton had lots of company in the disappointment department. Rusty Schmidt wound up with an old Watson chassis from Rolla Vollstedt, but just could not keep it running long enough to get through his exam. The same fate awaited the 3rd

Sneva brother, Jan, in John Mahler's Penske-copy-Offy. Other Incompletes awaited LeRoy Van Connett, the California sprinter, who simply disappeared after completing the first half of his test; Gary Irvin, whose promising-looking Swingler-Chevy arrived too late to be sorted out for an exam; Belgian Teddy Pilette, grandson of the 5th-place finisher in the 1913 500, whose old McLaren proved a year TOO old for Indy; and Dean Vetrock, who never got behond the preliminary warm-up-laps stage.

Others had troubles, but at least got through their tests. Desire Wilson's Theodore Eagle seemed to have an endless appetite for Cosworth engines; and Bob Frey, Tom Frantz and Phil Kreuger wrestled Chevy-powered machinery through the preliminary ritual. They, however, must have stared enviously at Dale Whittington, who became the 3rd of his family to be cleared, with amazing ease, after his brothers Bill and Don had easily made the show on the first day of qualifying.

Six members of the Class of '82 also made it on the first day. And leading the way was Chip Ganassi, whose 197.7 mph run raised as many eyebrows as any during the 4 days of trials. It landed him in the middle of Row 4, and proved to be good for the American Dairy Association's "Fastest Rookie Qualifer" prize, by one-100th of a second over 3rd-day-qualifying Dale Whittington. It was one row better than an all-newcomer 5th row comprised of Sullivan and Rebaque, sandwiching Herm Johnson's Eagle-Chevy. Rahal landed in Row 6. and Roger Mears took a safe-looking 194.1 on Opening Day, and wound up sweating out the last 2 hours of qualifying as the slowest to make the race at all.

The remaining successful rookies all made it on Day 3: Whittington joined on Row 8 by quiet Georgian Jim Hickman. And Chet Fillip, with former Goodyear Racing man Bud Poorman as his team-manager, became the final tyro in the field, in the middle of Row 10.

Sadly, that left 8 approved rookies for whom the final grade was "A" ... for Almost. Leading that list was Desire Wilson. Her final engine let go on the final day of qualifying. Patrick Bedard, the Car & Driver columnist, couldn't find the speed in Lee Brayton's Wildcat. Same problem faced Frey in the Jet Eagle, and Tom Frantz, in what was A. J. Foyt's Coyote a year ago. But at least their cars wound up in one piece. Not so Steve Chassey, who crunched the Hubler/

WFBQ Rattlesnake on the last day of trials; or Krueger, who did the same a day earlier in Joe Hunt's cobbled McLaren-Chevy. Poor Phil Caliva launched his only engine on his very first day on the track, and never got another ride. But Chip Mead got the Hard-Luck Trophy for the Class of '82. His 193.9 was allowed to stand by his crew on opening-day and return Chip next year as a THIRD-year rookie.

So 9 newcomers would answer Duane Sweeny's green flag on May 30th. At the request of veteran drivers, the 9 even agreed to carry their rookie stripes on Race-day. But 2 of them never SAW the green. As the broken cars of Kevin Cogan and Mario Andretti slid to a halt at the Start-Finish Line, Dale Whittington's March was jumping all over Roger Mears' PC9B, eliminating them in the pre-start melee. Mears was quick to criticize what had seemed to him like a reckless jump of the gun, in the incident. What neither Mears nor anyone else knew at the time, was that all 3 Whittington Brothers had been in the company of plainclothes Indiana State Police the preceding 2 weeks, after an attack-victim in Florida told police that the same men who had tried to kill him, were out to get the Whittingtons.

Once the damage was cleared, and the 7 remaining rookies took the green, it quickly became evident that there was only one who was really competitive: Hector Rebaque. The former Brabham Formula One driver spent more than a fourth of the race riding just off the blistering pace set by the leaders. Unfortunately, he would join the majority of his classmates on the sidelines ... victim of a fairly-innocuous-looking pit-fire ... only moments after his team-mate, Sullivan, had become the day's final wall-banger on Lap 148. Before that, it had taken 60 laps after the green flew, before the first of the rookies had left the race: Chet Fillip slowed suddenly when he had come upon Danny Ongais' 2nd-turn excursion, and was hit from behind by Jerry Sneva. Chip Ganassi's engine failed him at Lap 147. And Bobby Rahal's semi-competitive day came to an end with engine-trouble at Lap 174.

That left 2 rookies to finish the race. And heading that list, as quietly as he had done everything else all month, was Jim Hickman. He stated later that the handling of the car had been a mess all day long. But the engine held up while so many others did not, and his 7th-place finish was rewarded with the American Fletcher National Bank's Rookie-of-the-

Year Award. Two places back of him, came the only finisher of the 5 stock-block starters in 1982, Herm Johnson, who did a good, if not competitive, job all day long for 9th.

So nine drivers returned from whence they had come, knowing they no longer will bear the sometimes-derisively-used title, Rookie. The other 21 went (or, in some cases, stayed) home to contemplate the age-old Next Year. No doubt, a few of them won't be back. Those who do, will be joined by others who "would." and the process will begin anew, of inducting another class into the "University" of Indianapolis. ⟜

Desire Wilson

Chip Ganassi

The Forsythe Racing Team

Danny Sullivan

The Forsythe Brothers, Jerry and John, came to Indy last year as sponsors and figured out what the place was all about. This year they brought their own team with Hector Rebaque and Danny Sullivan, a pair of rookies at Indy who proved their mettle without difficulty. Jerry and John are the principals of Indeck Power Equipment Co., a Wheeling, Illinois based firm that is credited with maintaining the nation's largest inventory of package boilers and auxiliary equipment. By looking over their racing operation it was easy to see that they spared neither time nor expense to arrive with the best possible equipment. Even their wire-wheeled 18 wheeler transporter was detailed as though ready for a car show. Their name is relatively new at Indy, but one that will have to be reckoned with in the future.

BACK ISSUES

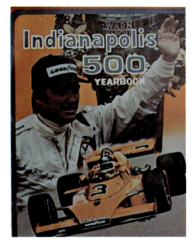

1974
Regular $11.50
Hardbound $16.95

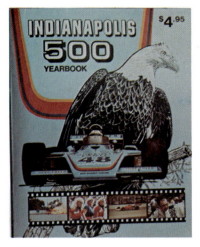

1975
Regular $11.50
Hardbound $16.95

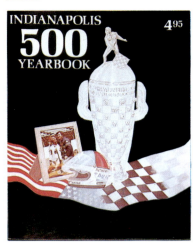

1976
Regular $11.50
Hardbound $16.95

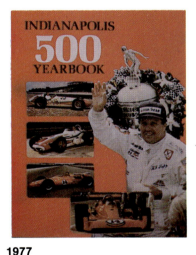

1977
Regular $11.50
Hardbound $16.95

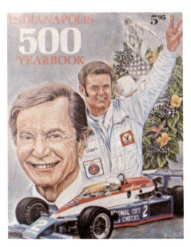

1978
Regular $11.50
Hardbound $16.95

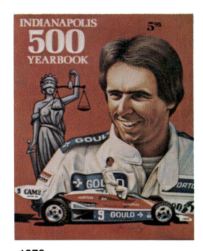

1979
Regular $11.50
Hardbound $16.95

1980
Regular $11.50
Hardbound $16.95

1973
Regular ...... **One hundred dollars**
(Only a few left — Never reprinted).

Back issues of each Carl Hungness Indianapolis 500 Yearbook are still available. Supply is short on some years however, and none will ever be re-printed. Order soon. Prices postpaid.

1983 500 YEARBOOK Advance Order
Regular $11.50
Hardbound $16.95

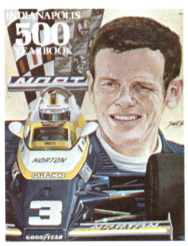

1981
Regular $11.50
Hardbound $16.95

What! No McDonalds!!!

by Jack C. Fox

How do you live when you come to the races? Fly in and stay at the airport? Stay in one of the luxurious motels near the track? Eat at one of the better restaurants in Speedway or the environs? The fans (and racers) today have very little conception how it was not too many years ago when the Speedway was on the outer edge of Indianapolis and there weren't the facilities available that they find today.

Living ... well, you had only one choice near the track ... rent a room or a basement bed in the town of Speedway. This is still a viable alternative and many of the home owners can convert their basements into living quarters for the month of May. Crews often stay there and fans who do get a taste of Hoosier hospitality. It is and was common to invite strangers into a home ... "Why, if this happened in California they would probably rob you blind ... or worse." As open as the town is to strangers you hear of very little trouble. Of course there is the occasional rent-jumper pit man but less than there used to be. Racing people living in Speedway, is a tradition as old as the town's existence. It is doubtful that there could have been a race if the town's residents hadn't been so trusting. Of course there was one "racers' hotel" The Riley but that was downtown, across the street from Methodist Hospital, and the big money boys stayed there. It was sold out, always before the race fans hit town. Some of the really high-rollers stayed at the Lincoln, Claypool, Marott, or Antlers (Cotton Henning used to LIVE there). All of these have either closed and fallen to the wrecking ball or just closed

and are awaiting the wrecking ball. Others have secured rooms at the Indianapolis Athletic Club or the Columbia Club but you have to be either very wealthy or a Republican or preferably both, to swing that. So a list of the drivers' addresses usually showed that they had found a room in Speedway. Fans staying more than a day or two did likewise. Your writer remembers his first trip here in 1951. I'd heard of the Riley Hotel but on checking it was full to the rafters so I settled for the Washington ... a fine ediface on the street of the same name. Rooms were large and, while not exactly elaborate, they were even then a fine bargain for $4.50 per night. Of course they charged $20 a night for the day before the race, the day of the race and the day AFTER the race ... and you had to take them ALL! If you wanted to go home right after the race it was still $60! Maybe it's still that way but after the next year I, too, moved in with people in Speedway.

The night before the race, like many others (I was adventurous at that early age) I joined a friend and slept in his '46 Chevy (or was it a '39 DeSoto) lined up on Sixteenth Street (three abreast, yet) until the the gates opened on race day morn. Those lines of cars used to be traditional and as the race drew near they would extend far east of Lafayette Road over White River to the ballpark.

What happened if you got hungry in those days before Ho-Jo's or White Castle or Taco Bell. Since the track closed at night and you couldn't eat at a concession stand (you had enough of

THAT during the day.) It was Sportservice which handled the track's concessions in those days). The restaurants in the vicinity were limited ... the gourmet restaurants NON-EXISTENT! Most of the racers, and a lot of fans ate at Marianna's (an old house — long since raized — at 16th and Livingston) saw the dish "stuffed Mangoes" on the menu and wondering how that tropical fruit would taste (and stuffed with what).

I ordered them. To my extreme disappointment they served me stuffed BELL PEPPERS! "Where are the MANGOES?" I immediately asked. "On your plate ... THOSE are mangoes" was the terse answer. That was my first lesson in ordering "Hoosier-style."

I was in for another surprise or should I say surprises. Down Main St. was a little cement block building (at that time MOST Indianapolis restaurants were built of cement blocks, with cement block decor inside as well as out) with a big sign "CONEYS". There I was to learn that coneys were something like hot dogs and that Hoosier-style chili traditionally contains spaghetti. Not that that is bad but its a little unexpected. Oh yes, the waitress was tatooed! Another shock in 1952.

There was another place to eat in Speedway. Don't remember the name but it was right in front of Kepler's Speedway Garage where most of the boys kept their midgets, dirt champ cars not entered at the IMS and one or two sprint cars. The sprint cars were not so popular then as now although there were a few

Rosner's Drug store ... first commercial building in Speedway.

Whitt

Kepler's Garage ... only the landscaping over the door has changed.

Whitt

The B & B used to grace these premises during the 50's.

Where once the foreign car garages stood is now the Speedway Motel. The Myers/Cagle house is now used by the Hulmans.

races, at Winchester, at Salem and at Dayton. These were responsible for a rather large turnover in race drivers. Only a few BRAVE souls dared run the high banks and even someone as brave as Bill Vukovich (the elder) would have NOTHING to do with them.

The aforementioned eatery was connected to Kepler's by a rear door as Kepler's entrance was in the alley parallel to Main Street. The food was rudimentary but convenient. There was also Myrt's Lyndhurst Inn (or Tavern or whatever) but I never had to eat there. Most of the race gang who didn't eat in Speedway went down to Washington St. and Bob Chapman's Silver Fountain. The restaurant is still there with the SAME menu although it has gone through several owners. Chapman is long since departed as is the little bus boy, Scotty, who later bought out Chapman.

For those more affluent there was a supper club called the B & B down Sixteenth Street. It was, I'm sure, the only place I ever saw Wisconsin lake turtle on a menu. It was excellent, too. The B&B is long gone; Gene White's Firestone store replaced it many years ago. I've often wished it were still there . . . that TURTLE! Yum! That was just about IT. The crowds were almost as

large then so you wonder where they DID eat. Probably over in Terre Haute.

One thing that we did have was nightlife. There was the B&B and then there was MATES' WHITE FRONT! It hasn't always been Mates' but apparently it has always been the WHITE FRONT. (They also served food.) It wasn't always cement block. It was once just a nondescript frame building, in which Dick Somers now has a speed shop. Not quite on the same site. Sometime after the war it was modernized into the present appearance and location although, I'm sure, it didn't change much. The Mates boys, Nick and Mike, took it over from their parents and really made it a watering hole for racers. Their T-shirts are still collectors' items (Dr. Tom Lucas, I know, still has one). The first time I was there, racing writer, Jimmy Yano, was running some of his Eastern racing movies. Here, I surmised, was a real Indianapolis-type racing hangout at its best (although some of the habituees were albeit a bit seedy.) Several years later my particular gang — Jimmy Reece, Jack Zink, Dick Miller, George Amick and/or Bob Eichor used to go there and hear the Three Flips and a Flop. At adjoining tables would be Mari Hulman (long before she added the George), Ted Hollingsworth, Stoogie Glidden and

others of the gang. The musical group would usually end the evening by playing something called "Flying Home" which seemingly lasted for hours. I know nothing of popular music and I'm sure I was thoroughly revolted by the Three Flips etc., etc. but compared to some things that I've heard lately their music was pretty creditable.

The only other means of entertainment in or near Speedway was a little movie, long since gone, which was near Kepler's Garage. Pretty rough decor but popular in May. That means there were fifteen or twenty people in the house. On the off season . . . who noticed. I guess someone did because it folded up in the mid-fifty's.

There was also Rosner's drug store. It has stood at Sixteenth and Main since about 1915, (oldest building in town) and shows no signs of going under. The Rosner boys used to have a soda fountain (where Pete and Sally DePaolo got a soda the night of his Speedway Victory) but that is gone now . . . as is their booth for scalping race tickets. The Clymer and Hungness 500 Yearbooks are still for sale at the same counter . . . which is all that really matters to race fans, I'm sure.

When not watching the big cars at the Speedway you could go over right across the street from where the Speedway Motel now stands and see the AAA

At the corner of Georgetown and Sixteenth are a number of fast-food restaurants catering to the visitor.

The White Castle, dispenser of mini-hamburgers, holds the pole position on the corner of Sixteenth and Georgetown.

[143]

The White Front, watering-hole for the racing gang for nearly 50 years advertised their new location in 1954. Inset; the White Front as it looks today . . . Not too much change.

Whitt

midgets run. The night before the race on the big track, Sixteenth Street Speedway held some of the best midget shows in the midwest. THREE OF THEM! Starting in the morning the boys (sometimes close to 100 cars) would start warming up for the afternoon show. That run they would start warming up again for the evening show and then after that would come the two a.m. performance. The track would finally shut down along about dawn. It was a good place for drivers who didn't qualify for the big one to make enough to keep them from starving during the long, hot summer.

That was just about all there was to Speedway and its environs in those day, not even a railroad underpass on Sixteenth Street. The New York Central streamliners from Chicago just crossed the road and you had to take the tracks with the utmost safety as they hardly slowed down. If you didn't watch them, there was John Conkle's Mortuary just down the street from Rosner's. Most of the drivers' funerals were held there if they hadn't watched it on the track.

It wasn't like it is now. Not even the Speedway Motel was there to rest thy weary bones. But in many ways it had charm. The charm of a small country town. Not as Carl Fisher dreamed, but certainly representative of what was running across the street. There were no rear engined race cars that looked like missles. No CART-USAC problems; No Holiday Inn Northwest; No Classic Motor Lodge; No Taco Bell; No Bonanza; No Denny's; No McDonalds . . . what? No McDonalds!!!

Bill Freeman & Mike Chandler

For a time, car owner Bill Freeman and Mike Chandler could have sworn that the powerplant being bolted in their new Eagle was more suited for demolition work than racing. Plagued by what can only be called bad racing luck, the team had very few miles on the track before qualifying. They'd begin to get up to speed and would experience a minor explosion in the engine department. Preparation finally met opportunity and Chandler enjoyed the task of making the most competitive field ever assembled at the Indianapolis Motor Speedway.

California car-owner, Bill Freeman, enjoyed a successful year in his debut at Indianapolis and there's no doubt that with the aid of sponsorship he'll be a front-runner.

Colonial Baking Co. and Payless Stores

Colonial Baking Company's Jim Esco and the Payless Stores Larry Contos had a successful introduction to the world of Indianapolis 500 racing last year with rookie Pete Halsmer. The two Indiana based businessmen continued their involvement for the 1982 "500" and the likeable Halsmer once again put the team's clean entry into the program. While not one of the most heavily funded teams running, they were in the starting line-up when some of the so-called top names were watching from the grandstands. We hope they come back.

A traditional sight in the 500, the Purdue Golden Girl.

Rotund Willie Davis down by the creek timing cars.

Mike Chandler picks up a king-sized check for having the fastest Chevy in the field.

Driver-TV commentator Sam Posey talks with old friend Dan Gurney.

Carl Robertson, has a drop of the bubbly. Must have either qualified or it's a warm day . . . possibly both.

Bob Frey in the pretty No. 64 Chevy.

Formerly a controversial figure, Salt Walther keeps a very low profile these days.

25... and Counting

by David Scoggan

Once upon a time, two young Capricorns headed north to become Kings. One came from Tupelo to Memphis, the other from Houston to Indianapolis. One began his career known as "The Pelvis", the other carried the nickname "Fancy Pants". Both eventually found fame and fortune, stardom and royalty."

Of one King, Elvis Presley, we have only memories, but of Anthony Joseph Foyt Junior, the legend grows with every day. The 1982 Indianapolis 500 marked the twenty-fifth consecutive year that A. J. had competed in the world's greatest race, a record that may never be surpassed. Love him or hate him, boo him or bow to him, there will never be another like Super Tex.

His racing achievements are well-documented; the only four-time ('61, '64, '67 and '77) Indianapolis 500 champion, Daytona 500 winner (1972), co-winner of the 24 hours of Le Mans (with Dan Gurney, 1967) in his sole attempt, seven-time USAC national champion, victor of seven other NASCAR superspeedway events, pole sitter at Indy four times ('65, '69, '74, '75), 67 career champ car conquests, two-time IROC champion, six-time Hoosier Hundred winner, ad infinitum. A complete list of his midget, sprint, stock car, sports car, dirt car, and champ car victories would resemble a mid-size town's phone directory. Foyt will likely remain the only driver to win Indianapolis in a front- and rear-engined car, as he is the last to win with a front-motored Offy roadster (1965). Sixteen years have passed since A. J. has so much as spun at the Speedway — a wind-assisted practice crash on the first day of qualifications in 1966 (not counting his bounce off the south chute wall on his 1981 time trial run). Promoters know that A. J. Foyt's name on their entry list has the same result as a "Free Beer" sign on the marquee — instant box office. Even though the stats may show otherwise, A. J. doesn't consider himself in a league apart from less victorious racers. "I don't picture myself being above any one particular driver, even in today's (500) field, because they're all good or they wouldn't be here. I'm just out there to do a job." Quite unlike another famous Capricorn, Muhammed Ali, whose "greatest of all time" line could easily describe Foyt (who coincidentally earned the moniker "Cassius" during the mid-60's for his similar boasting).

While some consider Super Tex's four Indy 500 triumphs as gifts received from other drivers misfortunes, one need only remember 1969, when A. J. dominated until a leaking turbocharger manifold cost 22 minutes in the pits, or 1974, '75, and '76, when Foyt had everybody "covered so bad it was pathetic." Various woes from faulty oil pumps, to fuel expiration, to rain, to broken sway bars (and more rain) kept the Gilmore Coyote from its rightful spot in Victory Lane. Or 1979's last chance gasp that ended a silent engine and second place. If A. J. was as lucky as, say, Richard Petty has been at Daytona, he cold easily lay claim to seven or eight Indy crowns. On reflection though, Foyt admits, "I'm just glad to have won as many as I have!"

Recent years have seen the poppy-red #14 in fewer and fewer championship car events as A. J. winds down his reign, dulling the fine edge needed to win consistently. After qualifying for this year's 500 at a great 203.332 in a new, untested March, Foyt observed that "Penske was doing his homework (testing the PC 10) while I was home healin' (from the Michigan wreck)", but the truth is Tex hasn't come to the Speedway ready to race "off the trailer" since 1979. "I kinda lost interest in racing about three years ago when everybody started squabbling, fighting and arguing (CART vs. USAC) . . . that came closer to making me retire than anything, to be honest." He only competed twice in 1980 champ races (Indy and Pocono) with an outdated Parnelli chassis, and his 1981 Coyote turned its initial practice lap mere days before the first qualifying weekend at IMS. Of course, when you've accomplished as mush as A. J. Foyt has, the pace at Churchill Downs looks much more inviting than the hectic schedules of the Patrick and Penske teams.

A. J. had come close to missing the month of May only twice in his career and surprisingly from racing the safer NASCAR stockers. At Riverside in January of 1965, Foyt's brakes evaporated, but continued to keep his Ford with the leaders, when a car ahead of Junior Johnson (whose driving skills A. J. could trust enough to run brakeless) made an error. Johnson slowed abruptly, leaving A. J. two quick choices — hit Junior violently or take to the infield. Foyt cut to the right and bounced through deep embankment at 150 mph, flipping erd for end. He suffered extensive chest and back injuries, cracked vertebra and a broken left heel, plus numerous bruises and contusions. Supposedly to be sidelined for an indefinite period, there was A. J. gingerly squeezing into his Lotus two months later at Phoenix, with the pole at Indy to follow. Daytona 500, February 1978, found Foyt again taking flight. Slowing his Buick to avoid Benny Parson' shredded tire debris, a boot in the rear by Lennie Pond caused Tex to flip frighteningly down the tri-oval. At first doctors feared head and back injuries, but only a sore left shoulder (from the harness digging in) and abrasions were reported.

Hospitals are not an unfamiliar location for Mr. Foyt, as anyone with almost thirty years of competition would realize. One week after losing a new Lotus in the disastrous 1966 500 start, A. J.'s just-purchased, ex-STP Lotus' suspension broke, flinging him into the Milwaukee wall. It burst into flame, severely burning Foyt's hands (and his face and neck to a lesser degree). He returned less than a month hence to compete at Atlanta. A trip to DuQuoin one day after the 1972 Indy 500 ended with A. J.'s dirt car torching on a fuel stop; diving to safety, his left ankle was shattered by the car rolling over it, sidelining the facially-burned Foyt until Labor Day Ontario 500. The unexplained Michigan accident of last July was definitely the most serious of the

Whitlow

[149]

King's illustrious career. He told interviewers from his hospital room that had he not changed from a thicker, stronger driving suit back to his normal type during the pit fire red flag that it "probably would have torn my arm clean off." Clotting and severe headaches lingered from his head striking the guard rail. A. J. could still make light of the situation, saying Danny Ongais had phoned him and chided, "Just 'cause I cut a car in two (at Indy) doesn't mean you've got to do the same thing!" Then this May, answering a query about side effects from the crash, A. J. joked, "Well I lost a little weight on my arm, gained it in my stomach and lost it in my foot — other than that everything's fine."

Twenty five years would suggest numerous peaks and valleys and Super Tex has found some low ebbs himself. the 1966 season contained such dismal luck (one sprint and one midget win total), a columnist named Bob Garner opined in the National Speed Sport news after the Sacramento dirt show that "the star of Texas has burned out. He's no longer the big threat that he was. That almost sure thing, top qualifier, come from behind charger . . . it's not there anymore." (Presumably, Mr. Garner awaits his next shipment of hula hoops.) Half a year later, Foyt claimed his third Indy 500, conquered that "little ol' country road" in France called Le Mans, and culminated the '67 season by nailing down the USAC points championship.

Foyt has flourished through the Watson roadster period, the rear-engine revolution ("Funny cars — like sitting in a bathtub full of gasoline" — 1964), the European invasion (he referred to Graham Hill as a "foreign midget driver" for his perceived contribution to the 1966 starting fiasco), the turbine scare ("It's just a damn ol' airplane. It ain't no car and it doesn't belong here!" — 1967), turbochargers, big wings, small wings ("A wing is a crutch." — 1973), pop-off valves, women drivers, ground effects, and underexperienced drivers. Of the latter two items A. J. warns, "I can set my (1982) race car up and get somebody that just knows a little bit about racing and he can probably run just as fast or maybe a little faster than me. But the difference is, can he feel when he starts to get in trouble?" Foyt's been the fastest qualifier at Indianapolis and he's been the slowest (1973, when his engines kept expiring like Kleenex). He's been lucky ("people make their own luck"), but he's made mistakes (probably his biggest professional blunder was not at Indy, but leaving the Wood Brothers NASCAR team after dominating the 1971 and '72 seasons because he didn't think a Chevrolet dealer could drive a Ford product in good conscience). After 25 years, at age 47, the Living Legend is still on top.

The streak almost ended in 1958.

A. J.'s very first competitive lap at Indy presented him the grisly picture of Pat O'Connor's car upside down and burning. "It was one of the worst feelings I've ever had. Pat had helped me a lot . . . I really didn't know if I wanted to race or not. But I already was in it too far (to quit)." Rookie Foyt finished 16th that day, compiling the first of 9,282.5 miles to date.

"Racing's given me about everything I have, " which includes all the personal luxuries of any multi-millionaire. A. J.'s prize and endorsement money has evolved into more than 1,000 acres of Texas ranch land ("my biggest relaxation is clearin' land and workin' 24 hours a day on my bulldozer"), thoroughbred horse racing (over 100), banking interests, the A. J. Foyt Chevrolet dealership, even partial ownership in the Houston Astros (the only thing on the team quicker than Nolan Ryan's fastball). With tongue firmly in cheek, A. J. recently told Paul Page, "I don't have a lot of money, but I've got enough to go out now and buy a cheeseburger, where I used to have to get a grilled cheese." Foyt's born-again loyalty to USAC during the early rounds of the power struggle with CART led him to confess, "If it hadn't been for USAC, we (drivers) would probably all be diggin' ditches and workin' on a chain gang!"

Many pieces comprise the puzzle which is A. J. Foyt. He has played the villain, feuding with sanctioning bodies, promoters, series sponsors, drivers, the press (definitely the press!) — anyone running afoul of the Gospel According to Foyt. But he's also been a philanthropist, helping fellow competitors in dire straits; a patriot, choosing to run the bulk of his races for his fans in the "Yew-nited States"; both a mechanic and car owner, placing four of his cars in the 1970 500; a family man (and grandfather-twice). How about A. J. the comedian? When word surfaced that Janet Guthrie would take a ride in the backup Gilmore Coyote on 1976's last qualifying day, scuttlebutt had Foyt receiving X-thousands of dollars from Goodyear to make the effort. A. J. discounted the tale, adding, "Hell, if I need money, I got friends that'll loan me some!" Accepting an award for the construction of his new Coyote at the 1981 drivers meeting, Foyt gave full credit to his crew, admitting, "My welding looks like mud daubin."

It won't seem right to gaze through the pits someday at Indy (or Pocono, or Daytona) and not see a uniformed A. J. Foyt, working a piece of Spearmint double-time, ribbing the other drivers, giving a malevolent stare to an appropriate party. Since he came from an era when "seat of the pants driving" meant more than reaching into the back pocket of your Calvin Kleins for a checkbook, an eventual heir to the Foyt

driving role would surely come from the same rim-riding, mud-churning heritage, perhaps Sammy Swindell, Doug Wolfgang, or Al Unser Junior. There most assuredly won't be second (third?) generation Foyt to compete against the likes of Michael Andretti and the Unser cousins, as A. J. would prefer his sons to stay with horse racing or other less volatile vocations. "They would probably have pushed my son in newspaper articles and on TV and expected him to do overnight what it took me 25 years to do, and I'm quite sure they'd have buried him pretty quick." Evidently for Foyt to begin grooming a future replacement at this time would be: (a) detrimental to his own effort and (b) an obvious indicator of impending retirement. A. J. guarantees that, "The day I quit — it may be a practice day, I don't know when — you can be sure of one thing. I'll never step back in another race car. I don't care if I'm broke or whatever they offer me to go back. That's one thing I admire about Jackie Stewart . . . He was offered many millions of dollars a few years ago to get back into Formula One, but he told me 'I've quit, A. J.'" Also, "I've had too many friends of mine through the years say, 'I'm going to finish out this season' (then retire) and they never make it." Foyt has always maintained he would continue as long as his eyesight remained sharp and he still enjoyed the sport.

And what will A. J. do when he finally hangs it up? "Sit out by the lake and learn how to fish. I've never been fishing — where people can't bother or get around me (chuckling)." His crowning post-driving achievement would be for a horse from the Foyt stable to win the Kentucky Derby; imagine winning mankind's greatest auto race *and* horse race. Any chance of becoming a member of the IMS brass (as has been rumored)? "No, the Hulman's are just very good, close friends. I've got enough problems down in Houston."

So the second quarter century begins with the 1983 Indy 500, still chasing victory number five, still breathing fire — mellowed or not ("It's according to what time of day and what mood I'm in if I've mellowed", says A. J., and we need only ask Kevin "Coogan" for verification). In assessing his milestone this May, A. J. kiddingly stated, "Joe Cloutier congratulated me on my 'Silver Anniversary' and I told him, 'Please don't say that, it sounds terrible' . . . It means I've been lucky for 25 years, I guess." But then he did later concede "It's nice to accomplish something like this, because many people don't make it 25 years in marriage, let alone racing for 25 years — it's about the same thing!"

A. J., it's been a fantastic twenty-five years and thanks for those "custody visits" every May!

A.J. Foyt, Jr.

25th ANNIVERSARY

The record books chronicle A.J. Foyt's 25 impressive years in Indianapolis racing. But, they really don't tell the whole story. It can be heard in the roar of the fans whenever his name is announced... or, in comments made by many of his rivals on the track. Words like courage, integrity and respect underscore his competitive spirit and driving ability.

There are many winners in auto racing, but none like A.J. Foyt. I'm proud of my association with him and the whole racing team.

Jim Gilmore Jr.

ONLY 4 TIME INDY 500 WINNER

GILMORE/FOYT
RACING TEAM

JIM GILMORE ENTERPRISES:
GILMORE BROADCASTING CORPORATION
WESTERN OHIO CABLEVISION
ANTHONY ABRAHAM CHEVROLET, MIAMI
JIM GILMORE CADILLAC, PONTIAC/DATSUN, KALAMAZOO, MICHIGAN
FLORIDA AUTO RENTAL, MIAMI/ORLANDO/TAMPA/FT. LAUDERDALE
GREEN TURTLE INN & GREEN TURTLE CANNERY, ISLAMORADA, FLORIDA
JIM GILMORE ENTERPRISE FARMS, RICHLAND, MICHIGAN
CONTINENTAL CORPORATION OF MICHIGAN

1961   1964   1967   1977

by Fritz Frommeyer

The Six-Wheeler:

Ask people whatever happened to the six-wheel Pat Clancy Special that raced in the 1948 and 1949 Indianapolis 500s and you'll get a variety of interesting answers. There seems to be two camps of opinion on the matter: one says the car was retired as a six-wheeler after a crash while the other believes that the car was converted to a traditional four-wheel racer.

Here are several versions of the fate of the unique car that was driven at Indianapolis by Billy DeVore in 1948 and Jack Holmes in 1949:

- In 1949, several months after the 500, Mack Hellings was running second at Trenton in the car and crashed so badly that nothing was really left but parts. Pat Clancy took the parts back to his home in Memphis and eventually sold them. The six-wheeler could never have been rebuilt as a four-wheeler because it was designed for six wheels only and would have not handled the more conventional four wheels.
- Following Hellings' crash, the car was rebuilt as a four-wheeler and driven in the 1950 Indianapolis 500 by Jimmy Davies. (There was a conventional Pat Clancy Special in 1950 and Davies drove it.)
- Another railbird recalled the same story about the car, adding that only the tail section was rebuilt to handle two, instead of four wheels.
- Another version has Hellings running third when he crashed at Trenton and the car being rebuilt in time for Davies to drive it at Syracuse as a six-wheeler. A new four-wheel car was built for Davies and he drove it to win the 1949 race at Del Mar, California, that claimed Rex Mays' life.
- The final tale is similar to the one above, except that Davies drove the rebuilt six-wheeler, minus two wheels, in his Del Mar win. The car was rebodied for the 1950 Indianapolis race. Davies drove it to 17th place and, several years later, to victory at Springfield. Finally, about 1957, Diz Wilson bought the car and converted it to a sprinter. It was involved in an accident and it is not known whether it ever was rebuilt.

Whatever its fate, the blue six-wheel Pat Clancy Special was one of the more unusual cars to compete at Indianapolis and is likely the only one entered with more than four wheels. Six-wheel cars also appeared in Europe. Mercedes Benz and Auto-Union used dual rear wheels on a single axle for hillclimb events in the Thirties. In Formula 1 racing, there was the Tyrrell with its four tiny front wheels and later a March that more resembled the Clancy car. All of these cars had one

"I've got a race car" Pat Clancy said to Billy DeVore. "It's a little different . . . It's got SIX WHEELS!"

Indianapolis Motor Speedway Photos

goal: to use the additional wheels for improved traction and stability. Some of these cars worked well, while others did not, but none worked well enough to inspire a proliferation of the concept.

If we are not quite sure about what happened to the Clancy car, we do know how it all started. Billy DeVore tells the story.

"I was involved in promoting an AAA championship race at Arlington Downs, Texas. I also made a deal with Louie Bromme to drive his highly respected car in the race.

"One day when I went out to the track there was someone sitting around near the office. He was dressed in brown work clothes. I asked him if there was anything I could do for him."

"I've got a race car," the man, who turned out to be Pat Clancy, said.

"What kind of car?", DeVore asked.

"It's a little different. It's got six wheels," Clancy responded.

"He showed me a picture of the car and it looked OK," DeVore says. "We were short of entries for the race and I asked if he had a driver. He didn't. I volunteered to drive it and asked for some money up front because the car was an experimental deal and because I would be giving up a good ride in the Bromme car."

The Clancy car arrived at Arlington Downs and DeVore took it for its first laps around the dirt track. Its Meyer

Drake engine powered all four rear wheels. Two midget rear ends were linked by a U-joint. Because of this power arrangement, the front end pushed and, if taken into a corner very hard, the car wanted to go straight. It was difficult to get the back end to hang out like a conventional dirt track car. Because of its unique handling, the driver had to run a high line through the turns.

DeVore qualified the car in the middle of the field at Arlington Downs. Before the race he noticed fuel leaking from one of the two tanks beneath the driver's seat. Clancy told him not to worry. He then put a piece of chewing gum in his mouth, chewed it until it was soft, plugged the leak with it, and told DeVore that a chemical reaction would seal the hole.

During the race, DeVore began to feel fuel on his legs and pulled the car into the pits. The "chemical reaction" did not take.

"It was lucky that I stopped when I did, because the body was going to come off if I raced any longer," DeVore says. "It was put together with metal screws and they had worked loose. I later learned that the car was built by some people Clancy knew at an Air Force base who were familiar with aircraft construction, but not race car building."

Despite the unsuccessful debut, DeVore felt the car had some potential and he signed to drive it in the 1948

[152]

A Bit of a Mystery

While it didn't work so well on the straightaway, it handles very well in the turns. It even lead the Novi on one occasion.

Indianapolis 500. As it turned out, that would be his last 500. He had competed in six other events, with his best finish being seventh in 1937. He started racing in 1931 as a riding mechanic for Deacon Litz and later rode with Fred Frame in the last race at the Altoona, Pennsylvania, board speedway. Billy's father, Earl DeVore, finished second at Indianapolis in 1927.

"When we got to the Speedway in 1948, there were a lot of arguments about whether the car would work or not," DeVore says. "The head of the Technical Committee tried to get it thrown out. He was an engineer and convinced that it wouldn't work.

"I was a friend of Wilbur Shaw (the Speedway's president) and I asked him to allow the car to race. After the debate over the six wheels was settled, the head of the Technical Committee then took issue with the car's magnesium wheels, saying they weren't as strong as the wire wheels used by the other cars. Wilbur again came to my aid and had the wheels tested by Firestone in Akron, Ohio. They found them to be a good deal stronger than wire wheels. I believe these were the first magnesium wheels ever used at the Speedway."

In practice, DeVore found the car did not handle better than a conventional racer in the turns. Better handling in the turns was supposed to have been an

advantage of the six-wheel design. And, much to his concern, DeVore found that the car would suddenly dart to one side on the rough brick front straightaway. The chassis would flex from the rough surface, causing it to dart sideways, reducing its straightaway speed. "You could feel the car bend. My only concern for the race was that someone would run over me. Thankfully, no one did," DeVore says.

Before the race DeVore told the Clancy crew that the car's tail pipe was weak and might come loose or fall off. His prediction came true and the car was black-flagged because the tail pipe was protruding from the side of the car. It took nearly 30 minutes to fix the faulty pipe in the pits. DeVore finally finished 12th, completing 190 laps. His prize money was $2,930.

After the race, he told Clancy he was no longer interested in driving the car, even though he felt it could be a dominant machine on the dirt if necessary changes were made to it. "I told them to put truss rods on each side of the chassis so it wouldn't flex so much on the front straightaway at the Speedway."

Jack Holmes (known as Jackie in his racing days) was signed to be DeVore's relief driver in 1948. He took his rookie test that year and needed five cars to get through all the necessary laps according to the *1948 Clymer Yearbook*. And,

while running fast enough to qualify, he had the transmission break in his car.

Before the 1948 race Holmes was allowed several laps in the Clancy car to familiarize himself with the unusual machine. He performed well during this run, turning one lap at 130 mph, and was later asked to drive for the team in the 1949 500. His services as a relief driver were not needed in 1948.

1949 was Holmes' first race at Indianapolis. He would compete in one more 500, in 1950, when he spun and hit the third turn wall on a very wet track after the rains came, stopping the event at 345 miles. Holmes was almost forced to become a race driver. He built a midget but could not find anyone to drive it, so he drove it himself. In 1949, driving Pop Dreyer's red and yellow sprint car, he won the AAA Midwest Sprint Car championship, improving on his runner-up spot from the prior year. He had his own airplane so he could race on Sunday afternoon, hop in the plane, and fly to a Sunday night event.

Back at the Speedway in 1949, Holmes practiced with the six-wheeler on the same set of tires that were used in running the entire race the previous year. "It reacted differently from other cars," Holmes says. "It handled better on the turns than it did on the straightaway. At first you couldn't tell where it was going on the straightaways. You had to pay attention to it. Those two rear axles made the front end wave back and forth. I always thought the car would handle better if the first set of rear wheels was disengaged.

"You didn't have to worry about spinning the car. It would have been very hard to spin," Holmes continues. "I think I could have run speeds of 140 mph if everything was right on the car. I did a couple of warmup laps at 134."

Holmes qualified the car at just above 128 mph, starting in the middle of the sixth row between Joie Chitwood and Troy Ruttman. The Clancy car did not run long that year, dropping out with driveshaft problems after 65 laps. Finishing 22nd, Holmes earned $2,410.

As Holmes drove the car during the month of May, its unusual handling characteristics became more predictable. "After you got on to the car, you knew what it was going to do," he recalls. "With some other cars, you never knew what they would do.

"On the first lap in 1949, I passed six cars on the north turn," he recalls. "I thought I was really moving until one of the Novis went by. Other cars had to slow down to go into a turn. I didn't have to slow as much because I ran a higher line down the straightaways and could get into the turns faster. The car would go about anywhere you wanted it to in the turns.

"I drove through the fire of Duke

The rear wheels were driven by a combination of two midget quick-change rear ends.

Nalon's accident, driving down into the dirt in the infield and back onto the track. This didn't bother the car a bit.

"We came to the Speedway in 1949 with a 270 Meyer-Drake engine in the car," Holmes says. "The engine broke after I qualified, so we borrowed a 255 cubic inch engine for the race. But it did not have enough power. By the time I would get halfway down the straightaway, the car was running as fast as it would go.

"After the Speedway, I drove the Clancy car at Milwaukee and finished second, I think," Holmes says. "However, I got into an argument over

the front axle not being heavy enough. Clancy said it was easier to change chauffeurs than it was to change axles. Later, the front axle broke and the car flipped end-for-end."

Today, Holmes and DeVore live on the westside of Indianapolis and both maintain an interest in racing. Billy DeVore is an avid golfer who, at 72, has a 15 handicap and shoots in the 90s. He also is working on the story of his career in racing. Jack Holmes, who always has been interested in electronics, operates the TV shop he opened in 1952. He is now 58.

The unusual has always kept the

Indianapolis 500 an interesting event. The six-wheel Pat Clancy Special certainly added spice to the Speedway. And, in each of its years, it had some extraordinary company among the other entries. In 1948, a 1931 Duesenberg was entered and, in 1949, a 1914 Peugeot was brought to the Speedway.

Today, despite the uncertainty about what really happened to the Clancy car, we do know that it was a capable machine, competing twice at Indianapolis and running well on the dirt. We bench racers can thank Pat Clancy for giving us the subject of some good conversation for more than thirty years.

After Billy DeVore, Jackie Holmes was Clancy's driver. He had the same problems with the car that Billy had.

Jim Davies drove the car after Wayne Ewing had rebuilt it into a one-man dirt machine. It performed particularly well on dirt tracks.

"Miller Pit Stop II"
1978 Indianapolis 500
30 x 30 ins

"Untitled"
1977 Indianapolis 500
30 x 30 ins

"The Champ And The Rookie"
1980 Indianapolis 500
30 x 24 ins

"When The Green Flag Drops . . ."
1979 Indianapolis 500
30 x 24 ins

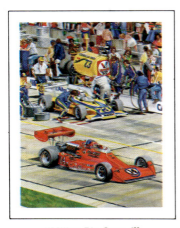

"Miller Pit Stop I"
1977 Indianapolis 500
24 x 30 ins

RON BURTON LTD.

Post Office Box 24342
Speedway, Indiana 46224
(317) 241-0490

"Bobby"
1981 Indianapolis 500
24 x 30 ins

All Limited Edition Prints $200.00

Desire Wilson

by Al Stilley

She is called Grand Prix Girl, The Fast Lady, and Lioness of South Africa. Those were the labels international racing star Desire' Wilson of Kent, England wore when she came to the Indianapolis Motor Speedway.

For a rookie, her international racing credentials were indeed impressive. She has driven for Tyrrell racing in the South African Grand Prix. In 1980, she won the British Formula One race at Brands Hatch and was first in World Championship of Makes endurance races at Monza, Silverstone, and Brands Hatch. In 1976, she won the South African National Formula Ford Championship and one year later received the South African "Driver-to-Europe" Award.

By the end of May when she left the Speedway, all her racing credentials were still intact, but she wore the uncommon label of utter frustration. The Perils Of Pauline were nothing compared to the Dilemmas Of Desire.

The dream of making the 66th Indianapolis 500 came to an end on the morning of May 23 in virtual silence at the north end of the pits. Away from the maddening crowd that stalked Janet Guthrie's every footstep in 1976, Desire showed no tears, no remorse, no bad temper. A mere shrug of the shoulders — that was the initial hint that it was over. Moments earlier, she had been victimized by another engine failure, the fifth (and last one) of the month.

Desire recalled her last lap vividly: "When I saw the gauges, I was hoping that I was wrong about the problem being the engine. In my mind, I knew it was over. We made a decision earlier that if anything went wrong with this engine, it would be all over."

After climbing from the ill-fated Theordore Racing Eagle-Cosworth No. 33 she was consoled by her husband, Alan, who later said, "All you can say is that Desire came to Indy and had the worst luck imaginable."

Desire was the focus of much attention from the press and the motorsports world at Indy because she was hooked up with the first class Indianapolis team of Teddy Yip's Theodore Racing and chief mechanic Derek Mower. Unfortunately, the Dilemmas of Desire began immediately during the annual rookie orientation when the first Cosworth engine blew. It was a bad omen of events to come during the following month.

Desire began slowly during May by getting in a portion of her 165 mph rookie phase on opening day. After replacing another engine, she eventually passed her rookie test May 11. Two days later, Desire's optimism peaked after going 193.4.

"The engine was very strong that day, but the car handled terribly," she said. "I almost got the car into the bends (turns) flat out. If you go through two and four without lifting, you're in the 195 bracket. I was confident that I could do it."

Desire made her only qualifying attempt May 15 with three laps around 191 before the run was waved off. After the crew struggled to replace the fourth malfunctioning engine, she clipped off a lap of 192.472 before spinning off the first turn on May 19.

"I thought the car felt good enough to go flat out and find the speed that I wanted," Desire recalled. "I was confident through turn one and left my right foot down, but the rear-end lost complete adhesion."

Misfortune struck again May 22 with the fifth blown engine which forced the crew to work overnight getting the Eagle ready for the final day's assault.

The strain began showing on the afternoon of May 22. Alan Wilson lamented, "The time element here adds to the frustration. You think you have three weeks to get ready, and now we have one whole day ... Optimism is not very high in my feelings right now. A sense of resignation is a better way of putting it."

He tried to hide his disappointment over the events at Indy by saying, "We've been racing for more than 15 years, and I've never seen anything like this ... This is the ultimate opportunity in her life. It's awful to have it go like this."

For Desire, at 28, the long trail to her first try at making it at Indy was coming down to a day of decision. Her fate at Indy would be decided in less than 24 hours. It meant nothing that she had already achieved more than any other woman in open wheel racing today. The trail from micro-midgets to Formula Vees, World class endurance races, Formula One and the Grand Prix eventually led to a tiny wooden garage in Gasoline Alley at the Indianapolis Motor Speedway.

Desire appeared perplexed over her dilemma of having only one day left to prove herself at Indy to the motorsports world: "We're running out of time. I was excited a few weeks ago, but I'm running at a disadvantage now. Nothing is going right."

Lady Luck ultimately and undeservedly shut the door on the Wilsons on May 23.

"I hate missing it," Desire lamented just a few hours after losing the fifth engine of the month to knock her out of making any attempt to qualify again for the 500. "I'd be silly if I didn't say I was very much disappointed ... That is what

fate is all about. I came here with quite a bit of confidence. I never lost it. I came here to prove that I am a competitive race car driver, and I feel I proved that to an extent."

In the face of his wife's greatest disappointment in racing, Alan Wilson praised her by stating, "She's a professional race car driver. We live racing seven days a week. That's why the frustration here hasn't led to a bad display of temper. She's a race car driver, totally capable of driving at Indy."

Later, Desire found time to talk about her month at the famed Speedway. The attractive 5'5" South African-born open wheel chauffeur was relaxed and more positive than she had been for a few days.

"The crowds, the officials, the press have all teated me good here," she said. "I really thought we would run out of bad luck. When we put that last engine in, we were sure our bad luck had ended. All you can do is shrug your shoulders. You can't look back. I have to trust my ability as a race car driver."

She continued, "I found out this track is not as easy as it looks to drive around. The top speed did not bother me. The big challenge is getting the car sorted out for the bends. There is no room for error, if you make a mistake here, you're into the wall."

She praised car owner Yip and the Theodore Racing team which "worked 24 hours a day for 15 days to get the car ready."

The Wilsons stayed for the pre-race activities and the 66th annual Indianapolis 500 prior to returning to England where he manages four race tracks and she works as administrator of the Brands Hatch racing school.

Alan expressed the hope that his wife opened "new horizons" for motorsports exposure by stating, "She opens new doors to the sport because she does more than merely appeal to the converted fan on the sports pages. Fifty percent of our clips come from women's pages — that's the sort of thing she can do for racing. There are very few drivers who spend the time with the press or the public that 'Des' does."

Desire expressed her long-range goal in the waning hours of the final day of qualification while walking slowly toward Gasoline Alley. She was convinced she had tried her best to conquer Indy. It was then she looked to the future: "I want the same opportunity to come back next year."

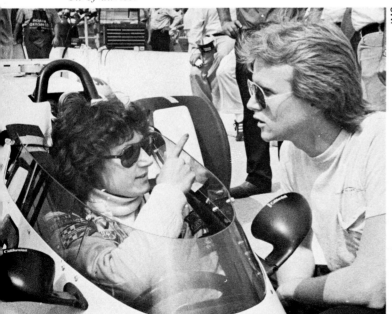

Gordon Smiley gave Desire some tips on driving at Indy. They were teammates.

Maybe Desire Wilson is the "rookie" but she still seems to be giving Kevin Cogan a bit of advice.

This conglomeration Desire is putting on her garage door is actually a South African good luck charm.

Desire tells Valvoline's Leonard Manley of her steady progress.

TWB III

The Greatest Name in Classic Cars
Thomas W. Barrett III
5601 East Nauni Valley Drive, Scottsdale, Arizona 85253
Phone 602-949-9946

Thomas W. Barrett III

Tom Barrett is one of those individuals who is in love with the world of wheels. While his name is not a household word to Indy 500 enthusiasts, those interested in the world's finest classic and antique cars recognize him instantly. His annual Scottsdale, Arizona antique auto auction is considered the premier event of its type in the world. He continues his interest in the Indianapolis 500 annually with a co-sponsorship and this year was a part of Desiree Wilson's team.

20 Years Ago...

Indianapolis Motor Speedway Photos

by Donald Davidson

The Indianapolis 500 mile race of twenty years ago ended with Rodger Ward winning for the second time in four races, having taken the lead at the two-thirds mark when pre-race favorite Parnelli Jones had been forced to slow his pace because of brake failure.

One of the cars in the race had its engine mounted in the rear, a Buick-powered creation entered by drag racing aficionado Mickey Thompson. Eight of the 32 front-engined Offenhauser-powered cars either had their engines placed completely on their sides, or virtually so. The remaining 24 starters had their engines installed upright, offset to the left and, with only a couple of exceptions, were housed in chassis either built by or based on the design of A. J. Watson.

Of the 33 drivers who lined up behind the Studebaker Avanti pace car on May 30, 1962, twelve of them are no longer living. Seven of the twelve perished in racing accidents, two within that summer, and the other five before four-and-a-half years had elapsed. Of the other five who are deceased, one was shot to death in a personal dispute, another died in a private plane crash, a third suffered a fatal heart attack, and the remaining two succumbed in hospitals, victims of chronic illnesses.

In a happier vein, not one of the 21 who survive, was forced to leave the sport through injuries, and in fact, at least two of them continue to race! A third, who has all but retired, made a qualifying attempt in 1981. Of the 18 who retired, each for all intents and purposes by his own choosing, seven were active in some form of racing, if not at Indianapolis, up into the 1970's.

It seems odd, in these days of long tenures and multiple winners, that the 1962 starting field should contain a mere four past winners, Troy Ruttman, Jim Rathmann and Rodger Ward, who were shortly to retire, and the phenomenal A. J. Foyt, who would win three more and still be trying for a fifth win in 1982. Other than Foyt, the only future winner in the lineup was Parnelli Jones, who would succeed a year later. All of the winners following Jones, with the exception of Foyt, made their debuts after 1962.

The following is a nostalgic look back at the competitiors in that 1962 event and an explanation of what became of them.

RODGER WARD

Repeat winners were not at all common when Rodger Ward scored his second "500" win in 1962, Tommy Milton, Louis Meyer, Wilbur Shaw, Mauri Rose and Bill Vukovich having been the only other drivers to win for a second time before that.

Rodger was delighted to return to Victory Lane, but he later claimed that he had been down on engine power, deriving not nearly as much satisfaction from winning in '62 as he had in 1959 or even in 1960, when, although ending up second, he felt he drove his geatest race.

The ex-P 38 pilot raced his way from a start with Midgets in 1946 to the Indianapolis Motor Speedway by 1951. Although he won a pair of Championship races (Springfield and Detroit) in 1953, his career was mainly marked by wild antics on as well as off the race track. After being involved in the accident that took the life of Bill Vukovich in the 1955 "500", Rodger made a number of changes in his personal life and relaxed his driving style, maturing into one of the greatest drivers of the post-war era. He won five Championship races for Roger Wolcott between 1957 and 1958, then moved into the newly-formed Leader Card team in 1959. Between 1959 and 1964, his "500" finishes in A. J. Watson-prepared cars

were first, second, third, first, fourth and second, the latter coming in a Watson-built rear-engine car. After splitting with the team following a stunning failure to qualify Watson's lastest creation in 1965, Ward finished out his Championship career with John Mecom's new team. Things didn't go too well at first, but in the spring of 1966, he placed second to Jimmy McElreath at Phoenix and won the rain-shortened April event at Trenton. He appeared to be running well in the "500", but suddenly pulled out claiming that his car wasn't handling when there was apparently nothing wrong with it at all. The following evening at the Victory Banquet, Rodger thanked his car owner, sponsor, crew, etc., then drew a breath and said, "A long time ago, I told myself that if ever racing ceased to be fun, I'd quit." He paused, and with his voice choking continued, "Well, yesterday, it just wasn't fun anymore. See you all." With that, he pulled a military salute, and returned to his seat with tears streaming down his cheeks. It was a moving exit for the normally cocky, swaggering wise-cracking Ward, stunning the Victory Banquet crowd as they have rarely been stunned.

Firestone installed him in a tire store on Crawfordsville Road, which later was turned over to the Andretti twins, and before that Rodger had dabbled in numerous other businesses, including a motoring club, a travel agency, talent agency, speed and sport shops in partnership with A. J. Watson, and service stations. He headed west and became Director of Public Relations for the Ontario Motor Speedway in its early days, and in fact was the first person to drive a race car around the track. That may have whetted his appetite for some further racing, and to the dismay of those who felt he had retired at or near the top of his profession, Rodger competed in some NASCAR Grand National-West events in 1973 without any success. He "re-retired," headed for Owosso, Michigan to manage a race track, and most recently was co-ordinating the activites of the power boat and Can-Am sports car sponsored by Circus Circus of Las Vegas. In 1980, he joined the Indianapolis Motor Speedway Radio Network as expert commentator, a role he had filled with distinction on televised races in the early 1970's. On the morning of the 1982 "500", now nearly white-haired and 62 years old, he made a parade lap in his 1962 winning car, an honor he greatly enjoyed. He then made his way up to the broadcast booth and spent the rest of the day imparting some of his vast knowledge in a most eloquent fashion, spotting incidents sometimes before they occurred and obviously completely up to date on the latest technical innovations.

LEN SUTTON

Len Sutton neither looked nor behaved as a race driver was supposed to!

He liked to travel, read books and discuss politics. He'd sit during a conversation clutching his knee with clasped palms, and when someone made a statement he didn't think he agreed with, he'd smile, tightly close one eye, stare off into space with the other, and pause, Dan Gurney-style, while forming his response.

Sutton came out of the Northwest from Portland, Oregon with a background of Midget racing to join AAA Championship racing at Sacramento in 1955. He crashed after passing his rookie test at Indianapolis in 1956 and raced mostly Midgets for the next couple of years, ranking 4th in 1957. He qualified for his first "500" in 1958 as one of the few drivers to have made their debuts there already having won a Championship race. He had beaten Tony Bettenhausen at Trenton in April.

The studious Sutton was another driver who seemed to do equally well on dirt or pavement, winning at Springfield on dirt in 1959 and in the Milwaukee 200 on pavement in 1960, in addition to frequent top five finishes on both types of surface.

In 1962, Len had by far his best run at Indianapolis, starting fourth, leading briefly and coming home second to teammate Rodger Ward. The prospect of winning the Championship had looked bright, but Len was injured in the very next race at Milwaukee and was sidelined until August. In 1963 he had a miserable year at the Speedway, getting "bumped", qualifying another car, and getting "bumped" again. Later, in tire tests, he drove the first rear-engine car to house an Offenhauser engine and became the first person to lap the Speedway at 155 mph. The following May, he had the car up to 4th place before dropping out.

Len unexpectedly retired after the 1965 Langhorne race, having decided to pursue politics for the next several years. He continued to represent several accessory firms as a salesman, and once owned as many as seven coin-operated laundries. He made the annual trek back to Indianapolis for several more Mays, joining Sid Collins on the IMS Radio Network as the driver expert commentator. He turned those duties back over to Freddie Agabashian in the early 1970's as

his involvement in politics increased.

It has been several years since Len has returned to Indianapolis, about his only connection with racing these days being as a frequent visitor of Portland car owner Rolla Vollstedt, with whom Len did much of his racing and through a continuing friendship with Jack Turner, the Turners and the Suttons having taken foursome vacations together, sometimes as far away as Europe.

EDDIE SACHS

Long before he qualified for his first "500" race fans knew who Eddie Sachs was.

Fun-loving, emotional, occasionally brash, and sometimes outspoken to his own detriment, Sachs was for the most part cherished by the fans. Sincere to a fault, Sachs had travelled to the Mid-west from Pennsylvania to pursue racing and washed dishes at Marianna's restaurant on West 16th Street in Indianapolis in order to be close to the track. He failed to complete a rookie test either in 1953 or '54, but was runner-up to Pat O'Connor for the Mid-West Sprint car crown in the latter year. His unfortunate speech at the season-end banquet in Dayton drew him a suspension for the first few months of 1955!

Back in the fold in '56, Eddie qualified as the first alternate at Indianapolis and won the Championship race at Atlanta shortly after that. In 1957 he qualified for the middle of the front row at the Speedway and ran with the leaders until dropping out at the halfway spot. He won the Hoosier Hundred in 1958 and the season's Mid-west sprint car title, after having been runner-up for a second and third time in '55 and '56. He was a front-row "500" qualifier in 1959 and then won the pole for the next two years, stamping himself as more than just another comical braggart.

He was narrowly defeated in the 1961 "500", electing to stop to change a badly worn tire only three laps from the finish while leading, and crossing the line in second place only eight seconds behind A. J. Foyt. The following year he came close again, coming from a second weekend 27th qualifying slot to third at the finish.

In spite of his disappointments, Sachs could always bound back grinning,

agreeing to pose for yet another gag shot. He joked about both a Jewish and Catholic upbringing, noting frequently that for luck he wore not only a St. Christopher medal, but also the Star of David. He admitted to weeping during the singing of "Back Home Again In Indiana" on race morning, and even marched down the straight with one of the bands one year.

Out of turn four on the second lap of the 1964 race, Dave MacDonald's car spun around entering the mainstraight. It slid into the inside wall, burst into flames, and ricocheted across the track into the outside wall. The beloved Sachs, driving a new rear-engined car which, like MacDonald's, was using pump gasoline, plowed into the inferno and erupted in a fearful explosion, snuffing out his life on the very race track he loved so much.

DON DAVIS

Don Davis was a "Buckeye" who moved to Arizona with his family just before he started racing in 1951. He won numerous titles in his adopted state during the nineteen fifties, but was hardly known outside of it. When the USAC Championship division arrived in Phoenix one year, Don toured the pits with an enthusiastic backer who wanted to see the local driver in a USAC car. "I'll tell you what", the backer propositioned one cautious car owner." You put Davis in your car and I'll give you $5,000 in sponsorship money." The owner considered his mediocre equipment and shot back, "Buddy, you make it $6,000, and I'll give you the car, the trailer, and the whole works. *You* can be the owner, and *you* can put him in it."

In 1960, Don ventured across the state line enough times to beat Danny "Termite" Jones out of the CRA Sprint title, and he moved into USAC at the end of the year. He made his Indianapolis debut the following May, hopping in and out of several cars before qualifying Gil Morcroft's roadster. He brushed the outside wall exiting turn four on his 50th lap and spun down the main straight to a halt. He climbed from the car and, apparently stunned, strolled at a leisurely pace across the track directly in the path of oncoming race cars. A. J. Shepherd didn't know which way to go, darting one way and then another before locking up, missing the stunned Davis and sliding

around to nail Bill Cheesbourg, who had passed the stationary Davis car on the other side. Roger McCluskey, who, like Davis and Cheesbourg, was from Arizona, was also involved, and Jack Turner, who was running his best "500 race ever, hit Shepherd and flipped.

Davis started out 1962 in magnificent fashion by winning the pole at Trenton with the Racing Associates dirt car, and then drove the ex-Johnny Thomson 1959 pole sitter to fourth at Indianapolis. He returned to the dirt car at Milwaukee and led the race until a wheel bumping incident with A. J. Foyt forced him to spin out as the crowd booed their disapproval of Foyt. Don was tied with Parnelli Jones for second behind Rodger Ward in the Championship standings when he lost his life in a Sprint Car. He scraped the outside wall at New Bremen on August 5 after taking the checkered flag, flipped badly, and succumbed to his injuries two days later.

BOBBY MARSHMAN

Bobby Marshman was only 24 and looked like a baseball player when he drove in his first "500". He already had been racing for several years, following in the footsteps of his father, and had been runner-up in the 1957 URC Sprint Championship in the east, scoring most of his points before his 20th birthday. He visited Indianapolis several times, hoping to land a ride, only to leave disappointed, and 1961 was no exception. He had already returned to his home in Pottstown, Pennsylvania when he received a telephone call asking him back to take a rookie test. With time running out, he breezed through the test and sqeezed into the lineup on the outside of the last row. He made it all the way up to seventh at the finish and split the Rookie-of-the-Year balloting with Parnelli Jones.

In September of 1961, Bobby really attracted attention when he qualified next to A. J. Foyt on the front row of the Hoosier Hundred, then followed Foyt home to place second. The next May the boyish-looking easterner with the closely-cropped hair qualified next to Parnelli Jones and Rodger Ward at Indianapolis and had his best finish of his four races there, placing 5th. He won the accident-marred Phoenix race at the end of the year, and placed fifth in the

Championship standings. Two years later, Marshman hovered on the brink of greatness.

Daily in May of 1964, Bobby Marshman would break the unofficial track record, and on the morning of the first qualifying day, he became the first person to exceed 160 mph for one lap. He bobbled a couple of times during his qualifying run, but still ended up in the middle of the front row. He took the lead on the seventh lap and began to build his lead at the unheard-of rate of two-and-a-half to three seconds per lap, having lapped almost the entire field when he was forced out at 39 laps. Some of his inside passes had been so low in the turns that he had ripped the draining plug from underneath his oil tank, running out of the supply.

Tire testing for Firestone during the summer, he continued to lower the Speedway lap times, raising the speeds to almost 163 mph. His rear-engine car continued to break down after qualifying well in races, but on dirt, Bobby was runnerup four times, beaten only by Foyt on each occasion.

Tragically, after the 1964 season was over, Bobby and his crew stayed over at Phoenix to run some more tests. He crashed during one segment, suffered severe burns, and died several days later, never having attained the greatness that had seemed inevitable.

JIMMY McELREATH

Jimmy McElreath had already been racing for seventeen years when he showed up at Indianapolis for the first time in 1962. Twenty years after that, he was still racing!

He had rarely ventured from home until 1960, content until then to lay bricks in the Dallas area by day and drive at the nearby Devil's Bowl whenever there was a race. At the urging of friends, he finally decided to try racing up north, so he set off for Indiana in the company of a 22-year-old area driver named Johnny Rutherford. In no time at all, Jimmy was winning super-modified events in the Mid-West, soon becoming a leading point scorer in IMCA Sprints.

He siezed upon an opportunity to drive in the 1961 Hoosier Hundred and made his USAC debut a memorable one by finishing 3rd. The following May he had his first Indianapolis start, and amazed

everyone by coming from seventh to second by 20 laps, driving the second oldest car in the race, only to drop back as mismanaged pit stops kept him from a better showing. He still was able to place 6th, winning the Rookie-of-the-Year award by a unanimous vote.

Soon to be equally at home in Championship events whether they were on dirt or paved tracks, he finished 3rd in the USAC standings behind A. J. Foyt and Rodger Ward in 1963, and after making a successful transition to rear-engine cars, was third to Mario Andretti and Foyt in '65 and runner-up to Andretti in '66 after finishing 3rd at Indianapolis. He was third yet again after winning the inaugural Ontario 500 in September, 1970.

During the mid-1970's, his son, James McElreath, began to succeed in Sprint Car racing, and Jimmy's ambition was to be the first driver to race against his son in an Indianapolis "500". James passed his "rookie" test in 1977, but did not qualify fast enough to make the race, and then, tragically, was fatally injured late in the year.

Rather than quit when his ambition was crushed, Jimmy decided to keep on racing and unintentionally found himself with another record. When he qualified for his fourteenth "500" in 1980, he was three months past his 52nd birthday, and records fail to disclose a "500" qualifier any older! Still he wasn't done, and in 1982, at the age of 54 and looking at least ten years younger, Jimmy McElreath was still an active driver at the Indianapolis Motor Speedway, trying to get a car into the race.

PARNELLI JONES

Parnelli Jones looked like he meant business.

Possessor of a wide grin when he'd display it, but more often than not scowling or dead-pan, Parnelli was as tough as nails. His desire to win was as intense in his makeup as it was in anyone's, vented by occasional fits of violent temper. His thinning hair was cut in a spikey crew cut and his hardened, tanned features were once described as being carved out of granite. His eyes were steel blue.

He had eight years of racing under his belt when he first visited the Mid-West. He was an immediate success, placing

second in the Little "500" at Anderson, Indiana, winning the Mid-West Sprint Championship and almost winning the Milwaukee 200 mile Championship race in August.

As one of the most highly touted "rookes" ever to come to Indianapolis, Parnelli had a better than average shot at winning first time out, and even led the race for several laps. He was struck in the eye by a rock, struggled on with blood trickling into his goggles, leaned out the fuel mixture, burned a piston and rolled home a thoroughly disgusted 12th. He had come to win.

The Mid-Western and Eastern Sprint titles were combined for the first time to form a National Sprint Championship in 1961, and Parnelli won by a convincing margin over Jim Hurtubise. In 1962, he won it again, but then began to drift away from Sprint car racing. In May 1962, Parnelli became the first, and for that year, the only person to qualify with an average of over 150 miles per hour. In fact, he was the only person to officially record a 150 mph lap, and he did it on all four of his qualifying laps. The race was unquestionably his for 300 miles, until he began to slow with brake failure, eventually nursing his car home in seventh place. In 1963 victory finally became his, but not without some controversy. A tiny crack developed in his oil tank, causing oil to be sprayed onto the track until the level fell below the bottom of the crack. Jim Clark, who was closing and within about four seconds of the lead, elected to back off slightly and play it safe, settling for second while a huge hue and cry went up as to whether Parnelli should have been black-flagged or not.

He led the 1964 event before static electricity is believed to have caused an explosion in his fuel tank during a pit stop, and he was runner-up to Jim Clark in 1965. In 1967, Parnelli almost repeated as an Indianapolis winner, dominating the race with the controversial STP turbine until a bearing failed only four laps from the end.

Quite possibly the most prosperous of all the Indianapolis winners, Parnelli invested virtually all of his winnings in real estate and business. He joined Vel Miletich as a partner in a huge Ford agency, operated dozens of Firestone stores on the West Coast, and entered into several business arrangements with J. C. Agajanian. He dropped out of Championship racing after deciding not to compete in the 1968 "500", but raced in Trans-Am events successfully for Ford for a few more seasons and continued to compete in off-road racing events long after he had retired from everything else. In a surprise move in March, 1978, he stepped into a USAC Stock Car in a 200 mile event at the Ontario Motor Speedway and placed 9th, approximately

ten years after the last time he had driven one.

The Vel's Parnelli Jones Racing team, which started in 1968, became known as "Superteam" in 1972, when Mario Andretti, Al Unser and Joe Leonard all competed for the vast organization. VPJ constructed their own cars for use in Championship, Dirt, SCCA Formula 5000, and even Formula One events until withdrawing as an entrant in 1977.

There are those who feel that Parnelli Jones may have been the finest race driver ever produced by the United States.

LLOYD RUBY

Slow-talking Lloyd Ruby should have won the "500" at least once. Everybody would have been delirious with joy had he done so, and nobody would have wanted to go home. But never having won it, he'll ever be remembered as racing's hard luck driver.

Actually, he fared much better than most people recall; several of his breakdowns came late enough in races that he ended up salvaging a decent finish. In 1960, his rookie year, he was running third with six laps to go when he had to stop for fuel, dropping to seventh. He was eighth in 1961 and '62, after being the second fastest qualifier in '61, with the car vacated by the fatally injured Tony Bettenhausen. Lloyd crashed while running second in 1963, and came home third in 1964. He dropped out late while running in the first five in 1965 and led more laps in 1966 than any other driver. He took the lead away from Jim Clark by passing him on the mainstraight and was in front for a total of 68 laps before being black-flagged twice because of an oil leak. In 1968 he was leading with 25 laps to go when an electrical failure forced him to the pits. Instead of giving up, his crew diagnosed the problem, replaced a faulty coil, and sent him back out to finish fifth in a race he might have won.

Nineteen sixty-nine is the year most people remember best. Tooling along in second, he moved to first when Mario Andretti pitted just past the halfway mark. Lloyd then made his stop. Chief mechanic and car builder Dave Laycock had designed the car so that both the left and right side fuel tanks could be filled from the left side, eliminating the necessity of a crew member running

around to the far side and thereby saving a couple of seconds. The filling points were placed one in front of the other. The front was disconnected on the fateful stop, but the rear one was not as Lloyd eagerly inched forward. The hose became taut and strained as a crew member tried in vain to get him to stop. Lloyd moved forward another inch and the side of the fuel tank was ripped completely out, allowing the fuel to pour onto the track from the gaping hole.

In 1970, Lloyd blew six engines before finally getting qualified. He came from 27th starting position to the lead in 50 laps before an overstrained rear end erupted in flames. In 1971 a similar thing occurred late in the race after he had led, and while he was comfortably riding in the first five.

More disappointments came, including lasting a mere seven laps with a works McLaren in 1975, and crashing out of the '77 race after climbing from 19th to seventh inside of 34 laps.

In 1978 his longtime friend Gene White purchased a car from Interscope Racing, but it was wrecked by Danny Ongais during a shakedown run. His career, which began when he was a teenager driving a Ford-powered Midget in 1946, and led him to become one of Ford's top endurance drivers of the 1960's, with financial remuneration beyond his wildest dreams, quietly came to an end.

Accompanying his wife in many of her civic involvements in Witchita Falls, Texas, Lloyd also like to travel in a Greyhound Scenicruiser he converted several years ago. He is as nice as they come. Unspoiled and unpretentious, he was always the perfect gentleman. Lloyd is a Texan through and through, always making jokes about his slow speech, and confounding others with his ability to "turn it off" and take a nap no matter how much pressure is in the air.

JIM RATHMANN

Poker-faced Jim Rathmann was considered by many to be the best paved oval track driver of his day, his 1960 Indianapolis win following no less than three runner-up finishes.

He borrowed his brother's driver's license and identity in order to start racing at 16, and qualified for his first "500" in 1949 two months before his 21st birthday. He placed second to Troy

Ruttman in the 1952 "500", by which time, in spite of being only 23 years old, he hardly had a hair left on his head. A shrewd businessman, a race track thinker who rarely let an opportunity slip by, the non-smiling Jim was financially secure through sound investments even before he won the "500". He was runner-up to Sam Hanks in 1957, won all three heats of the Monza "500" in Italy in 1958, and was runner-up to Rodger Ward at Indianapolis in 1959 before engaging in the greatest extended two-car duel ever staged at the Speedway. Rodger Ward, who was out to win his second straight "500" stalled on a pit stop and lost valuable time to the leaders. He caught the pack, which one by one were eliminated, until only Rathmann was left. Rathmann and Ward swapped the lead back and forth for most of the last half of the race, never more than a few feet apart from each other. Ward was leading with three laps to go when he noticed the white cord of his right front tire beginning to show through. Rather than risk having it blow out, or waste time by stopping, Rodger reduced his pace and nursed his car home second while Rathmann finally scored his long-anticipated win. He stood in his car in Victory Lane just as he had at Monza two years earlier, managing an open-palm, shoulder-high wave, his helmet still on his head with the straps hanging down, and the barest trace of a smile on his face.

Although Jim achieved very little after that, he was extremely competitive in the '61 race, which he led for several laps. In the meantime, the Rathmann Xterminator had become the leading Go-Kart of the day, with 15-year-old Bobby Allen winning the "World" Championship in Rathmann's product. Years later, Allen became a leading super-modified driver in the East.

Rathmann announced his retirement just before the track opened for practice in 1964 and never drove after that except for a brief incident which took place in 1966. Jim had become a car owner in partnership with Gus Grissom and Gordon Cooper, the astronauts, who were good friends of his. One quiet practice day, Jim pulled on a uniform and helmet and sneaked out for a few laps until officials flagged him for running illegally without a competition license!

Jim lives comfortably in Melbourne, Florida with his wife and adopted children, near the huge Cadillac and Oldsmobile dealership he has run for several years. In 1982, he drove the pace car, a duty he has performed without fanfare on numerous occasions.

JOHNNY BOYD

If there was to be an award for the driver in the 1962 lineup who has

changed the least, it would probably be won by Johnny Boyd, who is virtually unchanged from his appearance as a rookie in 1954, let alone 1962!

John visited the track in 1982, tanned, barrel-chested and wearing exactly the same hairstyle as he had throughout his racing career. He relaxed in the Champion Spark Plug room as he had hundreds of times before, holding court and spinning yarn after amusing yarn.

John was from Fresno, and a prominent Northern California Midget driver of the early 1950's, winning the 1951 BCRA Championship for George Bignotti. He was at the Speedway in 1954, assigned to a car, then replaced by another driver before he could climb into the cockpit. He stooged for Bob Sweikert on race day. A brief but successful fling in Sprint Cars vaulted him permanently into the championship ranks, and in 1955 he qualified for his first of twelve consecutive Indianapolis classics.

John's best shot was in 1958, when he led several laps, stopped near the end while running second, and still made it home third in a George Bignotti-prepared Bowes Seal Fast entry. He had already placed sixth in '57, and, after burns suffered at Langhorne in June 1958, came back to place 6th at Indianapolis again in 1959. In June of '59 he placed second in the 100 miler at Milwaukee, a track where he frequently qualified well. He won the pole position three times at the Wisconsin mile and even drew it a fourth time for a rain-delayed program that was finally scrapped in 1966.

He placed fifth in the tragic 1964 event and began to curtail his activities somewhat. He qualified rear-engine cars in 1965 and 1966, dropping completely out of racing after stepping out of a car on the final qualifying weekend of 1967. In the mid-1970's, John was treated for cancer, but beat the dreaded disease, and later made some Fresno-area television commercials on behalf of the American Cancer Society. He makes light of the fact that there are grey hairs on his head. In reality, there can't be more than half-a-dozen, and Johnny Boyd just doesn't appear to be approaching 56 years old.

SHORTY TEMPLEMAN

Clark "Shorty" Templeman was somewhat of a late bloomer in

Championship racing, enjoying his greatest success at the age of 41.

A free-living individual who packed 175 pounds into only five feet seven inches, he had raced Midgets from the earliest of the post-war years in the Pacific Northwest and his name was to become synonymous with Midgets nationally by the mid-1950's. He was third in the Midget point standings in 1954 and runnerup in 1955 before enjoying three consecutive years as Champion in 1956, '57 and '58. The separate National, Mid-Western and Pacific Coast titles were all won by him in 1957 and a year earlier, he had gained considerable notoriety at the old West 16th Street Midget track. On the night before the 1956 "500", there had been three consecutive Midget programs topped by a 100-lap, 150-lap and a second 100-lap feature respectively. Each program was run separately, complete with qualifying, heats, and even a thorough clearing of the grandstands after each feature so that fresh tickets could be sold for the next program! The bottom line is that Shorty Templeman won all three features, which, considering the practice sessions, qualifying and heats, represented quite an exhausting night's work!

Templeman's initial Championship start at Phoenix in 1954 resulted in his posting the fastest qualification time, but he was still several years away from becoming a front-runner in this type of competition. He had been in three 500 milers (1955, '58 and '60) when he tied up with Bill Forbes and a young mechanic named Dave Laycock. They placed fourth at Indianapolis in 1961 and also fourth in the USAC Championship after several good finishes, including seconds at DuQuoin and Syracuse.

A new Watson roadster was purchased for 1962 and Shorty became one of a handful of drivers to have been unofficially credited with a 150 mph lap on the morning of the first qualifying day. Race day was a disappointment. He was involved in a spinout and had to have his car towed back to the pits, eventually to complete the distance in 11th place.

Shorty came to a parting of the ways with Forbes shortly after that, slipping to the back end of Championship fields once again. He couldn't stay away from Midgets. On August 23rd, 1962 on a tiny track in Marion, Ohio, a huge accident at the start involved eleven of the eighteen starters, seven of which flipped end-for-end at the same time. The life of up-and-coming Jim Hemmings was lost in the accident and so was that of Shorty Templeman. Eleven days earlier, he had turned 43.

Several years later, his son, six-foot Clark Templeman, began racing mostly in California, but making excursions to the Mid-West in the late 1960's and again in the mid-1970's. In June, 1982, Clark was fatally injured at Ascot, California, just a couple of months short of the twentieth anniversary of his father's demise. This was believed to have been the first instance in which both a father and his son perished in racing accidents on American tracks.

DON BRANSON

Don Branson was another late bloomer, enjoying his greatest success after the age of 40.

He had raced sprint cars for years when he first competed in Championship cars in 1956, but it was not until 1959, at the age of almost 39, that he stepped into a car at Indianapolis for the first time. He competed in the "500" every year through the remainder of his life, placing 4th in 1960, qualifying for the front row in 1961 and 1963, and coming within a dozen laps of placing third with a rear-engine car, which he detested, in 1964. He was much more at home in Sprint cars, winning the Mid-Western title in 1959 and the National Sprint Championship in '64. He won Championship races at Trenton and Langhorne in 1962, and when he wheeled his roadster into the victory enclosure at Phoenix in March, 1965, it was to be the last occasion on which a front-engine car won a Championship race. He won the Springfield dirt car race in 1966. In his final Championship appearance, at Sacramento in October, he won the pole with a thrilling, rim-riding performance. A few nights, later he perished in a Sprint car accident at Ascot Park in the final Sprint race of the year.

There had been rumors that Don would retire at the end of the year to take over a management role with Goodyear's Racing Division. There was also the fact that he had been trying to pressure his longtime Champ crew chief and Sprint car owner, Jud Phillips, into constructing a new lightweight front-engine car for Indianapolis.

Don often appeared to be in a grumpy mood, hiding behind dark glasses, and trudging around pits, chewing gum. He had sarcastic answers for inane questions and seemed to laugh loudly only after he had just escaped being injured in an accident. Actually, he is credited with having befriended many young drivers and giving them tips. Of the drivers who are still active in 1982, Johnny Rutherford and Larry Dickson have frequently expressed their admiration both for his skill and for the assistance Don Branson gave them when they were newcomers.

JIM HURTUBISE

Unless a racegoer has followed racing for more than ten years, or has at least read of racing exploits before that, it is quite possible he has no idea that Jim Hurtubise was once one of the leading half dozen race drivers in the United States. To many he is known only as the jolly, occasionally outspoken fellow who likes to drink beer, laugh, and bring out a long-since outmoded front-engine car at Indianapolis.

Although the front-engine car is no longer entered at Indianapolis, it was as late as 1980. Every time it came through the gate, a cheer would go up in the stands, the people would yell, "Hey, Herk!" and the round-faced Hurtubise would wave back in recognition. In the early 1970's, the cheers were for Hurtubise's continued efforts at giant killing. Eventually they came merely because cheering Hurtubise had simply become the traditional thing to do. Once, they had cheered him out of sheer respect, first for smashing the one and four laps qualifying records as a rookie, and later for making a phenomenal comeback after near-fatal injuries.

Nineteen sixty was the year that Hurtubise caused one of the greatest sensations in the history of the track. On the final weekend of qualifying under menacing skies, he exceeded Eddie Sachs's qualifying records by two-and-a-half miles per hour, at a time when records were only broken by fractions. He was sideways through much of the run, and missed breaking 150 mph by, as Eddie Sachs put it, less time than it takes a human to blink an eye.

"Herk," as he was already known, had finished second in IMCA the year before

and had joined USAC Championship racing at the end of the year, winning at Sacramento third time out. A front-row qualifier at Indianapolis in 1961, Jim led the first 36 laps of the race, and two years later, led a lap and ran second for many more with one of the brutish Novis.

He dropped out of the "500" in 1964 while running third in a car he and his brother had built. A week later, at Milwaukee, he was horribly burned after hitting the wall while less than one second out of the lead. Chances of his survival seemed doubtful, and yet the following spring he was back in a car at Phoenix finishing fourth, probably the most remarkable comeback in all of racing.

Jim met with a medium degree of success for the next three years, but it began to diminish in the late 1960's. It appeared that Jim's career might have been complete in 1981, until he surprisingly jumped into a car on the last qualifying day and made an unsuccessful attempt. He was back again in 1982, this time as an onlooker, his antics of recent years sadly overshadowing the fact that some twenty years earlier on the nation's Sprint car and Championship dirt track circuits, Jim Hurtubise had had few peers.

EBB ROSE

It was very rare, even in 1962, for any driver with a road racing background to even *try* to drive at Indianapolis. Ebb Rose was an exception. Slight of build, soft-spoken, but with a Texas accent so thick you could cut it with a knife, Jesse Ebb Rose, son of a successful businessman, arrived at Indianapolis in May, 1960. He had raced with stock cars, but gained most of his notoriety by winning a series of SCCA regional sports car titles, which in those days were strictly run as amateur events. The "roundy-rounders" hardly knew the "sporty car" set even existed, and vice-versa.

Having arrived at Indianapolis, Ebb incurred even further disdain by purchasing his own car from John Zink. In those days, "buying your way in" was an unpardonable sin. It took him a while, just as it had Ray Crawford a few years earlier, but Ebb earned his spurs, so to speak, by racing an occasional Midget, and by qualifying for the '61 "500". Ebb was so sincere, gracious and laid back

that he eventually broke down all but a few barriers. He placed a distant 14th in the '62 "500" and qualified A. J. Foyt's backup after being bumped in his own car in '63. He was accused, once again, of buying his way in, but Foyt always contended that it was his own decision to offer the car to Ebb. In January 1966, following a downtown banquet, Ebb threw a party at his gorgeous Houston home which drew a cast of characters that most race organizers would have loved to have had as participants. Roaming around Ebb's home were Foyt, Rodger Ward, Lloyd Ruby, Bobby Unser, Jim Hurtubise, Jimmy McElreath, Bob Christie, Mario Andretti, Paul Goldsmith, Hap Sharp, Clint Brawner, Al Dean, Gus Grissom, Gordon Cooper, Red Adair (the famed oil drilling fire fighter), Jud Larson, who played the organ while Ebb sang, Johnny Rutherford, and countless others.

After accidents at Indianapolis in 1964 and '65, Ebb sat out the '66 season, but decided to try it again in 1967. A little-remembered fact is that Jim Hurtubise actually built two Mallards that year and that Ebb had the second one. He wrecked it heavily in practice and never raced again, reasoning that at the age of 42, he had better heed his wife's plea. He later sold the wrecked Mallard back to Hurtubise so that Herk could cannibalize it for parts.

Many years later, word travelled through the Garage Area that Ebb was going to drive a Foyt Coyote, evidenced by the fact that he had visited the infield hospital for a physical. High above the second turn in the VIP suites on the morning of the final qualifying day, his only comment while watching the track was, "I talked to him about just taking a ride in it, that's all." He never did.

BUD TINGELSTAD

The friendly, black-haired driver from Dayton, placed third behind Don Branson and a young A. J. Foyt in the 1959 Mid-West Sprint car standings and was 9th as a rookie at Indianapolis the following May. He failed to make the 1961 "500" lineup, but he did not miss it again until 1970, when he passed on making an attempt. In September of 1963, he showed up at Trenton without a ride, hooked up with the Federal Engineering team and finished 2nd to

Foyt. The following year, he placed 6th at Indianapolis, 5th in the Championship, and won two Sprint Car races, at Winchester and Salem, subbing for an injured Roger McCluskey.

On some days he would display flashes of greatness. On Labor Day, 1966, he won a 100-mile dirt track event at DuQuoin. In 1968, he drove a rear-engine car at Langhorne, in the words of an official, "Like a man possessed by the devil," placing second to Al Unser. At Indianapolis in 1965 he had taken the very first of the Speedway Lolas up to third before a wheel broke off and sent him into the wall.

Bud was a reliable finisher and his prize money was substantial. He was a neat dresser, and he purchased a Cadillac every year as an indication of his prosperity, but he suffered some personal problems in the mid-1960's and spent considerable time in a Speedway tavern, sometimes for hours on end, in a dark corner, drinking alone. A much happier Tingelstad emerged in 1966 when many of his problems were resolved, but some of them began to return as his career drew to a close. When he stepped out of his car to allow Salt Walther a qualification attempt on the final qualifying day of 1972, it was the last time Bud appeared as a participant. He expressed great enthusiasm for a stunt driving show he had become involved in for the rest of the summer, but it was less than he had hoped for. He was injured performing a difficult stunt, and that phase of his career ended about as quickly as it had begun.

Although he never tried it, Bud believed that he could still race, buttonholing anyone he recognized in the garage area and claiming that he could still do it. His hair turned grey and the annual Cadillac was replaced with a tiny, beaten-up Honda. He died in an Indianapolis hospital in December, 1981, succumbing to a combination of tuberculosis and sclerosis of the liver, remembered by a few as a daring driver who on certain days could race with the best of them.

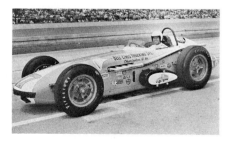

ROGER McCLUSKEY

Roger McCluskey had a good shot at winning the 1962 Indianapolis "500". At the very least he should have finished 3rd, just as he should have a year later. But

over the years, his fortunes at the Indianapolis Motor Speedway ranked along with those of Lloyd Ruby.

Roger, driving in his second "500" in 1962, led briefly during pit stops, and was engaged in a wheel-to-wheel duel for second place with Len Sutton when he overcooked it in a turn and spun out of the race. In 1963, he was running third as Parnelli Jones took the white flag. Trying to get into the same lap with Parnelli, he spun through the second turn and out of the race about four miles from home.

In 1969, as a teammate to A. J. Foyt, he ran second for several laps, dropped way back when he ran out of fuel just before making a stop, and still made it all the way back up the ladder to third before dropping out late in the race.

He seemed to score at every race track except the Speedway, winning the USAC Sprint Car crown in 1963, and coming back from a broken arm to win it again in 1966. Once out of Sprints, having decided there was nothing left to win there, he embarked on a tirade of USAC Stock Car racing and won that title twice also. In 1972 he won the third annual Ontario 500, and a year later, the USAC Championship for Indianapolis cars, having sought that title for fourteen seasons.

McCluskey raced until 1979, winning the August Milwaukee 200 in his 230th Championship start. During the winter he began more and more, at the age of 49, to consider the post of USAC Director of Competition, which had been offered to him on several occasions over the years. He decided to accept it, and in 1981 did something that he had avoided throughout his racing days: moving permanently from Tucson, Arizona to the Indianapolis area.

Having built racing cars in addition to driving them for better than thirty years there is little that McCluskey does not know about racing, his lengthy career coupling with his friendly rapport with people in all phases of the sport to make him one of racing's most respected officials.

ELMER GEORGE

It has been said that racing Sprint cars on the steeply-banked, paved half-mile ovals at Dayton, Salem and Winchester separated the men from the boys. In 1957, the acknowledged master of the

"Hi-banks" was Elmer George, a tough customer from Salinas, California who bore a striking resemblance to singer Andy Williams.

Elmer arrived in the Mid-West in 1954 with a driver named Johnnie Key, who was fatally injured later that summer and for whom a memorial race is still conducted in northern California. By 1956, Elmer had become the third-ranking Sprint car driver of the Mid-West, scoring points on dirt, but having adapted amazingly well to the all-out 30-lap blasts around the above-mentioned tracks. He drove HOW specials in Championship, Sprint and occasional Midget races for Mari Hulman, who happened to be the daughter of Speedway owner Tony Hulman. Early in 1957, Elmer and Mari were married.

Elmer qualified for his first of three 500 mile races that May, but was eliminated when he rammed a car driven by Eddie Russo while lining up for the start during the parade lap. Elmer won the Syracuse Championship race that September and finished 10th in the Championship standings in addition to winning the Sprint title. He had a short temper and ran into occasional conflicts with officials, the most serious of which cost him a one-year suspension from mid-way through 1959 until 1960.

Although he was one of the leading Sprint car drivers and an outstanding Championship driver on dirt tracks, Elmer just didn't have a happy time of it at Indianapolis. It was five years before he qualified for the second time in 1962. The car lasted 146 laps, but not before A. J. Foyt and Paul Russo had both driven relief laps in it and given up. Elmer was in the lineup again in 1963, but around for only 21 laps. He gave up entirely after waving off an attempt in 1964, and although he half-heartedly took his helmet and driving apparel to the Rossburg Sprint opener in April 1966, he never drove again.

Elmer headed up a variety of departments at the Speedway, finally settling with the Radio Network, of which he was director for several years. In a bizarre domestic dispute at his home in Terre Haute on the evening of the 1976 race, Elmer was shot to death by an employee.

TROY RUTTMAN

The Troy Ruttman who came all the way up to second before dropping out at Indianapolis in 1962 was a considerably slimmed-down version of the Troy Ruttman who had won the race ten years earlier. Bespectacled, thin and studious looking now, the six-foot, three-inch Troy had ballooned to 245 pounds when he won the 1952 race, competing there for the fourth time, and at the age of only 22.

Ruttman had begun racing with an

altered birth certificate and probably had achieved more by the age of 17 than most drivers could in a career. He won the California Roadster Association title in 1947, repeated it in 1948 and added the URA West Coast "blue" title for Offenhauser-powered Midgets the same year. He led the 1949 Arlington Downs Championship race, won in his first-ever Mid-West Sprint race, wound up second in the season's points, qualified for the front row at Sacramento, and had driven in his first "500", all before he was out of his teens! Then he became the first driver to unofficially lap at Indianapolis at over 135 mph, won the Mid-West Sprint Championship, the Pacific Coast Sprint Championship, and the "500", all by the time he was barely 22.

A freak arm injury in August of 1952 kept him out of racing for almost two years, and he was never after able to attain the success he had prior to the accident. But he still continued to be a tough contender at Indianapolis, leading in 1957, '60 and '61 before breaking down each time, driving the cars to the limit.

Finally in July, 1964, Troy announced his retirement from racing after almost twenty seasons, the truly remarkable thing being that he was still only 34 years old!

He never relented once he had hung up the goggles, but not long after that his teenaged son began to race, tragically to be fatally injured in 1969 at the age of only 19.

Several years later, another Ruttman came to the fore, Joe Ruttman, Troy's younger brother by eighteen years. Joe won the USAC Stock Car Championship in 1980 and then headed for the NASCAR Grand National ranks after eyeing Indianapolis himself quite closely.

After some stormy years during the late 1950's, which even drew a suspension for "conduct detrimental to racing", a mature 52-year-old Troy Ruttman now operates the family business, Ruttman's World on Wheels in Plymouth, Michigan, a huge dealership for motorcycles and snowmobiles.

BOBBY GRIM

Competing in the Indianapolis "500" was merely icing on the cake in the career of Bobby Grim. He was 34 years old when he made his first appearance there in 1959, and he had already been racing

successfully for more than twelve seasons.

He was the third-ranking sprint car driver with CSRA in 1948, and by the early 1950's became one of the leading lights with IMCA. After finishing as runner-up for several years, Bobby, driving the famous Hector Honore Bardahl "Black Deuce", won the IMCA title in four consecutive years between 1955 and '58. He decided to retire from IMCA at the end of the 1958 season, having won 183 feature events with the organization.

In his first USAC Championship start, at Sacramento at the end of '58, he qualified third, and in his first Indianapolis start, he wedged himself into the middle of the second row. During the event, he suffered an unusual injury. When his engine began to falter, he raised his arm to warn the drivers behind him of his plight and running at double the speed he was normally used to, his arm was pulled from the socket, causing him shocking pain. He managed to get back to the pits, but was through for the day. In spite of not finishing, he was declared "Rookie-of-the-Year".

Bobby was never quite able to adapt to USAC Championship cars as he had with IMCA sprints, but he held Tony Bettenhausen off to win the 1960 Syracuse 100, and was second and third in the Trenton 150 mile races of 1963 and 1965 respectively. He drove in nine "500"'s, placing tenth twice, and succeeded in 1966 in qualifying the last true roadster.

Bobby gave up racing in 1970 and still lives in Indianapolis. He makes a good living driving a gasoline truck, and keeps his ear close to the ground for racing news through the children he raised. Bobby, Jr. works for the Goodyear Racing Division, and drives Midgets from time to time. After the senior Grim's good friend, Frankie Luptow, a three-time IMCA Champion, was fatally injured in 1952, Bobby married his widow and raised Frankie's daughter. She is now married to dirt track specialist, Sheldon Kinser, and a happier father-in-law/son-in-law arrangement there could hardly be.

DAN GURNEY

Nineteen sixty-two was Dan Gurney's first year at the Indianapolis Motor

Speedway, and Dan was required to run through all of the "rookie" procedures, as with any first time entrant, in spite of having become one of the world's best-known drivers.

Born in New York state, the son of an opera singer, Dan formed an interest in cars and motorcycles at an early age and took up sports car racing in California in 1955, when he was 24. By 1958, Dan had become one of the country's outstanding drivers, winning the fledgling United States Auto Club's Road Racing Championship in a privately-owned Ferrari with such verve that he was invited to drive for the factory in Europe the following year. He made his debut in the 1959 French Grand Prix in July and was second in the German Grand Prix the following month.

His arrival at Indianapolis in 1962 was marked by several notable incidents. He was entered in the John Zink Trackburner, the first turbine-powered car to actually be entered for the race. The car he drove in the race, Mickey Thompson's Harvey Aluminum Buick, was the first American-built rear-engined car of the modern era and the first in many years to qualify with a stock production engine. Perhaps of greater significance was that Dan invited Colin Chapman of Lotus over to see the race, and even paid his passage. Chapman was so enthralled by the potential of a lightweight, rear-engined car at Indianapolis that he flew home, designed a car, aligned himself with Ford Motor Company for engines, reimbursed Gurney for the trip, and returned in 1963 with the stunning Lotus Powered By Ford team of Gurney and Jim Clark.

In 1965, Dan, who had now won three World Championship Grand Prix events, formed his own organization, All-American Racers, for the purpose of building and racing all types of cars. In 1967 he won the Belgium Grand Prix with his Eagle/Gurney-Weslake, and for the next two years was runner-up at Indianapolis, the initial one in 1968 coming behind Bobby Unser, who won in a Gurney-conceived Eagle.

Dan retired as a driver at the end of the 1970 season and continued to field cars for drivers like Bobby Unser (1971 through 1975 and again in 1978), Pancho Carter (1976 and 1977), Mike Mosley (1979 to date), and occasionally for Vern Schuppan, Jerry Grant, Wally Dallen-

bach, Jim Malloy, and others. In January, 1980, almost ten years after he had retired, he decided to compete in the Riverside "500" NASCAR stock car race "just for fun" and managed to qualify seventh!

Tall and exceedingly handsome, the fair-haired Gurney apparently continues to be embarrassed by public adulation. In spite of years in the limelight as an international star, winner of four Grand Prix, winner of the LeMans 24-hour race, and so many more; even at the age of 51, when he is recognized by an adoring enthusiast, Dan bows his head, grins, and blushes about as easily as anyone you've ever seen.

CHUCK HULSE

Quick-moving, quick-speaking, vibrant Chuck Hulse used to please dirt fans to no end as one of the last of the rim riders, placing the right rear tire right up against the outside guardrail and churning up roostertails of dirt.

He came from Downey, California, a sprint car standout who won the CRA title in 1959. It took him until his third shot before he made it into the Indianapolis field for the first time in 1962, on the Federal Engineering team, but his performances during the rest of that year earned him a seat with Dean Van Lines for '63. Chuck was the seventh ranking driver of 1963, placing eighth at Indianapolis, among other top finishes. The most notable was a second to Rodger Ward in the season finale, the last Championship race ever held at the Arizona State Fairgrounds one-mile dirt oval in Phoenix.

Chuck also finished fourth in the Sprint Car standings in 1963, much to the chagrin of Dean Van Lines chief mechanic Clint Brawner, who did not care for the dangerous cars. Against Brawner's wishes, Chuck went over to New Bremen, Ohio for a sprint race on May 3, 1964 and was one of several drivers to be hospitalized during the long afternoon. Chuck was soon back at Indianapolis trying to pass the physical, but his eyesight had been impaired so severely by the accident it took him two years to recover to the point where he could be accepted again.

In 1966 Chuck was back. Racing had changed quite a bit in two years, but he adapted to rear-engine cars quite well.

Whenever he got the call to drive a good dirt car, he was outstanding. Chuck was a friendly guy, talkative, helpful to new drivers, often chuckling a throaty chuckle, and grinning to display an exceptionally white set of teeth. He was also a good showman, turning his back to the crowd during driver introductions before the start of a race, and then turning around to wave with both hands as his name was announced.

For many years, Chuck was employed by Firestone and ran a tire store for the company in California. In the early part of 1968, he was offered the ride with the Myron Caves Gerhardt which, unfortunately was shod with Goodyears. Chuck ran a couple of races for the team but switched during May to the Leader Card team, which had brought him back in 1966. It also used Goodyears. Chuck caught the wall slightly once after a couple of days in the Leader card entry and decided he just didn't feel right racing anymore. Shortly after that, he was relieved of his Firestone store.

The word was out several years later that Chuck was considering racing again, but he did not. There is, however, a Chuck Hulse, Jr., who is doing quite well with CRA.

JIMMY DAYWALT

From Wabash, Indiana came Jimmy Daywalt, young, handsome, daring, and intense. He was outgoing, photogenic, friendly, and possessor of an occasional temper.

Only 24 when he made his Indianapolis debut in 1949 with the shoestring-budgeted Bill and Bud's Motor Sales Special, Jimmy had become well-known to Mid-western racing fans for his exploits in Sprint cars on banked tracks like Winchester, Dayton and Fort Wayne. It took until 1953 for him to make the lineup at Indianapolis for the first time, but he went the distance unaided, in atrocious heat, to finish sixth and win the "Rookie-of-the-Year" award. The following year, driving a new Sumar roadster for Coca-Cola magnate Chapman Root, Jimmy qualified for the middle of the front row and led eight laps of the race. Delayed by a lengthy pit stop, he banged his fists on the side of the cockpit in frustration. Later, while trying to catch the leaders again, he tangled with Pat Flaherty, who was relief driving for

Jim Rathmann, and two of them spun out.

Daywalt raced for several more years, but was never a front-runner after that. In 1955, Sumar entered a car which featured a fully enclosed streamlined body. Perhaps unnerved by not being able to see the wheels, Jimmy found that the more the streamlining was removed, the faster he could go, finally qualifying the car with virtually all of it removed. He finished ninth.

He crashed in the 1956 race, suffering some head injuries, and crashed again in 1957. In 1959, in an incident which virtually escaped unnoticed, Jimmy qualified on an "off" day with the third fastest qualifying speed of the year, driving one of the old Federal Engineering roadsters. In 1960 he qualified a car and withdrew from it after the pre-race "carburetion" runs, claiming that it had been changed so much since qualifying that he longer felt secure in it. Dempsey Wilson subbed for him on race day and was through in eleven laps.

Jimmy was back to drive in two more 500 milers before retiring after failing to qualify for the 1963 event. One of the original lecturers on the Champion Spark Plug Highway Safety Program, Jimmy hit the society pages in 1953 when he married a lovely lady named Carmelita, who played the piano and sang on a local television program. As dapper as ever in the first year of his retirement, he showed up on the first qualifying day in a dark suit, white shirt and tie.

In March, 1966, Jimmy was driving a truck to the West Coast when he became ill in Kansas. He was returned to Indianapolis, where he was found to be a very sick man. He lingered for a few days, yellow from a liver disease caused by cancer, week but still happy as he reminisced about a full life. He passed away on April 4, at the age of 41, having requested that the organist at his funeral play light popular tunes instead of the standard hymns. It was very moving.

A. J. FOYT

A. J. Foyt was the king of the roost in 1962, and while he does not win as often as he once did, he is still just that in most people's eyes, amazingly enough, twenty years later.

Foyt was the defending National Champion and race winner in 1962,

driving the Bowes Seal Fast #1 in his fifth "500". He had come up from Houston, Texas with some friends in 1953 to see the race, and returned in 1956, stopping off across the street the night before to compete in the West 16th Street Midget races. In 1957 he spent the summer in the Mid-West, following the Midget trail, driving Sprints wherever possible, and even making a quartet of Championship starts. Al Dean gave him a rookie test at Indianapolis in 1958 and Foyt made the lineup, something he would still be doing a quarter of a century later. In fact, when he did it for the 25th consecutive time in 1982, he qualified for the outside of the front row, and led the first 23 laps, lapping drivers who weren't even born when he started the race for the first time.

Foyt's 1982 "500" was his 287th USAC Championship start, his 67th win in that classification coming at Pocono in 1981. His prize money in Championship racing alone exceeds three million dollars, with another half million accounted for in other divisions of USAC. He runs a large Chevrolet dealership in Houston, has invested earnings in oil since the early 1960's, and is building a huge stable of race horses, which he sometimes blames for having stolen his attention from race car preparation.

Foyt's desire to win is incredible, and his acceptance of anything less than first is usually far from gracious. It matters not what the stakes are, or what the event is, for that matter. If there were no such thing as automobile racing, Foyt would be competing, and frequently winning, at something.

DICK RATHMAN

They used to call Dick Rathman the braver Rathmann, and that is no spelling error you have just run across. Dick dropped the second "n" of the family name when signing autographs sometime in the 1950's. And to add to the confusion, his name is not Richard, but James. Younger brother, Jim Rathmann, who won in 1960 and was three times runner-up, was christened Richard. They swapped identifications so that Jim (as we know him) could start racing at the age of 16. After he began to enjoy some measure of success, older brother James (Dick) thought he might have a go too.

Dick Rathman came to Indianapolis one year after Jim, driving the famous

City of Glendale "Pots and Pans" Special for a young A. J. Watson in 1950. After being the second person to drop out of the race, and not faring too well in the next few Championship events, Dick headed south to start competing with the new NASCAR organization for stock car racing. He became one of the top performers, placing third in the final standings ahead of literally hundreds of others in '53, and was also 4th in 1954 and 5th in '52. He had won 13 Grand nationals when he decided in 1956 to return to Indianapolis, after staying away for five years. He qualified for the inside of the second row and crashed in what was believed to have been the final lap. A recheck revealed that a lap had been missed, meaning that he had already finished the race in 5th place, moments before hitting the wall in turn one.

In 1958, his '56 car owner, Lee Elkins, took delivery of a new A. J. Watson chassis and Rathman left the owner he had been driving for in order to take it over. Daily he and Ed Elisian, a close friend, battled between five and six o'clock each night for the psychological advantage of turning the fastest practice lap. Elisian appeared to have the slight edge, and many believed that he had secured the pole position when he made his run early on the first qualifying day. While Rathman was unable to erase Elisian's new one-lap track record an hour later, his four-lap average was superior.

The 1958 opening lap was a tragic affair as Elisian took the lead from Rathman in the opening lap, lost control in turn three and was hit by the pole sitter. The resulting crash, which directly or indirectly involved most of the field, took the life of the very popular Pat O'Connor and eliminated seven of the cars right on the spot, including Elisian's and Rathman's, which was broken into two halves.

Dick, who was much huskier than Jim, never had very much to say and kept a pretty low profile. He qualified for the race each year until 1964, when he finished 7th in one of the last of the front-engined Offies, and then just drifted away, discouraged with the direction racing was taking at the time. He visits the track every couple of years or so, but goes virtually unnoticed.

EDDIE JOHNSON

Eddie Johnson's height was listed as 5 foot 5½ inches, which had to have been an exaggeration! High-voiced, and displaying a wide grin, Eddie was known as a reliable finisher, a qualifier of some of the oldest and most unlikely cars in the lineup, and later, for arriving without a car even assigned to him.

Eddie was born in Ohio, began racing after his family had moved to California,

and knew Johnnie Parsons before the two of them started their careers in Midgets before WWII. Parsons gives Eddie credit for several lines, including the phrase used when driving through an out-of-the-way location, "Man, this is 199th and Boondock."

Eddie returned to Ohio, specifically to Cuyahoga Falls, near Cleveland, and raced out of there throughout his "500" career. The only times he did not make the lineup between 1952 and 1966 were in '53 and '54, when he was the last person to be "bumped" (both times!) and ended up competing as a relief driver anyway. He was flagged off at the end in 1952, '55, and '56 and went the distance in '58, '59 and '60. The latter was his best shot, when he drove a Jim Robbins-owned car to sixth. He continued to make the lineup year after year, qualifying one of only four Offy roadsters in the 1965 race and finishing 10th with it. He holds the distinction (for what it is worth) of being the only driver to go from a roadster to a rear-engine car, back to a roadster and back to a rear-engine car in four consecutive years!

In 1966, at which time he was still making an occasional appearance in a Midget, Eddie drove in his last "500". Having avoided the huge first-lap accident and several others that followed, Eddie kept rolling along in the steadily depleting field until he, too, was obliged to drop out after logging in 175 laps. He watched the last twenty minutes of the race and still wound up seventh, figuring that at 47, that might be as well as he was ever going to fare. He had been working for a plastics manufacturer and was offered a very responsible position contingent upon his retirement as a racing driver. He accepted the post and turned down car owner Tassi Vatis's pleas to return in 1967.

On the evening of the 1974 Pocono "500", Eddie was flying his private aircraft in the Cleveland area and heading for the Cuyahoga airfield. He was caught up in severe weather and never made it home.

PAUL GOLDSMITH

In 1954, when Joe Leonard won his first of three AMA Grand National Championships on motorcycles, second place was taken by his Harley-Davidson teammate, Paul Goldsmith. The tall,

dark and silent St. Clair Shores, Michigan rider later gained fame as driver of Smokey Yunick's black and gold stock cars, and in 1958 scored somewhat of a sensation by adapting to the Indianapolis Motor Speedway, qualifying a black and gold Yunick roadster in his first try.

Paul was one of several drivers eliminated in the first-lap multiple accident that took the life of Pat O'Connor, and so was still little more than a rookie when he returned the following year. This time, driving the Demler "laydown" which had carried George Amick to second a year earlier, Goldsmith followed Rodger Ward, Jim Rathmann, Johnny Thomson, and Tony Bettenhausen home to fifth. In 1960, he advanced still further by placing third behind the epic Rathmann and Ward duel.

In spite of this, and in spite of the fact that Goldsmith drove in the "500" three more times after that, his total number of career starts in open cockpit cars was only eight! He drove six times in the "500" and twice ('59 and '61) in the June 100 miler at Milwaukee. The rest of the time, the reclusive Goldsmith was in Stock Cars, winning the last beach race ever held at Daytona (1958), winning the USAC Stock Car title twice (1961 and '62), and competing in a total of 127 NASCAR Grand Nationals.

His last appearance at Indianapolis was in 1965, when his non-competitive car was withdrawn on the final qualifying weekend, but he continued racing with NASCAR until 1969. He retired after a trio of third place finishes (the Atlanta 500 included) to concentrate on a number of businesses he was involved in with Ray Nichels, his Indianapolis crew chief of '59 and '60.

GENE HARTLEY

The psychologist who was trying to analyze the makeup of the average

Indianapolis driver would have been thoroughly stumped when he got to Gene Hartley! The Roanoke, Indiana second-generation driver claimed to be neither obsessed by a competitive spirit, a will to win, or any of those other handles that are supposed to explain the reason for race drivers doing what they do. In fact, Gene said he didn't even *like* racing, which wasn't really true, since he was occasionally noted as a spectator when he could easily have been elsewhere. But apparently he could live without it.

He came from a racing family, his uncle having been an entrant in the 1924 Indianapolis race and his father a driver from 1922 until he was well up into his 70's! Gene found himself in racing almost before he knew what was going on, and was able to make a living as a Midget driver while still in his early twenties maintaining that this was where his motivation lay.

Gene made it to Indianapolis in 1950, at the age of 24, and made it ten times in 13 attempts before giving up during practice in 1963. He never ran at the head of the pack, but had a reputation for "bringing them home", placing 10th once, 11th three times, and being around to take the checker a couple of other times as well.

Gene's great forté was midget racing, where he won the Championship in 1959 and was third place man for two years after that. He won 33 features under USAC sanction, and numerous others prior to that with AAA, having run in literally hundreds of Midget races during his career. The remarkable thing about his five consecutive top three rankings between 1957 and '61 is that he still only picked and chose races where he thought he could make a dollar. Never once, during his remarkable career, did he ever race on the West Coast, not even to try to grab an extra point or two, which might have given him another title. "For what?" he'd reason, "I never went anywhere unless I thought I could come back with more than I left with, and a trip out to California had to be a loser. So why go?"

Gene had a rather malicious sense of humor and was very positive in his statements. He seemed to take delight in shocking people with his observations, sounding almost as if he were simply saying them for effect, laughing after saying them, but ready to back up anything if challenged. Of his finest-ever Championship finish, a second to George Amick at Langhorne in 1956, he brushed it off, saying, "That's the only time I was ever there. I didn't care for the place, so I never went back. Look it up. I was never there again."

For several years, Gene and a long-time friendly rival, Leroy Wariner, operated the Indianapolis Speedrome track, but Gene eventually sold out his share. He did well as a sharply-dressed sales rep for an accessory company, moved to Florida for a while, and in typical Hartley style decided he didn't like it and in 1981 returned to Indiana.

PAUL RUSSO

Back in 1962, the tenure of the race driver was still not nearly as long as it is now, making the inclusion of Paul Russo in the lineup quite amazing at the time. The short, dark, gravel-voiced Russo was 48 years old, several times a grandfather, and had made his first Indianapolis start 22 years earlier in 1940!

Younger brother of four-time "500" competitor Joe Russo, and part of a huge family which produced several race drivers, Pudgy Paul was a leading Midget driver in the late 1930's. In the first post-war "500" in 1946, he made the middle of the front row with one of the strangest machines ever, Lou Fageol's oddity, which was powered by two Midget engines, placed sideways fore and aft of the driver, one powering the front wheels and the other the rear wheels. During the winter of 1949/50 he and Ray Nichels constructed the car known as Basement Bessie, so called because it was built in a basement and had to be partly dismantled in order to get out! It was no laughing matter on the track, however, Paul winning a race with it at Springfield and being a contender for the National Championship until incurring injuries two-thirds through the season. Even while recuperating, Paul campaigned Bessie with considerable success in the hands of Sam Hanks and Johnnie Parsons, and the car was still at championship races fifteen years later!

Russo gained his greatest notoriety at an age when most drivers had given up or been forced out of the profession. He was 42 years old when he signed on to drive the Novi in 1956, housed for the first time in a Kurtis rear-drive chassis. After starting in a disappointing eighth position, having been the only person over 146 in practice, Paul swept through the field to lead at 10 laps and was still there when a tire let go in the first turn of his 22nd lap. He smashed the wall but was unhurt, returning to lead the race again and finish 4th a year later.

The ferocious-looking, growling Russo, who was actually a friendly person, came awfully close to making the 1964 race at the age of 50, only to be bumped out late to the role of first alternate. He was even entered in 1965, but decided that due to a recurring back problem, he would not compete.

For many years, he was employed by Dana Corporation as a field representative for Perfect Circle piston rings, attending all the major races, making no bones about who he did and didn't like, and for the last years of his life driving the pace car at USAC Championship events. A couple of days after the 1976 Daytona "500", which he serviced, he was found in his hotel room, a heart attack victim at 61.

JACK TURNER

"Cactus" Jack Turner, two-time Midget Champion from Seattle, Washington, was another of those drivers who looked pretty stern in photographs but really wasn't. He was one of several drivers with a receding hairline, but the only one, for a while, to sport a pencil mustache. Jack's pouting lower lip and furrowed eyebrows disguised a very gentle person, who liked to travel, adored his family and preferred to pour his race track earnings into his Seattle home rather than visit the taverns. If he had a vice, it was golf and Jack was pretty good.

He had already won the Midget Championship twice and had a fine year of Sprint Car racing under his belt when he was brought to the Speedway to drive Ernie Ruiz's Travelon Trailer special in 1956. Having done most of the mechanical preparation on his Midgets for years, Jack was able to pitch right in and work on the larger Offenhauser engine in his roadster. He finished 11th in the 1957 race, and sadly, that was the last time this underrated driver finished. His car was badly damaged in the horrendous first-lap accident of 1958, and he subsequently pulled out, after struggling along for a few laps. In 1959, he defied superstition by driving a green car for Ernie Ruiz, and had it up to second at one point before retiring. He spun out while making a late qualification attempt in 1960, but came back to make the field again in '61 and '62. He was up to second again in '61 when A. J. Shepherd, Bill Cheesbourg and Roger McCluskey tangled with each other while trying to avoid the stunned Don Davis, who was strolling across the track as if in a trance

after wrecking his car. Turner had no choice but to run over Shepherd's car. He became airborne and flipped wildly in the air, becoming level at one point with the upper tier of the grandstands. He was helped from the car badly shaken, but able to walk away with some aid, suffering only an injured knee. The following year he was coming into the mainstretch when he found Bob Christie, Chuck Rodee, Elmer George and Allen Crowe spinning in front of him. Jack flipped again. This time, he climbed from the car, apparently uninjured. As he was helped into the ambulance, his foot slipped from the step and he broke his toe!

Back again in 1963, Jack was a teammate to Eddie Sachs. He was out practicing early on the morning of the second qualifying day when he lost control coming out of the fourth turn. What followed was one of the most incredible accidents ever recorded. The car turned partially sideways and then climbed up on two wheels. It then began to corkscrew through the air, nose pointed forward, turning over and over, then turned sideways and began to barrel roll. It was estimated that the total number of revolutions was in the region of sixteen.

Long-time friend Johnny Boyd raced to the hospital, expecting the worst. Jack was sitting up in bed, frowning, pouting, arms folded across his chest. He looked up, saw John and grumbled "I QUIT!"

He did, and these days he resides quietly in Seattle, a sales rep for several accessory companies and an occasional house guest and travel companion of Mr. and Mrs. Len Sutton.

BOB CHRISTIE

Blessed with a name like Bob "Caveman" Christie and hailing from a place called Grants Pass, Oregon, this sounded like one character you wouldn't want to tangle with. Photographs backed this up, as the thin-featured, balding Bob Christie looked a little on the mean side!

It was all an illusion.

Bob Christie was, and is, a delightful, easy-going person who never seemed to lose perspective of racing and his own role in it. He hung around the Speedway for years, and was one of those people who never ran at the front, but whom one was always happy to see in the lineup. After

failing to qualify in his first two attempts, he made the race eight consecutive times between 1956 and 1963, and was on the track trying to qualify as late as 1967.

Bob came out of the northwest with his stock car and competed with AAA in 1953, winding up third in points behind Frank "Rebel" Mundy and Don "Digger" O'Dell, a Chicago driver with whom Bob had his only major run-in. After a series of door-banging episodes with O'Dell, Bob became so incensed one night that he fell back a few feet, ran down through the infield to cut off a turn and headed for the outside wall, timing it perfectly so that he would tee-bone O'Dell. He got more than he bargained for as he almost got blinded with bright light. It transpired that O'Dell had illegally smuggled on board a small tank of nitro methane to give him some added zip when he needed it. His car lit up like an arc lamp when the contents spilled out in the crash.

At Indianapolis, he was one of several drivers who gained a reputation for "bringing them home" and was flagged off at the end of the race in 1956, '57, '60 (when he was tenth) and '63. He was running eighth in '58 with only eleven laps to go when he spun off into the infield. A year later, he placed third in the only Championship race ever held at Daytona International Speedway.

Bob gave up after failing to qualify for the '67 race in an A. J. Foyt backup, and for a short time, tended the bar at the Holiday Inn across from the Speedway, a job which he handled with entertaining grace and efficiency.

He went to work in a Sears automotive service department and was transferred after a while to the facility in downtown New York City. He spent a couple of years there, commuting from Connecticut by bus until he tired of that and moved to the W.G. Grace Company in Cleveland. He now lives in Columbus, Ohio and makes the trip to the track in May. His agile mind is always conjuring up amusing ways to circumvent the current rules, and memories of past accomplishments, his own included, remain pleasantly accurate.

ALLEN CROWE

Of all the drivers who competed in the 1962 "500", perhaps the least is known of a very pleasant individual from Spring-

field, Illinois named Allen Crowe. The unobtrusive Crowe arrived on the Championship scene in the summer of 1961, after ten years of racing stock cars in Illinois and Missouri, and had a brief run which ended with a fatal accident in June, 1963.

He competed in five Championship races in 1961, in addition to making his way into 29 Midget feature lineups, two of which he won. In 1962 he achieved his lifelong ambition by qualifying for the Indianapolis "500", but it unfortunately ended after only 17 laps, when he became tangled up in the Jack Turner, Elmer George, Bob Christie, and Chuck Rodee accident. He drove in seven other Championship races, making the top ten in five of them, including the Syracuse 100, where he placed 5th. A bad flip in the Hoosier Hundred just about wrapped him up for the season, but remarkably enough he ended up the 14th highest point scorer for the year. He was 8th out of 138 ranking Midget drivers, in spite of competing in little more than half the races, and also placed 11th in the Sprint Car division.

In 1963, Allen was back to make it into his second "500" lineup, but after 47 laps was involved in another accident. He headed back to the Sprint wars, where he had started the season in great fashion. He had finished 1st, 2nd, 3rd, 4th and 5th twice in his first six outings and was running second only to Roger McCluskey for the title. On the 13th lap of the feature event at New Bremen, Ohio, on June 2, only three days after Indianapolis, Allen flipped his Iddings sprinter and was injured fatally.

The pleasant Allen was memorialized by friends in a 100 mile USAC Stock Car race, conducted at the Illinois State Fairgrounds in August of that year, and which was scheduled to be held for the twentieth consecutive season in 1982.

CHUCK RODEE

Chuck Rodee was the professional racing name of a Chicagoan named Charles Rodeghier, who was one of the nation's top Midget drivers for almost twenty years, and who managed to find his way into the Indianapolis starting field on two occasions.

Diminutive, wiry, graying Chuck Rodee had twinkling eyes and a confident, bare suggestion of a smile on

his face most of the time, but not far under the surface lurked a temper which often became unleashed immediately after a race was over. It was just his way of letting off steam. He'd yell at an official or another driver, and after he'd said his piece, the twinkle and the "almost" smile would return.

Chuck was third behind Jack Turner and Shorty Templeman in the final midget season conducted by AAA in 1955, and runner-up to Templeman in USAC's initial year of 1956. He managed to finish 8th the first time he drove a Championship car, but the result was a little misleading. Only 13 cars had started the April Trenton 100 miler in 1958 and Chuck finished high based only on the number of laps he completed before he crashed and broke his arm!

He had three shots at Indianapolis before he finally made it into the field in 1962, driving the Ernie Ruiz Travelon Trailer roadster. He was out of it before 50 miles were reached, crunched up in turn four when Elmer George, Jack Turner, Allen Crowe and Bob Christie all had their accident.

It was three years before Chuck made it again, this time with Wally Weir's rear-engined Offy Shrike. He was still not destined to go far; engine trouble had him watching by 28 laps. In August of 1965, the Championship cars competed on the 1½ mile super speedway in Atlanta, Georgia for the first time, and in his best finish in this type of car, Chuck placed fifth.

Enjoying his best year in the Midget division in nine years, he closed the season in third place, and opened 1966 in fine style by winning three of the first four events. Chuck went through a period of being unusually moody and argumentative, so much so that USAC officials set him down for a month during the Spring of '66. He was back in the USAC office days later, having changed completely. He was bright, friendly and the word was out that he had called a meeting of the family and that profanity had been banned around his house.

A. J. Watson signed Chuck on to the leader Cards team in May, at a time when that operation was besieged with driver problems. In no time at all, Chuck gave the crew the biggest smiles they had worn in months. Looking for a good qualifying run with the best ride he had ever had at Indianapolis, Chuck never made it to the green flag. He spun in the first turn of his final warmup, backed into the wall with colossal force and succumbed a couple of hours later.

BOB VEITH

Bob Veith acquired the nickname "Traction" during the 1950's because his weight sometimes hovered around 250 pounds or so. On the surface, he seemed to have none of the attributes expected in a driver, appearing to be quite lazy, ambling around as if walking took just too much effort. Some owners even felt that he could have finished much higher than he did, believing that he rarely extended himself. Still, his record was pretty good.

Bob did most of his early racing in the northern California and made his first trip to the Mid-West in 1953. Rides were hard to come by at first, but he hung around, even serving as a crew member for Jimmy Reece in the "500" of 1954, until he eventually began to hookup with owners. Some good runs in Sprints led to Championship cars, and four good showings there vaulted him to 12th in the 1955 rankings. Federal Engineering gave him a rookie test in 1956, and having made the race, he cruised home to 7th and the Rookie-of-the-Year honors.

If Bob was guilty as charged by finishing 5th when he should have been 3rd, or 4th when he might have been 2nd, friends say that on the morning of the 1958 "500", there was rare determination in his eyes. He was starting on the inside of row two, only a tick slower than the pole sitter, and there was an aura of "winner" about him. It ended after three-quarters of a lap when he was unable to avoid plunging into the beginnings of the huge accident in turn three. He kept under control, but after making it around to the pits, the damage to the front end of his car was considered too severe to justify continuing.

Bob's next really spirited run came six years after that when he drove a rear-engined car for the first time in the 1964 "500". Discovering that his car possessed exceptional handling qualities, he made it all the way up to 3rd before dropping out. Inspired by this fine run, he arrived in 1965 considerably scaled down and was again moving toward the front when he had to drop out.

For the final years of his career, he gained the reputation for being able to qualify at the last minute with virtually no practice time. Inasmuch as he wound up driving at Indianapolis only, he would arrive in May not having driven anything for eleven months. He'd sit around the Champion room, listening to Freddie Agabashian and Johnny Boyd telling stories, then amble off to play a little golf. On the final qualifying weekend, he'd unobtrusively materialize in a driver's uniform, his hair almost completely white. He'd lumber aimlessly down the pit lane swinging his helmet, and park his equipment next to somebody's backup car. He'd take a few practice laps, sometimes less than a dozen, back the car up to the line, and qualify!

Bob's last stint as a driver was in 1970, when he practiced with Mike Mosley's backup car. But he made no attempt to qualify, hanging up his goggles at 45. On his last visit to the track a couple of years ago, Bob was armed with samples of souvenir laminated wall plaques he had become involved in selling, as he continued to make his home in California.

"Please Mister, May I Have A Badge?"

by Donald Davidson

One thousand dollars for a Speedway pit badge? You've got to be kidding!

It is no joke.

Those metal credentials issued to drivers, car owners, mechanics, officials and VIPs have become real collector's items in the last few years, allowing prices on the early ones to skyrocket to ridiculous proportions as collectors desperately strive to build complete sets. It is nearly impossible to locate any of the first four from the pre-war years starting in 1938, but died-in-the-wool collectors have been known to shell out in excess of $1,000 upon locating one. Even the 1946 badge from the first post-war race, which less affluent collectors have resigned themselves to accepting as a more justifiable starting point, seems to fetch $500 without much difficulty.

The price tag begins to tumble after that, the 1947 silver hovering at around $250, while the '48 and '49 silvers might go for $75. Most of the 1950's can be found from about $45 down to $25 or less, diminishing slightly through the 1960's and 1970's. Even so, other than those badges which are passed on as gifts once the most recent race is complete, it is hard to find anyone who will sell one for less than $10, which might strike the non-collector as rather amusing. After all, what can you do with the things once the race is over? It certainly won't get you anywhere. You'll be able to impress a few people with your pre-war acquisition, including some of the guards, who might even remember it when it was new, but as far as getting into the pits with it this year, forget it! The best you can hope for is to have the satisfaction of watching a few people with their tongues hanging out, or

better yet, finding someone who wants it so badly, he is prepared to pay you more than you paid for it yourself. Of course, if you sell, you'll no longer have it to show off and tantalize people with. And maybe the person you sold it to is making a beeline to a fanatic he knows who REALLY wants it. Check the classified ads in National Speed Sport News from time to time and you'll occasionally see an offer of a complete set priced at $10,000! Who knows? Collectors are sometimes motivated by the very challenge of trying to obtain something they've been told is next to impossible to find. The frazzled and exhausted hunter just might pop for the whole set.

The metal credential came about after more than a quarter of a century of standard cardboard pit passes, which were constantly being separated from their string attachments over the period of an entire month. The wear and tear on those used by participants, who had to tie them and untie them to their uniforms day after day, was just too much, and the trips to the registrar's office to apply for a replacement was a hassle for everybody concerned. Thankfully, in 1938, a sturdy metal badge was produced, depicting the old pagoda set inside a surround that resembled a wax seal. The '38 pin and clasp utilized approximately the same principal as was still being used in 1982, and from that year on, the only reason to return to the registrar's office was to replace one which either had been lost, or allegedly so.

The 1939 badge was oval-shaped; the 1940 resembled a police or fireman's badge; the 1941, an oblong; and the '46 based approximately on the shape of the track. These four carried the name of the Indianapolis Motor Speedway Corpora-

tion, and a serial number. In 1947, an impression of the 1946 record-breaking Novi was used, and since then a unique design of some sort has been used each year, including Speedway landmarks, revolutionary cars and so forth.

On several occasions, Speedway brass thought it would be appropriate to feature a likeness of Tony Hulman on the badge, and even had sketches made up for his approval. Genial Tony would predictably nix them preferring to see something else used, but he finally relented in 1970 when the silver anniversary under the Hulman regime was celebrated.

It took a while for the size of the badge to be fairly well standardized, reaching its largest and most cumbersome with a huge mounted Firestone tire in 1952, down to a tiny aerial view of the Speedway in 1964, before levelling off shortly after that to something a little larger.

As the cost of producing the badges increased, so the Speedway began employing outside assistance by permitting accessory firms to tastefully display either an example of their product or the company logo in return for underwriting the cost of the credentials. Monroe was first to do it in 1975, followed by Valvoline, Goodyear, and so on, with Chevrolet appearing on the 41st and most recent unit.

So if you are a one-time participant and you think you might have some old badges up in the attic, or you know someone else who has, it might be worth getting them out. The bronze badges usually go for $5 less than the silvers, except for the early ones, and if you have the raceday backup cards, some collectors are after those as well!

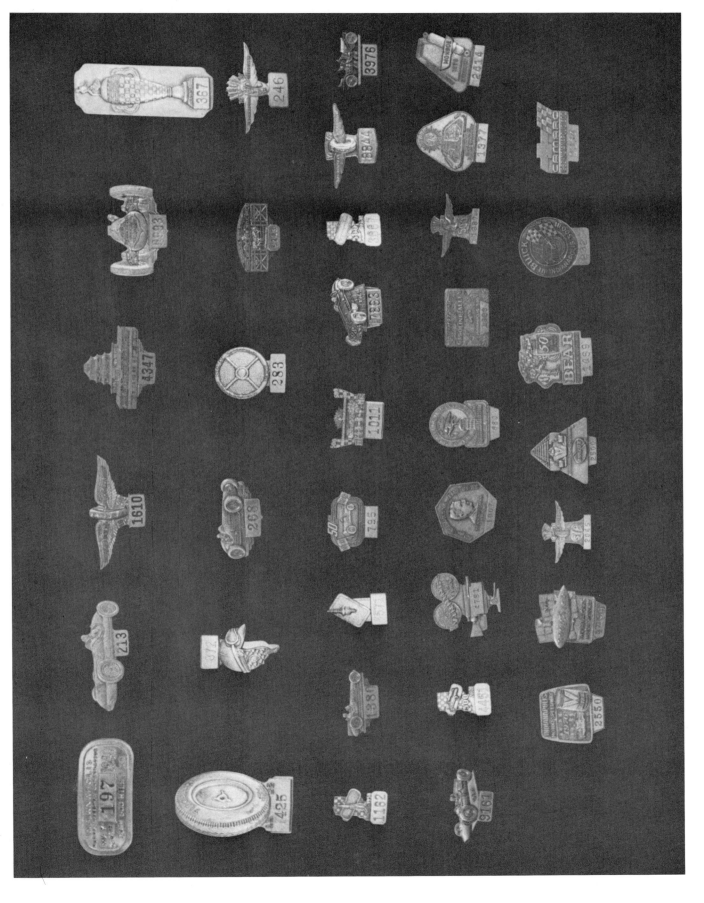

What Goes Up...

by David Scoggan

Remember the intro to the "Twilight Zone" TV show? Rod Serling would intone something like, "You're entering another dimension of space and time..." Not even Mr. Serling could have envisioned this year's breathtaking leap into the Zone by the Penske patrol of Rick Mears and Kevin Cogan.

From 100 mph, to the one minute 150 mph plateau, to the magic 200 mph mountain and all points in between, the so-called speed barriers at Indianapolis have fallen. Even repeated attempts by concerned officials to slow the new breed of Indy car have only created less powerful cars with faster average lap speeds. From 203, to 205, 206, 207, and finally an astonishing 208.7 MPH by Rick Mears — all at 48" of boost (assumedly) *and* a smaller turbocharger than allowed in 1981!!

Is there a "limit" to lap speeds at Indianapolis? Is there truly a "point of no return" where man or machine will refuse to cooperate?

After the tragic month of May, 1973, when unlimitedly boosted drivers flirted with (but failed to surmount the 200 mph mark,) USAC moved swiftly to tame the champ cars. Less turbocharger pressure (with the first pop-off valves implemented) and narrower wings drug 1974's hot laps in the low 190's. A. J. Foyt topped 195 mph qualifying for the 1975 classic (at the '74 boost level of 80"), but a rule revision to 75" found the 1976 pole speed below 190 mph. Again the pencil pushers bumped the legal limit to 80" for 1977 and the 200 mph bubble finally burst; first to Gordon Johncock in March tire tests then Mario Andretti, A. J. Foyt, and Johnny Rutherford in practice. Tom Sneva, however, was the only driver to officially top 200, twice breaking Rutherford's 4-year old track record of 45.21/199.071 mph with successive circuits of 200.401 and 200.535 (44.88 seconds).

By 1978 the 200 mph lap was commonplace for the high-dollar outfits. Top unofficial speed was nailed down by A. J. Foyt at 203.666, although some third turn watches had Tex at around 206 mph on one late afternoon test (he coasted through the electric eye at 202+ because of a yellow light). Once again, Tom Sneva pulled his qualifying rabbit out of the hat with an official lap in 44.20 seconds, or 203.620 mph. Sneva led a front row containing fellow 200 mph averagers Danny Ongais and some rookie named Mears.

Drastic restrictions by USAC (30" of boost reduction for the 1979 season — the first of the CART/USAC war) in attempting to equate the stock-based production engine with the purebred racing Cosworths created an approximate 10 mph speed drop until 1981, when the engine wizards regained lost horsepower through internal modifications and ground-effects chassis allowed the extra power to be put to the pavement. While straightaway speeds are still shy of the flat-bottomed, 850 hp days of 1978 (reportedly 224 on Sneva's 203.6 mark), cornering speeds are astronomically high. Rick Mears estimated his turn times at 205 mph during his top 1982 onslaughts.

The fastest lap in an Indy car on *any* race track set by A J. Foyt in the summer of 1974 on the steep banks of Talladega, Alabama. Foyt white-knuckled his coyote around the 2.6 mile tri-oval to a then-world's closed course record of 217.854, which stood until the late Mark Donohue cleared 221 mph on the same track with the awesome Penske Can-Am Porsche 917-30 (which A. J. later referred to as a "big ol' box with a lot of horsepower"). It is truly inconceivable that Rick Mears' 208.7 lap came within 9 mph of the Foyt Talladega mark on the comparatively flat IMS oval with a still-highly restricted engine.

Mears commented after his blistering pole run that "on a cool evening, with the right engine ... 210 wouldn't be a problem." When asked how fast the Gould PC-10 could travel with 80" of boost, Rick was non-commital. "We would have to change the car totally — wings, everything. It's built for 48" right now ... we'd be going faster, but ... it's hard to tell." (The mind boggles at the thought of a PC-10 running under the wide-open rules of 1973.)

Record holder, Rick Mears, at speed in Roger Penske's No. 1 machine.

[176]

Rick looks happy with his new one and four lap marks.

Texaco Tom Sneva was a little more specific estimating the potential of 200 more horespower in an '82 Indy car. "We would have to be running close to 220 mph. We'd have to be up to 235-240 down the straightaway. You would have to be looking at 1000 horsepower (at 80″ with today's advancements)."

Three-time pole sitter Johnny Rutherford waxed philosophically concerning the limits of speed at Indianapolis. "You really don't know . . . it's like asking how loud is loud or how high is up. You just don't know until you do it."

The tragic crash of Gordon Smiley has created a great hue and cry to again slow down the cars. Ban ground effects, go to a smaller engine formula, eliminate turbocharging; all thought well intended, but the Speedway is in a tenuous position. Spectators *like* to see high speeds and track records, at least in practice and qualifying, and just how can you expect people to pay $5 a head to watch the pole position go at a screaming 172 mph? As Johnny Rutherford stated, "It's show business . . . the mystique for 200 mph is here. When (spectators) read 180 mph headlines and say, 'Hell, they ran 207 last year' — will they be back?" Also, don't think the IMS moguls aren't aware that the NASCAR troops are right there in the speed department; Benny Parsons qualified at over 200 mph for the May race in Talladega. As of now, the Indianapolis Motor Speedway can claim the fastest closed-course racing vehicles in the world. Would they feel any fan effect if they suddenly lost that title?

Mario Andretti, who came closest to the Penske plateau with a 206.6 practice lap, told a local TV interviewer, "What's *too* fast? I'm sure that in due time something will have to be done so we remain somewhere around the 200 mph area and not too much quicker than that, because then it becomes a problem, I think, from a human standpoint."

Maybe that human factor should become a greater consideration than it is today. Trackside technology has lowered the needed driving skills primarily to an oversize breath-holding capacity; some have even suggested a trained chimp could run 190 in a ground-effects car (good luck finding a willing car owner). So is it more challenging to average 205 with ground-effects or 185 without? Do the fans care more about the amount of skill involved or how big the numbers on the stopwatch are?

Many Indy fans actually prefer the one-on-one confrontation of man and machine versus Brickyard of qualifications to the sometimes boring, frequently gut-wrenching 500 mile endurance run. To them, the paramount goal is the fastest lap, the baddest dude on four wheels, the most thrilling ride in motor sports. Will the speeds continue to climb, or will the legislative powers again red-pencil the cars to a "saner" level? Time will tell. . . .

It remains for dreamers to speculate just what the ultimate lap at Indianapolis could be. And as Johnny Rutherford put it, "How loud is loud, how high is up?"

Rod Serling couldn't have said it any better.

Three of the prime movers behind Indy car racing in the Eighties who have seen, and experienced jumps in speed are, from left: Owners Roger Penske, Pat Patrick and driver Bobby Unser.

"So's Your Old Man"

by Jerry Miller

Assignment: Do a story on Indy's second-generation drivers.

Immediate Problem: How many more stories on Pancho, Vuky, Gary B., Tony Lee, and Johnny P. can America take?

Method of Solution: If you've paid any attention to Jimmy Breslin — and very few have since Son of Sam — you end up forcing yourself to look for the obtuse angle, the hiddle seam, of the original assignment.

Eventual Conclusion: Hold on here, they're almost all second-generation drivers!

Think about it a minute, America. Race drivers don't spring up overnight, like dandelions after a good rain. They're more like perennials that bloom constantly in succeeding generations of flowering, 200-mph ambitions.

Sure, maybe the first generations only skin their knuckles at places like Illiana and Skagit, and never give up their jobs at the gas station or the construction site to play the big gigs at Indy and MIS. But they do sow the seeds — those wide-as-America, five-years-old eyes see everything — and the seedlings are likely to sprout up someday in the vicinity of 16th and Georgetown.

That is why "second-generation driver" is an almost meaningless phrase. There aren't that many first-generation drivers, when you get right down to it. At Indy, you probably could squeeze them all into the pace car.

Using the Breslin method of looking at things, also known as the Left Oblique, As-Seen-Through-A-Bourbon-Glass Method, you eventually discover that racing is as much a family tradition as big-city police and fire departments or the plumbers' union. The current crop of heavy foots hasn't fallen that far from the family tree.

So, with no disrepsect to Carter, Vukovich, the Bettenhausens, and Parsons — nice guys all, but too pat an answer for this assignment — the time has come to close the most overlooked generation gap around and open some of the family scrapbooks that don't have any old, yellowed clippings from the Star or News.

The First Digression: Pancho, Billy, Gary, Tony, and Johnny have had to make room for a new member into their particular club —Geoff Brabham. Vuky and JP's fathers put their faces on the Borg-Warner Trophy, but Brabham's dad, Sir Jack, changed the face of Indy racing forever when he showed up in 1961

with his little, green rear-engineed Cooper Climax. That was the first baby step in what became a short march (pun intended) to putting the engine in the rumble-seat instead of under the hood of an Indy-car.

Perfunctory Geoff Brabham Quote: "My father didn't encourage or discourage me. I used to go to all the races he was in, but he wanted to make sure, if I did go, it was my own decision. It took a long time to talk him into helping me, but he's tried to help me as much as he can from then on."

But the roots of Indy's drivers aren't planted only in old 500 year books. It doesn't take a genious to figure out, for example, that if there is an A. J. Foyt, Jr., there must have been an A. J. Foyt, Sr. There is, of course, and he drove some midgets in his day and helped make Victory Lane a family affair in 1967 and 1977 as Junior's chief mechanic.

And, out around Pikes Peak, the Unser brothers of Borg-Warner Trophy fame are still thought of as "the kids." It was father Louis Unser, Sr., and his brothers who drove circles around the old mountain, long before Bobby and Al knew which way was up. He also was the first father in modern times to put three sons in the Indy recordbooks, with older boy Jerry making the '58 race before being killed in a practice-lap crash a year later.

A Note on Brotherhood: What little brother sees big brother do, little brother invariably wants to do, too. A cardinal rule of child-rearing — and Indy racing bloodlines.

Dick Whittington didn't live long enough to see his three sons line up together at Indy, in the same 500 — a recordbook accomplishment that even the Unser brothers (or the Chevrolet brothers, for that matter) couldn't pull off. He only managed to have a reasonably good racing career of his own — and probably endured more cat jokes than Honor Blackman (think about it).

Dick (or R. D.) Whittington drove sprints and Indy-cars back in the '50s, and later owned some racing cars. Sprint car mechanic Willie Davis, later of Gary Bettenhausen fame, worked for him at one time.

So, scratch all three Whittington brothers from the "first-generation drivers" list. Just credit Don, Bill, and Dale with filling up almost a tenth of the '82 Indy field with Dick Whittington's progeny.

"When we were young, our father did a lot of racing," Don, the eldest, recalls, "so

he would be pleased. Our mother is very proud of us."

On the other hand, Ed Sneva may very well live long enough to see his sons not only equal the Whittingtons' Indy achievement, but better it. And, when Tom, Jerry, Jan, and Blaine Sneva all start the same 500, they can write stories about four "second-generation" racers from the same family in the same race.

Tom and Jerry have already planted the family name into the yearbooks, Tom beginning in 1974 and Jerry in '77. Jan has been on the entry list the last couple of years, and Blaine is skinning his knuckles in supermodifieds out around Spokane.

(A fifth Sneva brother, Babe, was killed in a racing crash a few years back.)

And, when it's four for the Indy road, Ed Sneva will know just where the road began. "They've been around racing all their lives," he says, standing along Indy's pit row this May. "They must have been three or four, and they'd sit in the stands with their mother."

The road never left Washington state for broad-shouldered Ed, however. "It got to be another job," he reflects. "It came down to working a full-time job and supporting the family or racing. There wasn't much choice."

"It's kind of nice to have your sons follow what you enjoy," he goes on. "You can be together and enjoy it more."

Rhetorical Question: How many of the last eleven Indy pole-sitters weren't second-generation racers?

Rhetorical Answer: None.

Which brings us to Bill Mears, father of both the fastest and slowest qualifiers for the '82 Indy lineup. Rick, the youngest and fastest, and Roger, the oldest and slowest, are both sprouts in a racing family's garden.

"I ran a bunch of jalopies at the fairgrounds track in Wichita," Bill Mears affirms.

And, after Bill gave up Kansas and racing for California and a backhoe business, he still built some of the racing buggies Rick and Roger tried their young racing legs with. "After awhile, they got in over my head," he says. "There was no way I could afford to stay in the business, but I would drive for them once in awhile."

Like Ed Sneva, Bill Mears was parked along pit row this May, in the pits of the Roger Penske stable Rick drives for. "Sometimes, Roger gives me something to do," he explains, "like hold the fire extinguisher or the electric starter."

He was, in fact, the man who

extinguished the fire that burned Rick during the '81 race.

Better part of Valor: We could run all this second-generation stuff in the ground, throw Johnny Rutherford in for good measure (or even Chet Fillip), but you've surely got the picutre by now.

Irresistible Mind-Boggler: If you put all the brothers Whittington, Sneva, Mears, Bettenhausen, Rutherford (Wayne's out there somewhere), and Carter-Parsons in an Indy field, you'd have a generation garden five rows deep! Toss in Foyt and Fillip, and you'd have half the field!

And it doesn't stop there — with the families who actually got some or all of their second generations in the '82 race. There were a lot of folks wearing driving suits most of May (up until race day) whose roots go deeper than a weekend at a driving school.

Desire Wilson: Indy's second woman driver wasn't playing with dolls when she was a girl. "My father raced motorcycles, and he always wanted someone to take over for him. I was pleased to do it."

Scott Brayton: The Michigan lad who made the '81 field followed in his father's footsteps. Lee was a sprint and champ-car driver for many years, but never made the field at Indy.

Rich Vogler: The sprint and midget master learned a lot of it from his dad, Don, who raced midgets and sprints around the Midwest for years until his death last year at the Indianapolis Speedrome.

Teddy Pilette: Perhaps the most interesting of all the family tradition tales, proving that Belgium grows more than Brussels sprouts. His father, Andre, drove Ferraris on the grand prix circuit, and, get this, America, his grandfather, Theordore, finished fifth in the 1913 Indianapolis 500! Even the Betten-hausens don't go back that far.

Mike Mosley, Larry Rice, Greg Leffler, Spike Gehlhausen, Salt Walther, and Steve Chasey: Except for Chassey, these are all former 500 starters who sat on the sidelines this May 30, but their fathers got the wheels of their ambitions rolling as race car owners and/or mechanics.

Now, a last, small gesture to fairness, objectivity, and all that other journalistic mythology. Not everyone in the '82 Indy field inherited their racing urge, like some family heirloom.

Winner Gordon Johncock didn't, for openers. And the fathers of rookies Danny Sullivan and Chip Ganassi are both in the construction business — Sullivan's wouldn't even come to his son's races until recently, in fact.

And Pete Halsmer's dad runs a flying service up in Lafayette, Indiana.

Clever, Convoluted Ending: But then flying on the ground isn't all that different from flying through the clouds (especially if the guy in front of you blows the engine). "Originally, I wanted to do skywriting, but I didn't have the finances to purchase the kind of planes you need," Halsmer relates. "I partially put myself through college by repairing cars, so I got involved in automotive sports as opposed to aviation sports."

Footnote: There are sometimes wide detours on the roads of the racing generations. The author of this story went to the race tracks with his father, who owned a couple of midgets in the old Hoosier Racing Association. But the first time he sat in a race car — Kenny Eaton's midget at roughly the age of six — he burned his arm on the exhaust pipe. So, like the kid who burns his fingers on the kitchen stove, he became a gourmet instead of a chef. But it's still the same recipe.

Gary Bettenhausen

Pancho Carter

Geoff Brabham

Billy Vukovich

Tom Sneva

[179]

Mario Andretti and Pat Patrick in happier days.

Rodger Ward, mellowed after his years of racing now does P.R. work for Las Vegas' Circus Circus.

Pat Vidan, who used to wave the flags over the field of cars.

Rick Mears finds that sun is HOT.

Jack Carey, arrived from Fresno with copies of a photo essay on Vukovich, Sr.

Bill Vukovich can't seem to find a competitive ride these days. "Mini-Vuke" his son, is doing very well in California midgets and one day may be the first third generation 500 driver.

Mr. and Mrs. Art Sparks. Art was active in racing for many, many years.

Stormin' Norman Hall, former driver and current car owner with driver Jim McElreath and chief mechanic, Ed Baue.

They can paint the walls but the skid marks stay all month.

Elmer Ostermeyer and Festival Queen, Julie Ann Smith, award the American Red Ball Trophy to Bill Alsup. It symbolizes the most significant contributions to racing. It is in the memory of Eddie Sachs.

Bill Whittington, who occasionally has trouble with the fence gets out of shape coming out of the first turn.

Bill nails the wall and his March starts to foul up.

The car scrapes the wall right behind where another unlucky soul has had the same misfortune.

The car slides to a halt.

THE HIGH CO$T OF RACING

by Dave Overpeck

You're wealthy. In fact you're filthy rich. You've just watched your first Indianapolis 500. And you're hooked.

Maybe it was the incredible duel to the flag between Gordon Johncock and Rick Mears. Or maybe it was the sensation — that indescribable thrill that went up your neck — when they came down to take the green flag. Maybe it was the pomp and color and all those 350,000-or-whatever people crowded into the Speedway. Or it could be the $2 million purse.

Probably it's a little bit of all of them and a little something else, too. Whatever it is, next year you want to be a part of it — and not just one of the hordes staring down on it from the grandstands. You want to be down there, *in* it.

You're 25 years and more than that many pounds past being able to consider driving in it. And while you're great at numbers, your mechanical skills pretty much begin and end with knowing which direction is up and which is down on your power window switch.

But, by God, there's nothing to keep you from owning one of those cars. You may not have youth and nerve and incredible hand/eye coordination, and you may not be an engineering or mechanical whiz. But you do have the one thing it takes to be an owner — money and a lot of it.

Come 1983, you're going to be down there in the pits watching *your* car battling with Pat Patrick's and Roger Penske's. Yeah, Patrick's and Penske's. Right up there in front, going for the whole ball of wax. You didn't get where you are in this world by being content with making the show. You play to win.

So what if it costs you $500,000. It'd be worth it to walk into your country club as the winning car owner in the Indianapolis 500. There are guys there who are worth as much as you are, including a couple who are worth more. There are also some politicians and movers and shakers who have their faces on television or in the newspapers regularly. But there are no Indianapolis 500 winning car owners. Half a mill? To stand out in that crowd, the price is cheap.

* * *

Sit down, fella. It's going to cost you a tad more — make that a lot of tads more. You are about to get a lesson on the economical facts of trying — just trying, no guarantees — to win the Indianapolis 500.

First of all, understand one thing. You're not talking about just Indianapolis. You're talking about the whole Indy car circuit. Sure, you can just enter Indy — there's no rule that says you have to run the other races. But you're not going to win, if for no other reason than you can't hire a driver who can win the big one just to run in one race a year. Besides, the cost effectiveness goes right out the window.

Now let's get down to some numbers.

First, you got to have a car. There are three ways to go about that: You can buy a used car, you can buy a new one from March or Dan Gurney or you can build your own. Let's examine all three alternatives — keeping in mind we're talking about the chassis only. No engine included.

Getting the used car is the economy way to go. Used is something of a misnomer. More than likely it is a new car built from a year-old design. Roger Penske has them available every year and you probably can pick up a PC-10 for around 90,000 1981 dollars. Patrick also sells his old Wildcats, probably at a slightly lower price.

A used car can be a good buy. They occasionally win races — Pancho Carter drove a 1980 Penske PC-9 to victory at the Michigan 500 in 1981, though in truth the race came back to him when the new cars either dropped out or experienced problems. You also can get stuck with a lemon. The Penske PC-9B won seven of 12 champ car races in 1981, including Indianapolis. Penske sold four of them to other teams this year. Only one even made the '82 Indy field — and it was the slowest in the 33-car field.

It might interest you to know that the last second-owner car to win Indianapolis was the Wynn's Friction Proofing Special that Johnnie Parsons drove in 1950. Let's face it, nobody is going to sell you his year-old car unless he thinks he's got something better.

Not interested in a used car, huh? Can't say that I blame you.

Now then, let's take a look at buying a car off the rack, so to speak.

At this point, there are two places to go to buy a new Indy car: The British March folks or Dan Gurney's All-American Racers. And the latter deserves a footnote in that Gurney didn't sell any of his '82 models to anybody. In fact, he barely got one done for himself — and then missed the show, mostly because of engine problems.

Both of these are good cars, though the

Eagle looks a lot better with a stock block engine than it does with a Cosworth.

There is no question the March is a potential winner. Tom Sneva was right up there battling with Johncock and Mears through much of the '82 race, and A.J. Foyt led in the early going with another.

The Eagle-Chevy combination seems to work pretty good in terms of performance. Mike Mosley came from last to first to win with one at Milwaukee and led early in the Michigan 500 in '81. But nobody, except maybe Gurney, is convinced a Chevy can win a 500.

Still, let's take a look at cost. The asking price for a fully assembled March in 1982 was $125,000. You could get an Eagle in kit form for $87,500 in the Chevy setup, $95,000 if you wanted to use a Cosworth. Assembly — getting it race-ready — will add another $20,000 easy.

There are a couple things you ought to know, though. The March factory is in England, so if you need parts or something there is a waiting period. Additionally, there is no March test program per se, and there is no March representative on the circuit, keeping up with developments. Engineering data comes from the competitors.

There is no question the March was a good car in '82. But that's no guarantee for '83. As the PC-9B proves, last year's bullet can be this year's bomb.

In the case of the Eagle, Gurney is on the circuit, he does have a test program (though not that extensive) and he does stay up-to-date. But in recent years, he's also had a lot of trouble meeting delivery schedules. In other words, you may or may not get your car when you need it.

The bottom line with an off-track car is that at best you're getting a car as good as the next guy's — but no better. You may win a few races here and there, but you're not going to beat Penske and Patrick consistently.

Not what you're really looking for, either? Okay, that means you're going to commit yourself to your own building program. If you're going to beat Penske and Patrick at their own game, you figure you got to play it the way they do.

If that's the way you want to do it, figure on budgeting something around $2½ million for next year. That's not a figure out of a hat. It's straight from one of the top Indy teams — and it's not as much as Penske and Patrick will be spending.

Here's where it's going to go:

First of all, you've got to hire a full-

time engineer to design and build your car. His salary is going to be in the $40-60,000 range. And he's going to need a full-time assistant, probably at about $25,000.

From there, you can go one of two ways. You can do your own development work without outside help or you make a deal with one of the European Formula One teams to share technological data and use some of their facilities. If you choose the latter road, $100,000 is the going price. But it'll probably be a bargain, because they're going to have a lot of data that's going to save you both time and money.

Also, try to get with one that has its own wind-tunnel facilities, preferably quarter-scale. There are several wind-tunnels in this country, but most of them are full-scale which means every test piece you make is going to cost you just about full price, even if it's a total flop. And wind-tunnel time is expensive — $300 or $400 an hour.

The wind tunnel time is valuable, though because it cuts down on track test time — and that's *really* expensive. Figure on about $6-7,000 a day. Even using wind-tunnels, you're going to need to test 30 or 35 days a year — and Penske will be testing twice that much.

While you're at it, you'd better throw in about $40,000 a year for travel between your base and England. Your engineer is going to have to be flying back and forth to check in with the Formula One team with which you're working and to do test work. (Pan Am is going to love you.)

What this is going to get you is a race car that is going to cost you about $100,000 for the pieces you buy or build. The number does not include labor. Nor does it include the engine — we'll get to that in a bit.

You can do all the building yourself. You'll have the people on the payroll to do the work. But it'll be as cheap and probably easier to get somebody like

$ $ $ $ $ $

Jackie Howerton or Grant King to build the major items like the tubs. It may even save you some money.

And don't figure on building just one car. Two is minimum and four is closer to ideal. That's if you only figure on running one car. Four may sound like too many, but it isn't for reasons we don't need to go into right now.

Now we come to the engine business. You can get a Donovan Chevy from Dan Gurney for about $26,000. A Milodon will go about the same. But if you choose this route, you've got a long, expensive development program on your hands. And there are plenty of people around who'll tell you it'll never get the job done.

If you plan on racing to win in '83, Cosworth is the only way to go. The basic engine lists at $42,500. Injectors are going to cost you another $3,500 and the turbocharger goes for two grand. Throw in a few other things to get it race ready, and the engine is going to cost you about $52,000.

You'll need at least four engines (but only three turbochargers) for a one-driver team. More than a few teams have six.

Now that you've got them, you've got to develop them and keep them up. Again, there are two ways to go. You can set up your own engine shop complete with dynamometer. Budget about $300,000 for that. Plus you'll have to have an engine man. A good one will cost you at least $50,000 a year. His assistant, about $24,000.

The alternative is to farm out the engine work to somebody like Ed Pink in California or McLaren Engines in Detroit. You'll pay them according to work done. In the course of the year, you'll pay them a lot.

Cosworths need to be rebuilt about

every 600 miles. Counting your test program and racing, you're going to need about 20 rebuilds a year at an average of $12,000 per.

You'll also want to run your engine on the dynometer for test purposes. That's $1,000 per run. Figure on about 25 or 30 during the year.

You've now got your cars and your engines. Now we come to operating expenses. Here's what it's going to cost to get 'em to the race track and keep them there:

Personnel (18 people)	$550,000
Shop	30,000
Office Expenses	25,000
Telephone	25,000
Insurance	25,000
Shop Expenses	10,000
Shop Materials	50,000
Entry fees	10,000
Driver expenses (per race)	2,000
Crash contingency	50,000
Cost of business	15,000
Spare (wheels, suspension, etc.)	50,000
Tires	50,000
Pit equipment and maintenance	20,000
Uniforms and maintenance	10,000
Transporter and maintenance	150,000
Travel expenses for cars, crew	175,000
Total	$1,247,000

And you still haven't hired your driver.

There are only about a dozen drivers around who have both the experience and the ability to do the development job you need done and to win Indianapolis with a new operation. Of that dozen, don't expect more than three or four to in any way be available for hire.

How you go about getting one of them can vary greatly and will involve salaries, percentages and expense allowances. But figure he's going to cost you from $100,000 to $250,000, depending upon who you get. Plus 40 percent of your purses — and maybe 50 when you win.

That brings you right up in the $2.5 million range.

But, you say, you can recover some of that from your purse earnings. Not nearly as much as you think. In 1981, Bobby Unser's car earned $404,674 for the season — best on the circuit. After paying percentages to Unser and the crew, Roger Penske cleared no more than 35 percent of that — $141,635.90.

But, you say, you also can recover some of that by selling off your cars after the year is over, like Penske does. Yeah, you can — if you have a track record. If your cars win a race or two and are competitive, you'll be able to sell them. But you very well might not win, and then the market is zero. Bobby Hillin has built new cars the last three years. In 1980 and '81, they didn't win. He couldn't sell them.

Sounds like you better get a sponsor to help you out, you say. It sure does.

Good luck.

No. 8 (Gary Bettenhausen) belongs to Lindsey Hopkins who had one of the first big buck teams and No. 52 (Hector Rebaque) a Forsythe-Brown entry, one of the most recent.

Mahoney

Museum in a Mortuary

by Jack C. Fox

Frankfort, Indiana is a typically Midwestern small town. There is nothing to etch it on the memory of a casual tourist. That is unless you pay a visit to the Goodwin Mortuary. Mortuary, you've got to be kidding!!! Oh yes, among its many rooms you find the usual things you find in mortuaries including cold customers; "cases" my mortician friends call them. But you will find a lot more in Goodwin's than "cases." Besides being a Mortician, William Goodwin is a COLLECTOR!

I don't know how dedicated Mr. Goodwin is to auto racing but race cars are one of the things that are collectible and he IS a collector. In one room, which almost defies description, are old passenger cars ... Duesenbergs, a Thomas flyer, an Auburn, a Bugatti, a National hearse carved in the fashion of 1910, a horse-drawn hearse (no the real horses are not there, they are carved,) a Tucker and bicycles of every description hanging like stalactites from the ceiling and in the middle of all of this is Jimmy Jackson's front drive Miller. The well-restored (VERY well, in fact) car has had a lot of ups and downs and competed until 1951 when it was owned by Tom Sarafoff, purveyor of sandwichs over in Terre Haute. (Tom used to have an old two man car set up for road use and the J. C. Agajanian "Old Smokey"... any one know their whereabouts?)

The Jackson has been restored to the green paint job and gold leaf numbers as when Jackson finished second in 1946. There is memorabilia enough in this one room to keep you fascinated for a week but this is not all!

In a hall leading to the "museum" are a number of Peter Helck paintings ... some of racing subjects and some not. On the walls of another room are letters written by Abraham Lincoln and other historical figures.

Across the street in a storage garage is the real gem of the collection ... Wild Bill Cummings 1934 race winner. The restoration isn't quite complete and the Miller engine under the hood is not the accurate size of year but to the uninitiated it is, from outward appearances, more than accurate. Goodwin hastens to state that it is far from complete and much work has to be done before it is shown. But the paint job is accurate, and the body and running gear almost so and there is evidence of much thought and accuracy.

Historic race cars have been found in old barns, garages, sheds ... with tree limbs growing through them, assembled and disassembled basket cases and whatever but did you ever think you would find a former winner in a MORTUARY!?

Jack Fox Photos

So You Want to be a Racing Photographer

by Jack Fox

Years ago we were walking the infield at the 500. In our hands was a small folding camera (a Voitlander, I think) and on our chest was a pit badge, proudly displayed. One of the great unwashed remarked "Hell, if that kind of a camera is all it takes to get a badge, I want one."

Well, so far as cameras go, that was all it took but there was a lot more involved with getting credentials to shoot the 500.

Al Bloemker is the man who issues the credentials for photographers and he is the one you have to convince that not only do you know how to shoot racing pictures but you have a valid reason to shoot them in Indianapolis. The Speedway has its own photographic staff headed by Ron McQueeny. In actuality he is REALLY the MAN. He heads a staff of over 30 men; professionals and non-professionals who can do the job to Ron's standards. Other than that maybe a thousand photo or press credentials are issued to people who work for newspapers or racing publications who incidental to their other assignments shoot occasional shots.

The life of a true racing photographer is not all that it is cracked up to be. Sure, he has a good vantage point (possibly the next best to a driver's) but being in this spot, remember, he often has to dodge race cars and on occasion can get hit by them. Personally, I've been hit, had my feet run over, been nudged, been chased and, on one occasion had a car stop after I had jumped on the radius rod with my hand on the cage. (This, however, was NOT in the 500 where I hope I never get close enough to get even a breeze from a car.) Even on the best days you have to stand out near the track in a broiling sun or shivvering in cold night air. Usually alone unless a driver loops out or gets on his head. Sometimes you find that you must be a good first aid man, fireman or both.

Charles Lytle, the late raconteur and racing buff used to tell of the time he was asked to take a man's picture. He said that he was an amateur and that he didn't charge for prints. The gentleman asked him if he wanted credentials for the race. (This was in older and happier days ... 1941) Charles said YES he would.

In making arrangements to ride out to the track, Charles contacted a Mr. Rose, who used to shoot for the then track photographer, Charlie Bell. Mr. Bell was a little under the influence at the time and had forgotten to give the proper credentials to Rose. When through an interesting, though irrelevant, set of circumstances the Speedway refused to duplicate them, Rose was without the tools needed to ply his trade while Lytle, a thorough amateur, had been given the credentials in payment. Charles said that, on this occasion he was NOT a gentleman and a photographer instead. Whether Rose ever did get in to shoot is unknown but that was the year of the garage fire and the speedway files have no photos of the burning buildings; only one shot of the levelled area taken at a later date.

Today things are much simpler or at least more organized. Photographers are contacted by card several months prior to the race and asked which credentials they want. Their publisher endorses the card and then Bloemker decides what they will be given. This seems to work quite well with only three or four thousand disappointed. Of course there are always those who come to the office and try to talk Bloemker (or someone) into the proper metal but these are rarely successful. One of the first things Al learned on his job was to say "NO!"

Photographing the 500 has a certain amount of prestige but it is not as adventurous as shooting the other circuits. Other than getting hit by shrapnel from a disintegrating March, the dangers at Indy are minimal. At old Southern Ascot you not only had to stand in eye-high weeds but had to dodge race cars with perhaps a bale of hay on their front ends and skip in and out of gopher holes while doing so.

Shooting Indoor Midgets there are no hay or gophers but the cars occasionally run over your feet. As a veteran of this type of racing I can say that you have never known terror until you have shot a race with Joe Leonard in it.

Joe, who won a national championship or two, couldn't see very well (so they said) and when he spun-out indoors he always kept his foot on the throttle. When the car lost enough momentum, off he would go at full bore. Over photographers, under photographers, in the right direction, backwards and forwards or straight up. It was pretty scary. And Joe was only one of forty others who might be doing the same thing to lesser degrees.

Believe me it takes a sense of timing to get that perfect photo. Someone once told me, "If you want that perfect shot, see what you want, then count to three and THEN SHOOT! You may not have a thing or you may have something really great." That was over 30 years ago and I haven't done it right yet. I usually forget to count at all or go "One, two, awh, to hell with it." That's why I'm no John Mahoney, Dennis Torres, Jim Chini or Ron McQueeny.

Occasionally a photographer gets to have the last word about something only he has seen well. One time at Indy, Jim Chini was shooting from an observer's stand, watching a great foreign star practice. This foreigner, in later years improved to the point where he was an almost competent race driver but at that time he was really a very raw novice to Speedway-style racing. During the long afternoon, he got his car way up out of the groove and hit the wall, totally demolishing the machine. As he extricated himself from the debris, Chini sauntered up. "The wheel fell off, the bloody wheel fell off" was the driver's vehement explanation. Jim was unimpressed. He had seen the accident perhaps better than the driver had. "Sure it fell off AFTER YOU RAN IT IN THE WALL, YOU SQUIRREL! It had been a long afternoon for both of them.

If you don't mind the elements, wild animals, errant race cars, low remuneration, high weeds, dirt dust, burned rubber, sunburn, frostbite and are generally just a bit crazy then racing photography might be for you. Maybe THEN you can con Al Bloemker out of a badge! 🔫

This is what it looked like to run behind Desire Wilson.

Wendt

Steve Krisiloff often comes in and puts a car in the race. Not so this year.

Dick Simon just couldn't get enough speed out of an old car.

Howdy Holmes is a very photogenic driver. Here he almost plays it straight.

Ken Hamilton's "Crop Duster" actually had some nice workmanship in its strange design.

Some of the prettiest girls in Indiana became princesses of the 500 Festival.

Tom Bigelow tries to determine if his cup is half-full or half-empty.

Pete Halsmer is, like Howdy Holmes, one of our more photogenic young drivers.

Missed The Show

Bill Alsup qualified this A B Dick Spl, but was bumped.

Early in the month Alsup had his old PC-7 out for testing.

A blown engine kept Kevin Cogan from qualifying in this car.

Pennzoil backup wasn't any faster than Rutherford's No. 1 car.

Gary Bettenhausen tested this car.

Chassey eventually put the Hubler II car into the wall.

Foyt pulls into the pits after a brief run in the backup.

The Vollstedt 17 had problems with veteran John Martin.

Vukovich gets ready to shake down Vern Shuppan's car.

Shuppan seems to be wondering what else can we try.

This No. 1 car was relegated to backup status by Bobby Rahal.

Pat Patrick's backup was shaken down briefly by Andretti.

Dick Simon practiced all month in this Watson.

Engine problems plagued Rusty Schmidt all through practice.

Jerry Karl's new ride was very pretty. but lacked speed.

Problems kept Desire Wilson from the field.

Enoch

Pat Bedard had this PC-7 out early in practice

Mount

But, most of his time was spent in the Escort Wildcat.

Mount

Brayton was recovering from injuries, so Shuppan tried it out.

Mount

No sponsor kept Phil Caliva from a qualifying attempt.

Enoch

Chet Fillip used this Wildcat for his rookie testing.

Mount

Greg Leffler's determination still didn't get him into the field.

Mount

West Coast sprinter Leroy Van Conett gave a good try.

Mount

Spike Gehlhausen tried this car out on the last weekend.

Mike Mosley ran out of engines and disappointed many people.

This marked Chip Mead's second year and he almost made it.

Garza put this March on the wall and had to qualify a new car.

Tom Bigelow blew the engine while trying to qualify this car.

Genesee Beer Wagon's twin was driven by Joe Saldana.

Billy Engelhart needed sponsor money before he could qualify.

Ken Hamilton's new car showed aerospace designing.

Hard work still didn't get Bob Frey qualified in this car.

Back again this year was Ted Pilette in the Mergard McLaren.

Dean Vetrock made only a few laps in his own car.

Roger Rager and Steve Krisiloff both tried to work this car.

Tom Frantz had Foyt's Coyote from last year with a Chevy.

It was told that Bob Harkey traded an airplane for this car.

Roger Mears practiced in his PC-7 in case he was bumped.

Billy Scott tried to qualify the Frito Lay Special.

Again this year Phil Krueger's bid ended against the north wall.

Enoch

Mount

Gary Irvin made another try this year, but the car failed him.

Jan Sneva drove this car before John Mahler took it over.

Mount

Mount

Grant King's car didn't handle properly for Jim McElreath.

Schuppan tried to get the aerodynamics right on this car.

As this issue was going to press Jim Hickman, 1982 Rookie-of-the-Year, was fatally injured in a CART race in Milwaukee. He slammed into the first turn wall in a practice session and died from massive head injuries. It is believed that the car's throttle stuck causing the accident. Although he had been associated with Championship racing less than a full season he left a host of friends in that division.

Susan Gilmore . . . her husband sponsors A. J. Foyt.

Tony Bettenhausen, uninjured but out of the race supervises the removal of his car.

George Bignotti discusses aerodynamics with Tom Sneva.

John Mahler catches the wall.

Rusty Schmidt just couldn't find any speed.

It's OK to "hike" a wheel but this is ridiculous.

Winner's Interview

The following interview with Gordon Johncock was taped shortly after the completion of the race. There has been very little attempt to edit it. This is just how he told his story.

JOHNCOCK: . . . Every lap that I'd push more and more and more; every lap. I had to drag down underneath the line, with all four somethimes to allow myself enough room. And when I went through three, I had all fours underneath and the bottom of the car hit and I almost lost it. And on three on the last lap, I am surprised Rick didn't come up along side of me at that time; maybe it bothered him at the time, I don't know where he was at at the time. But, when he came up beside me coming down for the white flag, I thought that was it. I thought definitely he would go on by me and go into the corner. But I knew that we were both going to go side by side because there was no way I was going to back off. I went through the corner like last year when the race was with Mario; we went through side by side. There are several of the guys out there I don't mind going side by side with.

Q. Coming down the main straightaway, and I presume it was the last lap you were talking about, you wavered a little bit. Were you trying to perhaps use some race trap or were you racing to the finish line?

JOHNCOCK: No, like I say, on the last lap, I really didn't know exactly where Rick was. I looked in my mirror, but I couldn't see him. Evidently he was on the left side of me, I guess. Because when I looked in my mirror, I couldn't see him, so I didn't know if he was directly behind me or if he was on the left side of me.

Q. Did you ever give any thought to '77 when you were leading the last 15 laps?

JOHNCOCK: I sure did. I thought about it with about 10 laps to go or so especially when the car started pushing. It seems, you know, throughout my career, it hasn't been meant for me to run 500 miles. There's been so many 500 races that we've been so close, yet so far away. I've even had a lap lead on the field before; like one time in California and had a tire go flat and wrecked. Another time, two years ago when Al and I was running back and forth, I was leading with three laps to go and ran out of fuel. It just seems like it hasn't been meant for me to run 500 miles.

Q. What is your summation of the race from the last pit stop to the checkered flag?

JOHNCOCK: I was running as hard as I could go every lap. You know I didn't slow down because I had eleven seconds on Rick. I guess that's what I had when I came out of the pit stop. I don't know why I had that unless he had a bad pit stop or something, I really don't know. I was awful fortunate myself, because when I decided to make my pit stop, there was a slow car in the way coming in the pits. He cost me some time; I was worried about that when I could see that I was going to come behind him coming in the pits. I thought, "Yow, here it is again."

Q. The same thing happened to Rick Mears. He had to really get on the brakes and smoke the tires to keep from hitting Herm Johnson.

JOHNCOCK: Roger!

Q. How much does this erase the memory of '73. You said before you would really like to go the 500 miles and win it.

JOHNCOCK: There's never been a feeling like this. Like I said out there, really my biggest victory and thrill is when I finally won the Michigan race. That was another one, that three or four times we were so close to the checkered flag and really had it, and one time cracked a rim and ended up in the wall and another time we ran out of fuel. But, there will never be another victory like this one we had here today. I suppose what really makes it that way is that it ended up with Rick and I as close as we was and the way we had to run — the both of us.

Q. Did it have any effect on you that you were out dueling a Penske car and that a Penske car had taken out your teammate?

JOHNCOCK: No, It had nothing to do with it. I never thought about that throughout the whole race. I have no hard feelings. An accident is an accident and they do happen. That never dawned on me thoughout the race whatsover.

Q. Where did you go during the accident? Where you able to go down lower; where did you go?

JOHNCOCK: I went high. I seen it starting to happen. I see Kevin get sideways and then get over and bump A. J. and then come back across the track and Mario hit him broadside. I swerved to the right. It's just fortunate for me there was nobody coming along the right side of me. Because if they had, I probably would have got in to them. But, you know, there is so much of that stuff that is all uncalled for, as far as I'm concerned. When we are in second and third gear and for somebody to come from the back of the pack and for accidents to continue to happen in the back of the pack, it is all uncalled for; that's all I can say. I don't know what all those guys think about. Instead of getting slowed down, they all could have come to a dead stop within 200 feet — no faster than they were going, but I just don't know what they think about.

Q. You read a lot and you can see it a lot in print that it is car against car anymore rather than driver against driver. But today it looked like on the race track, on the last few laps, it looked like driver against driver. How do you feel about that?

JOHNCOCK: Well, I suppose it was a lot, but really our crews, all the mechanics, the crews, the engine man and all them people really don't get the credit that they really deserve. You don't realize the hours and the time, and the thinking and everything that goes into making that car run like it does so I can drive it. Because if that car didn't work, I sure can't carry it and neither can Rick. It takes a combination of everything — the owner, the sponsors, the mechanics and the driver.

Q. Do you think, on the original start, the pace laps were too slow — and how fast were you going?

JOHNCOCK: Well, I don't know exactly how fast we were going. Yes, the pace laps were too slow — especially the first one. I was in low gear and my car was loading up and chugging along and I almost come going up beside the pace car and motioning for them to go on because they were running way too slow. And, also, I think the race was started too slow. I think it should have been started in third gear. I think any race should be started at a faster pace so the turbos don't have so much torque with the engine — the turbos don't kick in and get you sideways just like what happened to Kevin.

Q. What was the year of the Michigan race that you won the broken streak, Gordie?

JOHNCOCK: My wife says '76. I don't really remember.

Q. Why didn't you run out of gas or do something like you usually do, Gordie?

JOHNCOCK: Just believe me, I was

really thinking about it. I radioed into them several times and said, "Better have enough fuel."

Q. Did you take that one pit stop that you made during the yellow — just before your last main pitstop — when you were topping off — did you think that helped a lot with your stategy?

JOHNCOCK: Well, I don't know if it really helped a lot or not. It might have because it allowed us to run a little longer than Rick. And, I did really want to get away from him because my car definitely worked better out there by itself. Behind some cars, the turbulence was just so bad — I was having a pushing problem to begin with and then when I would get up behind somebody and get that dead air, I just couldn't do nothing with them. I had to try and run all fours underneath the line to get fresh air — clean air out there — to be able to get by out on them. There was three or four cars out there that had pretty good straightaway speed. It was tough to get by on them.

Q. Did you find anything between qualifying and race day in speed in your car, Gordie? In the practice runs you were able to make?

JOHNCOCK: Most definitely. We qualified on Saturday, the first weekend and then Sunday is when we found one of the things that was wrong with our car. We found it by accident we went out to get set up for the race. We found one thing that made the car a lot more stable and a lot more consistent. I would never have been able to drive the car today, I believe, if we hadn't have found that.

Q. What was it you found?

JOHNCOCK: No comment.

Q. After the last yellow went off and the green went on, where did you pass Rick on the course?

JOHNCOCK: If I remember right, I went underneath. Like I said I had to get clean air. I went underneath with all fours coming off (turn) 2 and got him going down the back straightaway.

Q. What kind of impact did the '73 victory have on your life?

JOHNCOCK: I really don't think it had any. I really never think about it. We were sitting in pit lane, you know, when they decided to call the race. It seemed like there was nothing to it.

Q. What is the normal speed you usually get on a pace lap and what do you think you were doing today on the pace lap?

JOHNCOCK: We couldn't have been doing over 70-80 miles an hour when we came down. I think an ideal speed would be anywhere from 110 to 120 to come down for the green flag.

Q. Gordie, could you have been any lower on the first turn when you went into the turn with Rick on the last lap?

JOHNCOCK: I don't think I was that low on that lap as I would had been on some other ones or I wasn't as low there as I was been in (turn) 3. I had all fours below the line up there and I hit a bump that I really never knew was there like that before I drove my car bottomed out and it got me a little sideways and for a second I was just a little bit worried. I was surprised that Rick didn't, if he would have had it just right, he could have come up besides me in the short chute because I had to get out of it at that point.

Q. When was that?

JOHNCOCK: On the last lap; going through three. I left a white mark up there because I seen it when I went back the next time around.

Q. Has all the bad luck that you've had made you more pessimistic than you are optimistic?

JOHNCOCK: Well, yes, you know like I said with ten laps to go, I just, in my mind, is it going to stay together? Is it going to stay together, you know? Especially after last year. I think about it all the time. You know, like last year I had six laps to go when all the belts broke on the car and put me out of the race. So, it was in my mind every second.

Q. The way your car was running, could you have held Rick off if you had another lap to go in the race?

JOHNCOCK: It would have been mighty tough! I don't know. I didn't have anything left, I know that and it was getting worse each lap. I think it is kinda where Penske has it over us. But like I said before the race started, I think we've caught up with them considerably from what we did the first two races. Because like down to Atlanta, I was second down there but, you know, Rick could have run 10 mile an hour faster down there at anytime he wanted to and I was just out there working and running for all I could go and he was just cruising, in Atlanta. But what we've found here the day after we qualified what cured a lot of that.

Q. Were you surprised that Rick was able to gain so much on you in the last 10 laps, which is probably about 10-12 seconds, I think. And he almost gained a second a lap for 11 seconds and he gained almost a second a lap and he really came right up to you then?

JOHNCOCK: No, because my car started pushing. If my car had handled like it did from lap 155 to 190, he would have never; I don't think he would ever gained on me. Like I said I worked better when I was out there by myself than I did with him behind me. A car running behind me really affected me also, you know when you run down below a car, it has a tendency to make you push. And when you run high on a car, on the rear, it has a tendency to pull the back end off and under it. There were a couple of cars out there, slower cars, that were running behind me trying to get by me that, boy, when I was having a pushing problem, it really affected the car so bad that I couldn't come out of the corner. I really had to get out of the throttle.

Q. Your mother has been kinda ill, Gordie, are you dedicating this race to her or something?

JOHNCOCK: Well, yes, I definitely like to. I guess I'm kinda ashamed of myself because of I had't thought about that.

Q. What causes the car to push? And, after you found out what caused you to gain so many miles an hour after you qualified. How many do you think you gained, by doing whatever you did?

JOHNCOCK: What causes the car to push is when the tire stagger in the rear goes away like it did one time during the race, there. I think I was leading it under a yellow, and three of them went by me and I was running fourth and the best I could run there for 20-25 laps was 185-186 miles an hour; the left rear tire just got hot and grew so big that it was cross-weightin' the car and it makes the car push so bad, that you can't come out of the corners.

Q. The second one was: after you made the change in the car the day after qualifying, how many miles an hour did you think it was worth to you — that change?

JOHNCOCK: It really wasn't worth that many miles an hour so much as it was to made the car consistent to where you knew what you could do with the car; you know, how fast you could run it and it wouldn't be first one time the front end loose, the next time the back end loose when you get on a bump. So, but what we found just made the car a lot more consistent. Of course, that is definitely what picked us up, I don't know, a few miles an hour, there's no question about that. But, the consistency of the car is what made it a lot better.

Q. Gordie, were you scared when you saw Sneva have his engine problem and were you afraid you might throw a yellow on you?

JOHNCOCK: I sure was. There were three or four within the last ten laps that lost turbochargers and I just knew there was going to be a yellow. Fortunately, there wasn't.

Q. Were you being told all the time on the radio how much he was gaining each lap on you during those last ten laps.?

JOHNCOCK: I was watching on the board.

Q. Besides the start and the part where the car was bottoming out, did you have any other close calls during the race?

JOHNCOCK: I guess I had one coming in the pits with a slow car; trying to sqeeze by him to get to my pits. And one time fairly close with Gary Bettenhausen.

Q. We would like to have an opinion from the pretty lady on Gordie's lap (his wife) and what do you think of his win.

LYNDA JOHNCOCK: I think it's great. '73 was my first year and I was young and I thought if I could make it through that year I could make it through anything. But, the last ten laps were tougher, today;

than ever. I mean I think it is the most wonderful thing ever because it was sad in '73. We didn't really have victory, we had no victory dinner. They mailed us a check and it was really sad. Today, to go 500 miles in sunshine — it's fantastic!

Q. *Why was there no victory dinner?*

LYNDA JOHNCOCK: It had been postponed for three days.

Q. *Tell us your name.*

LYNDA JOHNCOCK: Lynda, L-y-n-d-a.

Q. *You said you were running all out on those last several laps and, obviously, Mears was also running all out. Why was it, he gained a second or so a lap on a lap except the last lap? Why couldn't he gain on the last lap?*

JOHNCOCK: It's like I said it is a lot different when you — you can run so much easier and so much quicker — when you are out there by yourself in fresh air, than you can when you get up behind someone. I'm sure he had the same problem when he got up behind me, he got into the dead air and, you know, he just couldn't hold his race car. I was running down low because I needed all the room coming out because I was pushing so bad. If I had been running high on the race track, he probably would have drove right underneath me.

Q. *Gordie, there are so many young guys coming along; do you find it harder to keep racing or does this sort of solidify your position in racing?*

JOHNCOCK: Well, you definitely have some young guys coming on that down the line are going to be tough. There's no question about that, but there's something about it that you really need a few years around here. You know, I'm not going to say it is never going to happen for a guy, I suppose it has, but to come here the first or second year to win or something like that, but it's really tough to come here when your're young. I think the older guys definitely have the advantage. They've been here before and they kinda know how to run the race. I probably could have run a little faster the first part of race, myself. I was running close enough to them and really my car wasn't working all that well. There was a couple of times that I got into a little bit of trouble because, as hard as I was running, if I had run any harder, I might not have been setting here, I might be in a wall, or something. I think there's a lot of guys who really just don't know there limitations of their driving ability — you know — when they are out there running. But there is some young guys coming along that are going to be tough, there's no question about it. And there's a couple more, who aren't here yet, who are going to be tougher yet. And that is Andretti and Unser; Al and Michael, Jr.

Car owner Pat Patrick.

Lynda Johncock

Peeled Eye, *continued from page 6.*

Yesterday I think I made a couple of million dollars. Per week. Our new deal is the single most preposterous, simple program I've ever heard of in my entire life. I visited some of the world's largest corporations and outlined the plan to them. Now I walk into boardrooms, paneled offices and I wear the right three piece suit. Within a year I fully expect to have more dollar bills than I'll ever know what to do with.

But I hate to sell. I like to write. But my writing doesn't sell enough to build the little empire that I always thought I was going to have. I don't like the idea of putting out a book that is less than beautiful. And we've been guilty of publishing many books that can be judged mediocre.

I know most of the auto racing booksellers of the world and they all agree that we're in a small, close-knit little society. That's hard for me to understand when I see several hundred thousand spectators each race day at Indy.

This year I was supposed to write a detailed feature story on Roger Penske. I've read several stories about this textbook case business-man, but I really wanted to get down to the knitty gritty with him and ask, "Listen, you were in your late twenties and you wound up with this Chevrolet dealership. Then, wham-bam you were a car owner at Indy and you had lots of other businesses going. How'd you do it? Exactly."

Just when I was supposed to go back and set up the interview time, some executives called me and said they wanted to meet. It was good-bye Penske and hello dollar bills. On the trip to see the executives I wondered to myself if I was selling out. What was more important, doing a good story on the nation's premier car owner for an Indy Yearbook or obtaining the means to maybe become a car owner myself? Roger Who?

While this Yearbook is being produced your publisher is criss-crossing the nation working on a new advertising distribution program that just may revolutionize the industry. Maybe it'll work and maybe it won't. Either way, we'll be back at Indy in '83 and you'll have a Yearbook.

Duke Nalon, one of the greatest drivers to ever tour the track, listens to Argentina's Dr. Vicente Alvarez. Must be something about the Falkland Islands.

Herm Johnson just before he was rear-ended by Rick Mears.

Linda Vaughn has brought Hurst more good publicity than the Jaws of life.

Bob Berggren, editor of the popular magazine "Open Wheel."

Roger McCluskey, a veteran driver, and now USAC's Director of Competition.

A Race Car for an End Table

Ever use a race car for an end table? Well Wayne and Sandi Nowostawski do, and since it's quit leaking oil it has been quite serviceable.

The cubed Indy car is only one of many . . . VERY many, items of racing memorabilia which the pair has collected. The collection includes a complete set of Speedway Pit badges, uniforms, crash helmets, trophies, officials's arm bands, photos, art and parts of race cars. Anything, in fact, associated with motor racing in general and the Speedway in particular. The Nowostawskies, incidentally also collect cats, or so it seems with sixteen kitties roaming the premises. How they get along with the racing collection has not been reported.

The cubed race car . . . it was the one in which Mike Mosley hit the wall in 1971 and then ricocheted into Mark Donohue's machine was badly wrecked and after removing the engine, the owner had the remains cubed as are unwanted used cars. This amounted to a $30,000 piece of junk. Eventually it found it's way into the Nowastawski racing room. "It leaked oil for almost eight years but its all leaked away now," says Wayne. There is a photo on the wall of Mosley with his leg in a cast sitting beside the cube.

Sandi is the autographs-seeking member of the family and autographed pictures of racing's greats and near greats grace the walls. The pair, lifelong collectors started by collecting patches and then it went from there. Wayne, a photographer, started adding racing photos and Sandi had them autographed. Then it just sort of snowballed and now the house is full of all sorts of things which have racing connections. The collection as it now stands is valued at better than $100,000 and it is growing all the time.

Wayne's racing room is a converted garage in his South Bend home. His ottoman is a sprint car tire once used by A. J. Foyt. The model race cars and other mementoes of the sport are kept in showcases, bookcases and cabinets. They sit on windowsills and hang on the walls. In fact, they are EVERYWHERE! Possibly there are larger collections around . . . but don't bet on it!

PIT SAFETY

by Al Stilley

Steps taken by the United States Auto Club and the Indianapolis Motor Speedway greatly improved pit safety for the 66th annual 500.

A number of new refueling regulations were implemented by USAC to prevent pit fires like those that plagued the 1981 Indianapolis 500 and the CART-sactioned Norton 500 at Michigan International Speedway (MIS).

"I saw the MIS fire on TV and it was frightening," USAC technical supervisor Jack Beckley said. "We don't want anything close to what happened to Rick Mears last year happening again at Indianapolis."

The Speedway came close to a major pit disaster in 1981 when Mears' Penske-Cosworth erupted in invisible flames when methanol was spilled during a pit stop. The pandemonium that broke out in the aftermath of the fire will never be forgotten. It led to a full attack on safety in the pits at the Speedway in preparation for the 1982 event.

The Speedway installed a water line directly behind the pit apron wall to wash down a major methanol spill, not to extinguish a fire. Cuts were made in the frontstretch pit wall to permit emergency vehicles and fire apparatus with better access to the pit area. The pit wall was raised. And USAC implemented strict Nomex clothing requirements for all personnel in the pits connected with a racing team.

It was also required that all methanol tanks in the pits be bolted to the concrete to prevent tipping over.

USAC's requirements for 1982 called for: a positive shutoff valve, commonly called a "dead man's" valve; rigid requirements for refueling supply hoses and vent hoses; all pit personnel to wear fire-retardant clothing, including team scorers and the fuel man and vent man to wear Nomex-type footwear, all other pit personnel were required to wear leather shoes; manufacturers to certify all fuel coupling units; and pit crews to go through the refueling procedure prior to race day in the USAC impound area.

USAC also recommended that a drain tube be installed on the race car to force any fuel spills down to the ground as a preventive measure to prevent fuel overflows on the driver or hot engine.

"We wanted to make sure that everyone connected with refueling knew what was going on," Beckley stated.

CART also implemented more stringent refueling requirements for the 1982 championship car season. Both sanctioning bodies experienced some problems which caused Beckley to comment, "You can't eliminate human error."

That's exactly what happened at Atlanta in the CART event there in late April when Tom Sneva pulled away from the pits while his car was still being refueled. There was also a reported fuel spill in Al Unser's pit. Fortunately, there were no fires.

During the Indianapolis 500, there was a brief fire in Hector Rebaque's pit, a near-disastrous incident involving four-time winner A. J. Foyt, and a malfunction of the refueling system that cost Tom Sneva a major delay in his final pit stop. A major fuel spill was reported in Gordon Johncock's pit which turned out to be nothing more than water that had been tossed on the eventual winner to cool him off during the race.

When Foyt pitted twice shortly after the 150-mile mark, the veteran had to deal with an emergency that few spectators saw. After pulling onto the track, fuel began sloshing into the cockpit because of a faulty O-ring.

Car sponsor Jim Gilmore explained the frightening incident by commenting, "When A. J. made that second pit stop, he was soaked with fuel. I've never seen so much fuel come out of a car before. We were lucky it didn't go off like a bomb, but that's where his experience came in. He didn't cut the engine off because that could have produced a spark. He kept it running while we threw water on him and replaced the gasket."

Sneva's misfortune was caused by a screw which backed out of the fueling nozzle, forcing the fuel to keep shutting off. It couldn't have happened at a worse time for the hard-charging three-time 500 runnerup because he was in the lead chase with Johncock and Rick Mears when he pitted.

Beckley emphasized that the refueling training and review session for pit crews will take place again with the qualified cars prior to the 1983 Indianapolis 500.

"We went over how the new nozzle and vent functioned with each crew using their own equipment in the USAC impound area," Beckley said. "We had three major fuel sprays due to bad O-rings that were replaced. The session was a blessing because it gave us a chance to see if all the equipment would function properly.

Beckley reported that Dan Gurney's crew told USAC officials just a few hours before the start of the race that the O-ring on Mike Chandlers's Eagle-Donovan had failed during a pre-race refueling drill in the pits. Dave Ayers of Induction Systems, was paged from the stands to come to the pits to repair the system prior to the race, according to Beckley.

"We will strive to better the refueling system for the 1983 race," Beckley attested.

"You can never eliminate human error, especially in a race of this magnitude because the crews are so nervous. I certainly feel like we lessened the chance of human error in the pits during this year's race," Beckley concluded.

Johnny Parsons comes in for a pit stop.

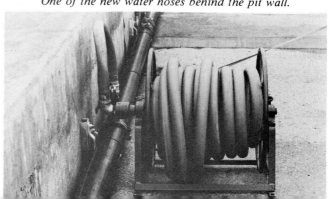

One of the new water hoses behind the pit wall.

Wealthy, international racer, Teddy Yip seems to enjoy his role of sponsor of Desire Wilson's car.

U. E. "Pat" Patrick saw his car win the race for the second time.

Welcome back, President Cloutier.

Bobby Rahal "at speed." Unhearalded here, he adapted to the track very well and was quite competitive.

Boris Kondroff and Bob Wyman of Mallory Electric maintain a shop in Gasoline Alley to assist car owners in their electrical needs.

After Ten Years In The Making...

GO!
The Bettenhausen Story
The Race Against A Dream

Is Finally On The Printing Press!

Constant readers of the Indianapolis 500 Yearbook will know that author Carl Hungness has been working on auto racing's most complete biography ever written. The life story of the famed Bettenhausen family is now in the production stages of completion. Type is being set, last minute photos are being selected. At this point we can't promise the book out for Christmas of 1982, but it should be ready for January delivery.

This book covers not only the Bettenhausen family's life from the early 1930's to 1982, but American auto racing as well. It has been aimed not toward the knowledgeable race fan, but the general sports enthusiast. Consequently, if you have a friend you've been trying to win over to become an auto racing fan, this work should do it.

Hundreds of photos are included in this one-of-a-kind biography in addition to complete racing records.

Please note that the language used in this biography may be offensive to some readers. It is not intended for young adults.

Book orders are now being accepted for January-February 1983 delivery. Pre-publication price is $14.95 (plus $1.50 postage).

Order from: Carl Hungness Publishing
P.O. Box 24308-EY
Speedway, IN 46224

Comments from the Winner's Wife

by Lynda Johncock

How does it feel?

Let me put it this way.

I remember when I was a little girl, stretched out in front of the television set watching the finals of the Miss America contest. There would be Bert Parks crooning "Here she comes ... Miss America."

And, I'd get all bleary-eyed ... dreaming and fantasizing that maybe ... maybe ... someday I might be Miss America.

Well, I'll never be Miss America. But, I'm Mrs. Gordon Johncock and the wife of the Indianapolis 500 champion and I'm content with that. To me, that's the ultimate.

I guess that there was a feeling all through the month of May that we — Gordy and his team — would win the race. Gordy isn't really superstitious, but he does firmly believe that good things happen to him when he drives for STP. He won Indy in '73 in an STP car and although he didn't finish first last season with STP, he was competitive in almost every race. So, he truly did believe this would be his year.

I don't think either of us realized what was happening immediately after the race. In my case, I was sitting in the STP lounge watching the race on closed-circuit TV. When the race neared the end, and it looked as if Gordy would win, the STP people wouldn't let me out the door and get to Victory Circle.

They had heard that Dolly Granatelli wouldn't let me leave the room in 1973 until the checkered flag dropped and they didn't want to jinx Gordy by changing the routine. So, when it was over and I started to run to Victory Lane, I couldn't get through the Tower Terrace area 'cause it was blocked off. The attendants wouldn't open the door.

There was some man right behind me who shook his fist at the guards and shouted if they didn't open, he'd personally break down the glass doors. Well, they finally did and this man pushed me through. To this day, I don't know who he was.

About all I remember in that mob scene was screaming to Gordy over and over, "You won Indy" and kissing him every time I said it. After Gordy went through the post-race interviews and we drove back home, I kept punching him on the arm and repeating,"You won Indy."

And that's something I want to stress right now. Gordy won Indy. Not me. I had nothing to do with it. It was his car, his team and his equipment — the best equipment that Pat Patrick could obtain for him.

It's true that I may have some influence on his personal life. At least, I hope so But that's all. I'm thrilled to share in his victory, but I'm not naive enough to think that I honestly contributed to his performance on the track.

The realization of what Gordy had accomplished didn't set in until we walked into the Pat Patrick/STP victory party that evening.

There were cameramen, television crews, floodlights and all and when we entered the hall, everyone rose and applauded ... sort of like a presidential press conference. We were so stunned that neither of us could say anything. Nothing like that happened in '73 when Gordy won, because of all the rain delays and tragedy surrounding the race.

We didn't stay long because Gordy had to appear live on the ABC race telecast that evening and right afterwards we got on Pat's private plane to fly to Hastings, Michigan, to visit Gordy's mom who was near death. We both felt that she was holding on until he won the race.

We couldn't land at Hastings because it was fogged in and had to go to Grand Rapids, Michigan. By the time that Gordy's sister drove over to pick us up and we got to Hastings, it was two in the morning. We stayed until four and left to go back to Indy. It was almost six in the morning when we returned and then Gordy had a 6 a.m. live television spot with NBC and then right afterwards one with CBS.

We stopped at McDonald's for breakfast on the way back to the Speedway and one of Gordy's fans recognized us and picked up the tab.

The official photo session at the Speedway was delayed until noon because of rain and when that was over we went back home and Gordy finally had a chance to nap until about four in the afternoon. I stayed up to screen the phone calls and work on his speech for the Victory Banquet. We hadn't slept since we got up at 5:30 a.m. on race day.

Oh, I forgot. Before we reached home we stopped at the Oxford Clothing Shop to pick up outfits for the banquet. We hadn't planned to attend but intended to fly right up to Gordy's mother's bedside after the race, so we didn't have any dress clothes. The owners of the shop agreed to open the place even though it was a holiday and five ensembles for each of us laid out to choose from. They were really neat people.

When we walked in the front door of our rented home after the banquet, the phone began ringing. It was Gordy's sister telling us that his mom had just died. Even though we were expecting it, her death was still a jolt.

We slept as best we could and Gordy flew back to Hastings on Tuesday morning and I followed by car after spending a few hours straightening out things.

I'd never seen Gordy cry before, but at the chapel on Thursday when we gathered for the funeral and he saw the race team members walk in behind Pat Patrick and Jim McGee and Ralph Salvino of STP, it really hit him hard.

Well, after things calmed down, I returned to our home in Phoenix on Saturday and Gordy remained in Michigan to tend to his business.

I really didn't begin to appreciate the attention that goes with the victory until after reaching Phoenix. When I stopped in at the local department store to buy some cosmetics, a sweet little lady named Barbara Verbanick ran up and hugged me and cried 'cause she was so happy. I worked with her years ago and still buy all my cosmetics from her. She doesn't have a family and she sort of adopted me as a daughter years ago.

The people at the dry cleaners, the travel agency and the grocery store all gushed and fawned over me. And when I stopped at a service station for gasoline the young attendant, whom I'd never seen before, noticed the name on my credit card and was impressed.

Being a racing wife isn't always fun. There've been years of struggle ... no privacy ... lots of travel and packing. There've been good times and bad. Stressful situations with lots of highs and lows.

But I wouldn't change anything.

May 30, 1982, made everything worthwhile.

Mahoney

Mary Hulman serves as Chairman of the Board and makes the important decisions.

Mahoney

Her grandson, Tony George, may someday be in charge of the operation as he is very interested in Speedway happenings.

Larson

What fun Rick Mears must be having as he pilots the Goodyear blimp over the track.

Photographs

If you would like copies of photographs in this Yearbook, most can be purchased from the photographer whose name appears in small type alongside the photo. Please address your requests to the individual photographer and not to the Yearbook.

John Mahoney
2213 Groff Ave.
Indianapolis, IN 46222

Phil Whitlow
1900 S. Walnut
Bloomington, IN 47401

Arnie deBrier
123 Barclay
Cherry Hill, NJ 08034

Roy Query
494 S. Hamilton Rd.
Columbus, OH 43213

Rick Whitt
P.O. Box 68374
Indianapolis, IN 46268

Bill Enoch
1725 N. Whittier Place
Indianapolis, IN 46218

Bob Mount
920 N. Grant
Lebanon, IN 46052

Don Larson
1013 Tuckahoe
Indianapolis, IN 46260

Gene Crucean
1215 Azalea Dr.
Munster, IN 46321

Doug Wendt
R.R. #3, Mass Lane
Danville, IL 61832

Dave Scoggan
5116 Elaine
Indianapolis, IN 46224

Any photo marked "IMS"
Indianapolis Motor Speedway
Photo Shop/Ron McQueeney
Speedway, IN 46224

Patrick Bedard seems to be bothered by the noise.

Bobby Unser helps tune Josele Garza's engine.

A packed grandstand. Part of the largest crowd in history watches the first turn action.

Don Whittington must have a small helmet.

Michael Warren and Charles Haid, of "Hill Street Blues" clown in Gasoline Alley.

Chet Fillip leads Tom Sneva down the front stretch.

YEARS AGO

Indianapolis Motor Speedway Photos

Race fans are lucky that such a fine photographic record of the 500 is on file at the Speedway photo shop. here are some historic examples which Ron McQueeney can furnish. Also ... *THE ILLUSTRATED HISTORY OF THE 500 is soon scheduled to be reprinted.*

One of the prettiest cars in 500 history, Joe Marks' red and silver Miller. Riding Mechanic, S. T. "Pinky" Donaldson, is still at the track almost every day. The driver Howdy Wilcox II, was ruled off the track because he was a diabetic although it was at first reported that he was an epileptic. Wilcox sued and won a settlement.

Joe Russo with his ride, a fine Duesenberg Model A.

The famed Cotton Henning works on Mike Boyle's cars prior to the 1932 race. That's Jigger Johnson helping.

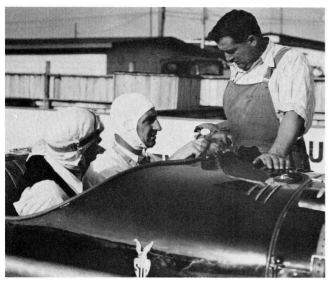

Raul Riganti came up from Buenos Aires to drive this Chrysler in '32.

A top race car for only $1200. This was Russ Snowberger's car in '33 and what it cost. Here Al Miller drives it on the dirt at Detroit.

Another Model A Duesey owned by Cotton Henning. Babe Stapp is the driver. The No. 13 . . . who knows?

Billy Arnold had a heavy foot but crashed in '31 and '32. It was a little hard on Billy and Spider Matlock not to mention the car.

This is what a stripped-down two-man car looked like in 1932.

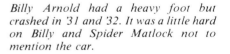

The Indy cars run the dirt at Detroit. Bill Cummings is on the pole.

Lou Meyer and his Miller before the 1931 Detroit race. Master mechanic Riley Brett sits on the wheel.

Start of the 1933 Championship race at Detroit.

Louie Meyer sits on the pole at Detroit in 1931.

A lot of interesting cars in the Detroit pits in 1931.

Louis Meyer has apparently just won the Detroit race in 1931.

An example of a home made engine of the 30's. This is the Morton and Brett 8 in 1931.

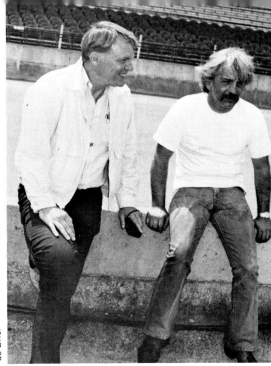

Jack Fox, your editor, has written The Mighty Midgets *and the* Illustrated History of the 500. *His next book detailing Sprint Car racing from 1895 until 1942 is now in the final stages of production.*

Al Singer, Detroit-based chief mechanic, is an expert on Volker engines and early sprint cars. Unlike a lot of mechanics he is a very gentle person.

Dan Gurney and first year mechanic, John Buttera. Each had his own car to worry about in practice. John's made it; Dan's didn't.

George Bignotti hasn't yet found the right combination for Tom Sneva. It isn't from lack of experience as his career working on race cars extends back almost forty years when his midgets used to clean up in the San Francisco Bay area.

Has it really been 34 years that Larry Bisceglia has been first in line to get a chosen viewing position for the race? When you reach the gates and see that blue van you know that "Larry's here, everything must be all right."

Prize Money

COMPLETE PRIZE FUND FOR THE 1982 INDIANAPOLIS 500-MILE RACE

Indianpolis Motor Speedway	$1,643,000.00*
Citizens Speedway Committee (Lap Prizes)	50,000.00
Citizens Speedway Committee (Parade)	10,000.00
Accessory Prizes	364,475.00
	$2,067,475.00**

*New all-time record: Previous record — $1,280,200.00
**New all-time record: Previous record — $1,605,375.00

ACCESSORY PRIZES

AFNB	$ 5,000.00	Motorola	2,000.00
American Dairy Assn.	5,000.00	NADA	10,000.00
Anheuser-Busch	10,000.00	Cecil C. Peck	1,000.00
Bell Helmets	5,400.00	Premier	1,500.00
Borg-Warner	5,000.00	PPG	66,000.00
Brodix, Inc.	1,000.00	PWS	1,500.00
Canon, USA	2,000.00	Raybestos-Manhattan	5,550.00
Champion Spark Plug	35,000.00	Rockwell	5,075.00
Ditzler	5,000.00	STP	16,500.00
Earl's Supply Co.	3,950.00	Sears	5,250.00
Esso	13,000.00	Sid Collins Award	800.00
Gould	3,500.00	Simpson Safety Equipment	5,550.00
Hurst Performance	5,000.00	Speed Pro Piston Rings	1,000.00
Ideal	2,500.00	Standard Oil Dealers	2,500.00
Imperial Clevite	2,000.00	Stant, Inc.	1,200.00
Indiana National	5,000.00	Stewart-Warner	1,750.00
Indiana Oxygen	500.00	Sun Refining	5,000.00
Indiana SAE	1,000.00	Sunnen	1,500.00
Ingersoll-Rand	5,000.00	Texaco	10,000.00
Koni Shocks	6,000.00	Total Seal Piston Rings	500.00
Knights of Columbus	1,000.00	Valvoline	16,000.00
Loctite	6,000.00	Vandervell	4,000.00
Machinists Union	6,000.00	Wheel Horse	1,000.00
Mallory	3,500.00	WRTV	500.00
Miller Brewing	43,750.00	WTTV/AMC/Jeep/Renault	5,000.00
Miscellaneous	1,500.00	UNO	10,000.00
Monroe Shocks	1,200.00		

TOTAL ACCESSORY PRIZES $364,475.00

Merchandise won by race participants included:

The Camaro Z28 Pace Car Replica
The Thornton Bardach Checkered Flag Ring
Tool sets from the Ingersoll-Rand Company
PWS Corporation Parts Washer
Rolex President Chronograph

Trophies were presented to race participants by the following companies:

American Dairy Association	Miller Beer
AFNB	National Automobile Dealers Association
Borg-Warner	Cecil C. Peck
Budweiser	Premier/DA Lubricant Co.
Sid Collings Memorial Fund	Raybestos-Manhattan
Indiana Oxygen	Renner's Express
Indiana SAE	Stewart-Warner
Loctite	STP
Machinists Union	WRTV-6

OFFICIAL SPEEDWAY RECORDS
AS OF
JUNE 1, 1982

Laps	Miles	Time	Miles Per Hour	Driver	Car Name	Year
			QUALIFYING RECORDS			
1	2.5	43.35	207.612	Rick Mears	The Gould Charge Penske	1982
4	10	2:53.91	207.004	Rick Mears	The Gould Charge Penske	1982
			RACE RECORDS			
	12.5	46.31	194.342	A. J. Foyt, Jr.	Valvoline-Gilmore	1982
2	5	1:31.86	195.950	A. J. Foyt, Jr.	Valvoline-Gilmore	1982
4	10	3:03.68	195.993	A. J. Foyt, Jr.	Valvoline-Gilmore	1982
10	25	7:41.62	194.966	A. J. Foyt, Jr.	Valvoline-Gilmore	1982
20	50	15:40.66	191.355	A. J. Foyt, Jr.	Valvoline-Gilmore	1982
30	75	24:18.94	185.066	Rick Mears	The Gould Charge Penske	1982
40	100	32:20.89	185.482	Rick Mears	The Gould Charge Penske	1982
50	125	42:16.91	177.381	Bobby Unser	Olsonite Eagle	1974
60	150	50:57.29	176.627	A. J. Foyt, Jr.	Gilmore Racing Team	1974
70	175	1:03:57.98	164.149	A. J. Foyt, Jr.	Gilmore Racing Team	1974
80	200	1:13:06.75	164.131	Al Unser	Pennzoil Chaparral	1979
90	225	1:21:14.76	166.162	Al Unser	Pennzoil Chaparral	1979
100	250	1:32:31.68	162.113	Gary Bettenhausen	Sunoco McLaren	1972
110	275	1:40:45.43	163.760	Gary Bettenhausen	Sunoco McLaren	1972
120	300	1:49:03.76	165.043	Gary Bettenhausen	Sunoco McLaren	1972
130	325	1:58:21.78	164.747	Gary Bettenhausen	Sunoco McLaren	1972
140	350	2:06:46.87	165.640	Gary Bettenhausen	Sunoco McLaren	1972
150	375	2:17:55.37	163.135	Al Unser	Norton Spirit	1979
160	400	2:26:34.49	163.739	Gary Bettenhausen	Sunoco McLaren	1972
170	425	2:35:57.25	163.510	Gary Bettenhausen	Sunoco McLaren	1972
180	450	2:46:23.97	162.260	Jerry Grant	Mystery Eagle	1972
190	475	2:55:01.16	162.839	Mark Donohue	Sunoco McLaren	1972
200	500	3:04:05.54	162.962	Mark Donohue	Sunoco McLaren	1972

TOTAL PRIZE MONEY EACH YEAR

Year	Amount	Year	Amount	Year	Amount
1911	$ 25,550	1935	$ 78,575	1961	$ 426,162
1912	52,225	1936	82,525	1962	426,162
1913	55,875	1937	92,135	1963	494,030
1914	51,675	1938	91,075	1964	506,575
1915	51,200	1939	87,050	1965	628,399
1916	31,350	1940	85,525	1966	691,808
1919	55,275	1941	90,925	1967	734,634
1920	93,550	1946	115,450	1968	721,269
1921	86,650	1947	137,425	1969	805,127
1922	70,575	1948	171,075	1970	1,000,002
1923	83,425	1949	179,050	1971	1,001,604
1924	86,850	1950	201,135	1972	1,011,845
1925	87,750	1951	207,650	1973	1,006,105
1926	88,100	1952	230,100	1974	1,015,686
1927	89,850	1953	246,300	1975	1,001,321
1928	90,750	1954	269,375	1976	1,037,776
1929	95,150	1955	270,400	1977	1,116,807
1930	96,250	1956	282,052	1978	1,145,225
1931	81,800	1957	300,252	1979	1,271,954
1932	93,900	1958	305,217	1980	1,503,225
1933	54,450	1959	338,100	1981	1,605,375
1934	83,775	1960	369,150	1982	2,067,475

500 OLDTIMERS

by Jack Fox

Veteran readers of this book will know what officially constitutes an "Oldtimer" for membership in the "500 Oldtimers' Club", but newer readers must wonder who they are. The elderly, and not so elderly, gentlemen who congregate in a large house trailer at the south end of the Press Building are really an elite group. They are the veterans of the sport of Auto Racing. The club is quite exclusive. No, just being a fan doesn't qualify you for membership! You must have been a driver who actually completed a qualifying run; a full-time employee of the Speedway, a riding mechanic, chief mechanic, a car owner, track official, an accessory man or a member of the press. And for a period of TWENTY YEARS or over!

Even Tony Hulman and A. J. Foyt had to wait their 20 years before being allowed to join. Every applicant for membership must be passed by the membership committee and they are TOUGH! The membership rolls are almost totally male-oriented due to the makeup of the sport but a few females have been given honorary membership. Long-time female employees of the track like Fran Welker, Francis Derr, June Swango, Glad Cagle, Jan Binford and several others. Janet Guthrie might be eligible along about 1997 or thereabouts. Of course this doesn't mean that a wife,

Two of the most vocal men of the 1980's . . . Art Sparks and Harry McQuinn.

friend, or historian is excluded from the trailer but visitors are rare and guest invitations to the Club's barbecue are very rare. Bud Hook, who supplies the barbecue and Dick Huddleston and Lew Worcel who supply the trailer are just about the only male honorary members.

Housemothers in the trailers are Marge Hauss and Mary Owen; Marge during the week and Mary on weekends. Other "regulars" during May include the ever-helpful Freddy Mangold, John Mangold, John Berry, story-teller Art Sparks, Myron Stevens, Matt Fairlie,

Someone must have said something good (probably Art Sparks). Harry McQuinn, writer Russ Catlin, and driver Henry Banks.

Billy DeVore, Clem Marvel, Emmett Carpenter, "Pinky" Donaldson, and your writer.

Each year special awards are given at the barbecue and this year they went to Leonard Manley (Valvoline), Norman Froesher, Dennis Bender (Champion), Clay Ballinger and racing writer, Russ Catlin.

Currently Jack Beckley is president, John Berry and Lou Meyer, vice-presidents and Bob Laycock is executive secretary and Jep Cadou edits the newsletter.

Unfortunately, the racing stories have been mostly replaced by tales of ill health, and instead of "Gentleman, start your engines", it seems more like "Gentlemen, start your pacemakers", but what can you expect from some members who are in their 80s and 90s. They are all great guys.

Mary and Marge are the "hospitality girls" in the Oldtimer's trailer.

Fox

Art Sparks, who always has something interesting to say, meditates over a fine book on Legion Ascot Speedway with Myron Stevens, driver and builder.

The first group shot of the club before the annual barbeque. Roy Harper set it up and Ron McQueeny shot it.

IMS-McQueeny

Joyce DeWitt, star of the show "Three's Company" is a graduate of Speedway High School.

Gary Bettenhausen occasionally visits the Snake Pit.

Jim and Susan Gilmore sponsor A. J. Foyt.

Dean Vetrock just didn't find the speed to pass his driver's test.

Jim Hall, of Chaparral fame, listens to a mechanic.

Paul Page used to do a little sporty car racing before he became "The Voice."

GREAT RACING BOOKS

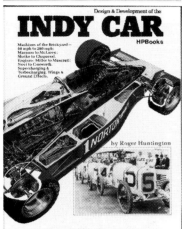

INDY CAR

Here's a great new book by noted author Roger Huntington that takes you on a trip through time and technology. Huntington discusses, in easily readable terms, engines from the Miller to the Maserati, Novi to Cosworth. He tells about rule changes and how Indy car influence has influenced passenger car design.

There are hundreds of great black and white photos along with some classic color plates that will make INDY CAR a welcome and classic addition to any race fan's library. 176 page paperbound. $14.95 p.p.

SPRINT CAR TECHNOLOGY

The first book ever written on the subject of Sprint Car technology. It's a must but for anyone who is interested in Sprint Car racing. This 160 page work covers everything from design to building and the facets in between. It will be interesting for the fan, too! Beautiful illustrations.

$8.95 postpaid

OUTLAW ANNUAL

After we attended the great Knoxville Nations in '77 we decided that the Outlaws should have an annual they could call their own. We called the best photographers we knew and they responded with some memorable photos, both color and black and white, that we've reproduced on the best paper money can buy. You'll see the world of Outlaw racing, on the track and in the pits, in full color.

You've heard their names: Wolfgang, Ferkel, Swindell, Patterson, Smith, Amati, Kinser and more. They're the guys who tow up and down the interstates all year long with no guarantees . . . just a Sprint car hitched up out back and the lure of another night of Outlaw racing.

MIDGET ANNUAL

If you're a Midget fan, here's a great book we're sure you'll like. The USAC Midget Annual chock full of stories, photos and statistics. You'll find a rundown of every race on the schedule that includes every heat race and complete feature results. It's a great argument solver. All qualifiers are listed too. We've also included a short story of each race with over 100 photos of all the Midget racers. We added several great full color pages of action photos. Just for fun, we put in pages called "Midgets of Yesterday". This annual is 48 pages, printed on the best paper and bound sideways, so it opens to a full 22" wide . . . . The cover is full color, and varnished to stay nice for years to come.

Official WORLD OF OUTLAWS
Annual 1978
Outlaw Annual 1977 Season
Please specify year
. . . . **each $3.95 p.p.**

1977 Season
1978 Season
Please specify year
. . . . **each $3.95 p.p.**

Order From: Carl Hungness Publishing   P.O. Box 24308-EY   Speedway, IN 46224

• Master Charge and VISA accepted.   • Indiana Residents add 4% sales tax.

BEAUTIFUL PRINTS & POSTERS

Set #1

Set #2

NOW — TWO SETS OF ACTION RACING PRINTS. Four 11x14 prints in each set, carefully lithographed on finest art paper and ready for framing. Set #1 in full color; Set #2 in handsome brown. Specify set. $4.50 ea. set p.p.

FULL COLOR CUT-A-WAY
Steve Stapp built Sprint Car

Beautiful FULL COLOR, finely detailed cutaway drawing of a Steve Stapp built sprint car. You can see every nut, bolt, hose and fitting. Printed on fine art paper. Size is a full 11X14. This impressive print is a great addition to your collection.

A.J. Foyt's 4th, Front Page Poster
Specify "Front Page" $3.95
A.J. Foyt, Full Color
Specify 'A.J.' $3.95
USAC Sprint Car Poster
20 Action Shots of USAC Sprints
in Full Color $3.75
Indy 500 Winners Wall Poster
All Winning Cars & Drivers
From 1911 to 1976, Printed in
Racing Blue & Black $3.95

Carl Hungness Publishing
P. O. Box 24308-EY
Speedway, IN 46224

• Master Charge and VISA accepted.
• Indiana Residents add 4% sales tax.

Speed Reading

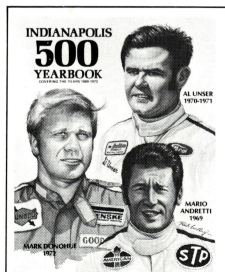

THE MILLER DYNASTY

A Technical History of the Work of Harry A. Miller, his Associates, and his Successors.

by Mark L. Dees

Here, at last, is the eagerly awaited book of the decade. Mark L. Dees has produced a complete and thorough history of the wizard of American Auto Racing — Harry L. Miller.

The disciples of Miller such as Leo Goossen, Riley Brett, The Winfield brothers, Art Sparks, Fred Offenhauser and Wilbur Shaw and their contributions to the Miller legend are descibed and illustrated.

This hardbound volume contains 528 pages and over 700 photos and original drawings. 20 years of research and discussions with experts from the Miller days have gone into this monumental work. It is expensive but no one who really loves auto racing will want to be without one.

$62.50 postpaid

Racing Cars

A Great Collector's Magazine

If you like in-depth, well researched feature stories on cars, drivers, mechanics who are involved in open-cockpit racing, then you'll enjoy our back issue of Racing Cars Magazine. We published Racing Cars as a quarterly for nearly three years and included coverage of some of the most famed names in open-cockpit auto racing. Each issue is chock full of color and memorable black and white photos. All back issues have become collector's items as publication of this great publication stopped in 1980.

There are profiles on some famed race cars, long, close looks at some of your favorite race tracks. There are award winning stories that bring you facts that haven't ever been published in another auto racing journal. We are sold out of issue number five (there were eleven issues in all) and we're in short supply on many other issues.

Back issue price is $5.00 each. Please add $1.00 postage per total order and specify the volume and issue number.

Order From: Carl Hungness Publishing   P.O. Box 24308-EY   Speedway, IN 46224

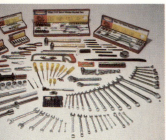